MW01008058

Health and Inequality in Standup Comedy

Health and Inequality in Standup Comedy

Stories That Challenge Stigma

Sean M. Viña

LEXINGTON BOOKS
Lanham • Boulder • New York • London

Published by Lexington Books
An imprint of The Rowman & Littlefield Publishing Group, Inc.
4501 Forbes Boulevard, Suite 200, Lanham, Maryland 20706
www.rowman.com

86-90 Paul Street, London EC2A 4NE

British Library Cataloguing in Publication Information Available

Library of Congress Cataloging-in-Publication Data Available

ISBN 978-1-66694-082-4 (cloth)
ISBN 978-1-66694-083-1 (electronic)

To Amanda, my greatest love and second wife:
Thank you for swiping right.

Contents

Acknowledgments   ix

Introduction   1

Chapter 1: Why Use Standup to Understand Stigma and Inequality   7

Chapter 2: Invisible Stigma from Least to Most Taboo   33

Chapter 3: Visible Stigmas that Define What People See   51

Chapter 4: Testing Social Boundaries   71

Chapter 5: Tactics to Manage Stigma   83

Chapter 6: Context Matters: Black and Latino Lives   99

Chapter 7: Cultivating Positive Outcomes   121

Chapter 8: The Structure and Culture of Inequality   141

Chapter 9: Lost Opportunities to Cope and Heal   167

Conclusion: Lessons Learned   187

Appendix A: Questionnaire   211

Appendix B: Supporting Table   215

Bibliography   217

Index   233

About the Author   239

Acknowledgments

I am deeply grateful to the comedy community for warmly accepting me and answering personal questions about their lives. Unfortunately, due to confidentiality concerns, I cannot name them, but their contributions were invaluable. I also want to thank the club owners who allowed me into their private businesses. A special thanks goes to the comedians who couldn't participate in interviews but still recognized the importance of this study and referred their colleagues. Without their generosity, this project would not have been possible.

This work was supported by the Department of Sociology at Indiana University—Bloomington as the final project for my graduate studies in sociology. I am grateful for the intellectual companionship provided by IU that helped uplift this project. My dissertation committee's support and guidance were crucial to making this work possible. I would like to thank Dr. Susan Seizer for her expertise as an anthropologist who has studied comedy. She challenged my perspective on comedy and enriched the analysis. I would also like to thank Dr. Koji Chavez for his eagerness to support a young sociologist trying something different. Dr. Bernice Pescosolido allowed me the opportunity to train under her tutelage as her graduate assistant. She not only guided me through the complexities of the discipline but also exposed me to the impactful work of sociologists outside the classroom through research-driven advocacy. Working with her and seeing her passion brought me a deep appreciation for the need to address stigma in all its forms. Finally, I would like to thank Dr. Fabio Rojas for recognizing the value in exploring health among standup comedians. Above all, it was always fun to chat with him about pop culture, which was a much-needed distraction from work stressors.

I want to express my most heartfelt gratitude to Dr. Amanda Layne Stephens, Esq. Our paths crossed during my first semester at IU, and she has been a constant source of support throughout my graduate school journey. Amanda has been an unwavering advocate for me both personally and professionally. She has provided invaluable intellectual companionship and has given me more feedback on my projects than anyone else. Most importantly, she has been there for me when I needed emotional support and has helped me prioritize my mental health. I feel incredibly fortunate to have her in my life.

Introduction

Rebecca was drugged and raped. Unfortunately, her story is all too familiar. The night prior, she was in a local tavern where she would often gather with friends, catch up on the week's events, tell jokes, and wind down for the evening. That night, she met a man who seemed like just another average-looking guy. But he was not. At some point, he slipped a Xanax into her whisky and water. She was raped twice, once on the walk home and once more when she got there. The next morning, Rebecca awoke with severe bodily injuries that put her through months of physical therapy.

Unexpectedly, separate from the physical damage, was the emotional distress she soon encountered. She discovered a second type of prolonged emotional trauma: stigma. Not only was she coping with the fact that somebody violated her body, but Rebecca also discovered that she now occupied a new social status: rape survivor. From that point forward, all her relationships changed. Friends, family, and even strangers perceived and treated her differently. Before the rape, people knew her as a strong, forceful, cheery feminist. Afterward, she felt eyes looking over her as someone now weak, fragile, and broken. She had lost the one thing that made her who she was: her sense of humor. Worse, everyone could see she had lost it. In this new world that Rebecca occupied, the word itself—rape—was so uncomfortable that it could barely be whispered, only ever hinted at as that "thing" that happened. She was no longer the person that everyone had grown to know. She was no longer the person she knew herself to be. And the stigma was too taboo even to be uttered.

Nevertheless, what Rebecca did next separates her story from those of most victims. Soon after the rape, she did the unthinkable. Rebecca stood on a comedy nightclub stage in front of an audience of strangers and told her story. She needed to prove to herself that she was still the same person, even with a scarred body. She opened with a couple of non sequiturs, got a few laughs, took a breath, and said the truth out loud: "Two months ago, I was raped." The air was instantly sucked from the room. Unprepared, the audience was silent. A moment later, she calmly and politely—as if comforting a group of victims—told them to take a deep breath. Rebecca then told some rape jokes.

She did not make light of the rape. Not at all. Rather, she ridiculed the justice system that allowed a violent predator to walk around while she was fighting in court. She made fun of her new uncomfortable family relationships. She even joked about being a super-feminist liberal who now sympathized with gun owners—but only the gun-toting women.

Throughout her set, the audience laughed. When she finished, they cheered. And at the moment of applause, Rebecca knew she was still herself and that she was going to be okay. Her identity was secure. For a time, comedy provided her a place to speak. Then she was silenced. And once again, comedy helped liberate her voice. Although she was bruised, she could look in the mirror and again see the person she knew she was. "It was like the world was hugging me," Rebecca told me with a smile.

While Rebecca is relatively new to standup comedy, performing at a club in her little midwestern town for only a couple years, on the opposite side of the professional spectrum is Treyvaughn, who stepped in front of the mic almost thirty years prior in the mid-1980s. Unlike many who struggle when they first begin standup, Treyvaughn was one of those rare gems in this performative art who spoke comedy like it was his first language. And his career started out with a bang, or "gong" to be more precise. One of his first standing ovations came just a few months into his career when he performed at the world-famous and historic Apollo Theater:

> When I got to the Apollo, they said, you can't say this, and you can't say that. That was my whole routine, so I thought, well, what am I going to do? I got out there, and I said, I'm just going to do me, and I got a standing ovation. But the ovation scared me. I took a few steps back because I thought the sandman was coming out to get my ass.

But unlike Rebecca, who was able to stand tall and truthfully disclose the most painful experience of her life to uplifting public support, Treyvaughn's personal life was met with scorn in comedy. As a gay Black man, he received little support in those early years to share his trials and tribulations on the standup stage. In a very short period, he was denied stages, eventually struggling with rent and food; homophobia quickly forced him out:

> A lot of male comedians, and when I say male comedians, I'm talking about African American males, they feel like I am not someone they want to associate with. And that's because of the stigma of being gay. We don't socialize outside of comedy and not even really in comedy. I took a break because I had to regroup. I had to think about where I wanted to go with this and what I was willing to do to succeed. I know comedians who have slept in their cars because they couldn't afford a hotel room. And I had to say to myself, am I willing to do that?

In recent years, thanks to the support of some very funny, very influential queer Black women, Treyvaughn has been able to return to standup. But despite progress of the LGBTQ+ community, Treyvaughn still largely remains in the closet onstage in front of Black audiences because attitudes have not changed that much in his community: "I don't have a lot of comradery with African American males, comedians. Right now, I don't feel like I'm that popular, and I have been doing comedy for thirty years." When taking the stage, Treyvaughn can talk about his life, but he has to disguise his sexuality. To talk about dating, sex, and his general daily life, he disguises his speech behind a caricature of an elderly woman. Most audience members do not know he is gay, especially because he never openly admits it.

Countless women, men, and children have experienced trauma and chronic stress, resulting in psychological issues such as depression, anxiety, PTSD, and even suicide. Rebecca and Treyvaughn's stories highlight an important point and the crux of this book. The violent trauma and homophobia they faced were only one aspect of their mental states. They also experienced a secondary trauma derived from the stigma attached to their experiences. Rebecca's friends and family were tiptoeing around her, trying not to harm or trigger her, while some avoided her and the uncomfortable subject altogether. Treyvaughn was shunned by his community, losing valuable social connections and eventually suffering financially. They both internalized the fear of being judged and avoided interacting with others, or retreated from the community altogether. This led to self-doubt and a loss of love for the standup stage. The distress from mistreatment changed their behaviors and closed them off from the world, creating new distress and exacerbating other health issues.

Their stories also emphasize that overcoming stigma is a journey that is not the same for everyone. Despite having only a few years of experience and less than two months after the incident, Rebecca was able to confront her stigma and largely eliminate the social consequences associated with her trauma. However, Treyvaughn is still struggling to come out of hiding, feeling sidelined and unable to fully express himself as a strong, gay, Black man. It's clear that the path to overcoming stigma is not a linear one, and each individual's experience is unique.

The negative impact of stigma has been extensively documented.[1] The main goal of this book is to raise awareness that stigma worsens people's lives. Once stigmatized, individuals face discrimination, social isolation, loss of income, and limited access to resources, often due to their fear of violence.[2] One of the most harmful consequences of stigma is that it makes unnatural things seem natural. Society conditions us to believe that being LGBTQ+ is deviant, that being a person of color means being dangerous, and that "rape" means broken. This normalization of inequality perpetuates discrimination and makes it seem like it's a natural part of life. The process of creating stigma is also used to justify inaction from both those who remain silent and those who silence others. Therefore, inequality continues to exist, and it is regarded as normal rather than a product of discrimination.

This book delves into one of the most effective ways to reduce stigma: social contact through open conversations. Rather than focusing solely on those who are unable to speak out, I explore the nuances of open conversations through a profession that revolves around discussing taboo topics: standup comedy. Over the course of almost three years starting in late 2018, I recruited ninety-nine diverse standup comedians from across the country, all of whom were given aliases to maintain confidentiality. From open mic performers who had only been onstage a few times to touring comedians who spend most of their lives on the road, and headliners who have performed on networks like HBO and shows like *The Tonight Show with Jimmy Fallon*, their voices provide a broad perspective on the hidden voices in the standup comedy world.

This book draws on over 175 hours of transcribed, structured, and guided in-depth interviews to answer three fundamental questions: (1) how do people disclose their stigmas in public, (2) what prevents some from having open conversations, and (3) what do people gain even if they cannot openly discuss their stigma? In the following chapters, I report the findings on emergent themes from the interviews and argue that the scope of stigma resistance is not solely a product of an individual's skills, but is defined by the prejudices of those who stigmatize. Resisting stigma through open conversations is an incredibly unequal endeavor, making it virtually impossible for most to fully liberate their voices. I will argue that despite what anti-stigma advocates would like, having open and productive conversations like Rebecca's, many will never be able to find full equality and will remain closeted to some degree like Treyvaughn. I will discuss the importance of intermediary processes (i.e., building conversation skills and finding friends), especially for those who embrace the limits of conversations. But I will also argue that if the onus of responsibility to address stigma lies solely on those who are stigmatized, then stigma will not change, discrimination will not decrease, and inequality will persist. To help people access their voices, institutions, including standup comedy, need to implement policies that decrease segregation, a fundamental component of stigma. Drawing on the experiences of standup comedians, this book asks us to reconsider what an individual can realistically achieve in the fight against stigma and what structural changes need to be made to make a difference.

NOTES

1. Graham Scambler, "Stigma and Mental Disorder," in *The Sage Handbook of Mental Health and Illness*, ed. David Pilgrim, Anne Rogers, and Bernice Pescosolido (London: Sage Publications, 2011), 218–38, https://doi.org/10.4135/9781446200988.n11; Bernice A. Pescosolido, "The Public Stigma of Mental Illness: What Do We Think; What Do We Know; What Can We Prove?," *Journal of Health and Social Behavior* 54, no. 1 (2013): 1–21.

2. Jack K. Martin, Bernice A. Pescosolido, and Steven A. Tuch, "Of Fear and Loathing: The Role of 'Disturbing Behavior,' Labels, and Causal Attributions in Shaping Public Attitudes toward People with Mental Illness," *Journal of Health and Social Behavior* 41, no. 2 (2000): 208–23.

Chapter 1

Why Use Standup to Understand Stigma and Inequality

The stigma that prevents people from disclosing their problems and seeking care has been identified as one of the most critical challenges of our time.[1] The most comprehensive study on the societal cost of the stigma attached to mental illness comes from the military. A 2008 study estimates that stigma costs the United States $6.2 billion in the first two years after deployment from direct medical care and lost productivity.[2] What's frightening is their research only estimated stigma affecting about 300,000 service members. But in 2019, an estimated 51.5 million Americans lived with a diagnosable mental illness, which increased to about 58 million in 2021.

To address stigma, many organizations, both federal and private, are taking up the fight with aggressively expensive effort. For instance, in 2022, Congress passed the Bipartisan Safer Communities Act, which dramatically expands investments in our nation's mental health services over a decade, including up to $5 billion for broader mental health programs and $120 million for other miscellaneous mental health awareness training.[3] Part of this law funnels $240 million to Project AWARE to provide training for school personnel and other adults who interact with school-aged youth to detect and respond to mental health challenges. Similarly, in 2021 the National Alliance for Mental Illness, the nation's largest grassroots mental health organization, spent $23.3 million on programming, marketing and communication, education, and advocacy.[4] In 2017 alone, the United States spent an estimated $162 million on direct-to-consumer advertising for mental health and addiction services, an 8,000 percent increase from $2 million in 1997.[5]

Unfortunately, despite hundreds of millions of dollars that have been pumped in mental health training, services, and awareness campaigns, the mountains of money have not seemed to put a dent in either the rate of mental illness or the stigma attached to it. Evidence suggests that educational campaigns alone do not have any stigma-reduction value. Education can cause some short-term attitude changes, but long-term discriminatory behaviors don't change.[6] These education campaigns are particularly ineffective in eliminating the stigma attached to race, gender, and sexuality, where biases are subconscious and automatic. And the problem with stigma seems to be getting worse. Three decades of research tracking attitudes toward those with mental illness has found that although the public is much more aware of mental illness than ever before, discriminatory behaviors have not substantially changed. While the desire to social distance against those with depression has slightly decreased, the perception that people with mental illness are dangerous has increased.[7] A likely culprit of these alarming attitude shifts may be in part to the constant connection that the media makes between gun violence and those with mental illness, despite the fact that those who are mentally ill are more likely to be victims of crime than perpetrate it. All of these stubborn statistics on stigma partially explain why: In 2019, approximately 19.86 percent of adults in the United States experienced a mental illness,[8] which is higher than any year before.

There is only one known effective measure against stigma: social contact.[9] If you are close with someone who has a stigma, you are more likely to be friends, coworkers, or even welcome into your family another person who has that stigma. People cannot simply be told that a stereotype is inaccurate and harmful to the stigmatized person (i.e., those with mental illness are not dangerous), they need to experience reality firsthand. Many organizations are finally taking notice of the evidence on direct social contact. In the fight to eliminate stigma attached to mental illness, Bring Change to Mind is embracing the efficacy of social contact through interactive educational interventions.[10] The National Alliance for Mental Illness and the American Psychiatric Association are developing campaigns around the idea of breaking or ending silence.[11] And organization like the W.K. Kellogg Foundation's Truth, Racial Healing & Transformation even have turned their attention to racial healing through open conversations within communities.[12] They have resources to help people create productive conversations around relationship building. For all these campaigns, the key is talking and listening through direct exposure between those who stigmatize and those who have been stigmatized. Those who stigmatize have deeply held stereotypes expelled, and those who are stigmatized experience a less threatening world.

WHY STUDY STIGMA REDUCTION IN COMEDY?

To understand why so many people silently live with stigma, I sought out a group who actively talks about taboos and asked how they do it. Standup comedy provides us with that opportunity because of its long and robust history of taboo conversations. In fact, many of the participants in this study praised comedy for its ability to have unfettered conversations. Lora, one of the longest-performing and most professionally successful comedians in this study, explained, "You can say whatever you want so long as it's funny."

Indeed, standup comedy has a robust heritage exploring a wide range of topics including issues of death and dying, human rights, addiction (to food, drugs, or alcohol), women, racial and ethnic minorities, incarcerated people, animal rights,[13] and even sexual assault.[14] On topics of race and inequality, there are many important contemporary examples of comedians spearheading these conversations including Dave Chappelle and Wanda Sykes, who discuss Black lives; Ali Wong and Joy Koy, who explore the intricacies of different Asian experiences; and Latino comedians, who include such personalities as Gabriel Iglesias, George Lopez, and Anjelah Johnson. More recently, issues like mental illness and homophobia across different communities have come into the fray. For instance, Hannah Gadsby made national headlines for her one-woman show *Nanette*, in which she discussed violence, living with mental illness, and being LGBTQ+.[15] A few years later, Jerrod Carmichael used the stage to explore his identity as gay man in the Black community.[16] And indeed, the diversity of participants in this study barely matches the diversity of the stigmatized experiences that they are discussing onstage, because, as described by some researchers, comedy is an increasingly successful mode to engage with question of social difference, division, and power.[17]

The diversity of topics discussed by participants is crucial because the impact of stigma extends beyond mental illness, despite stigma scholars often concentrating on this topic. Even if a person has a diagnosable mental illness, it's not necessarily what they're dealing with when they initiate conversations with others. Instead, they're attempting to combat the stigma that leads to discrimination that makes it hard to have their voices heard.

To illustrate the point, let's reflect on Rebecca and a few other participants. When Rebecca took the stage, she was struggling with being labeled a "rape survivor" and how people treated her differently. The rape had harmed her both physically and psychologically, but she explicitly described trying to change the public and personal perception of being a "rape survivor." Although Rebecca may have experienced more severe symptoms of depression and anxiety due to the trauma, she was actively trying to dispel the negative public perception that was holding her back in silence. Like Rebecca, many people are not just coping with mental illness; they are also trying to overcome negative public perceptions of their identity that cause them distress. Let's consider three other comedians I interviewed for this project. The first is Nora, a white mother, who describes in graphic detail the effects of her recent childbirth on her body in her comedy.

The process of having babies is such a mystery to people. The way it is portrayed on TV is so hilariously vague and off base that people don't know what happens. But people it happens to, they are in on the joke. They are in on the experience. We know. To be able to say it out loud in a microphone is great. And it's not like I am giving away trade secrets. People should know! This is what happens when you have a baby. Why don't we talk about it? Well, because it's gross. A lot of people don't want to talk about it. After I have this baby, I am going to bleed for six weeks.

Nora describes how being a mother leads to others treating her differently, causing her distress as many people instantly perceive her as weak, including her comedian peers:

I've been pregnant most of the time I have known these comics, and they have sort of treated me with kid gloves, which is kind of weird. Getting me chairs and stuff, like I'm fragile. They sort of pick at each other and tease each other, but they won't do that to me. Is the joke is going to hurt my unborn baby? Like mothers are so precious. We are tougher than you give us credit for.

Next up is Holly, a comedian from Canada who identifies as transgender. Her comedy largely centers on her experiences as a trans person. She openly shares stories with her audiences about being bullied as a child, her dating and sexual encounters, and her thoughts on her identity. "I pretty much share everything. There's not much I haven't shared," she says. Recently, her comedy set has focused on her struggles with finding romantic relationships as a transgender woman.

And when we first met, our relationship was very peripheral. Organically, over the years, we got closer and closer. And then our friendships went deep. And I started to fall in love with this person. And he was falling in love with me, or at least he was saying so. He would say things like "I am so obsessed with you; I want to know everything about you." I really relied on him for a feeling of security and safety. I thought we were experiencing this thing together, but then he started dating someone else. And I fell apart. And everything unraveled. I really felt like he led me on as a trans woman.

Next up is Booker, a young Black man who frequently discusses his experiences dating a white woman. A key aspect of Booker's comedy is his effort to dispel negative stereotypes often attached to Black men in interracial relationships. One stereotype that particularly bothers him is the notion that Black men are lazy and seek out white women for financial security or as mere sexual objects:

Everyone wants to say, as a Black man, dating white women is the ultimate goal for some reason. Some people may start to think that I believe this woman is a trophy. I'm not coveting this person. They are not a pair of shoes. I actually love this person. But that's just the stigma; it's not. Like I told this joke: "I don't know if you all know this, but I am really into white women. I know it sounds crazy to be into white women as a Black man. But I am not into it because you think that I am into it. I like fuckin' with white women because their fathers are racist. And I know it may sound a little weird, but racist dads really do it for me."

So far, none of the five comedians we've discussed are dealing with a mental illness. Instead, each of them has described the distress they face due to their social status or negative experiences they've endured. Rebecca is trying to dispel perceptions of rape survivors, Treyvaughn is navigating the hate toward gay Black men, Nora is trying to break free from the stereotypes attached to mothers, Booker is trying to overcome the perceptions of being a Black man in an interracial relationship, and Holly is trying to combat the perceptions attached to her as a trans woman. This book will explore how successful each of them has been in combating these stigmas.

In addition to the breadth of stigmas being tackled by courageous comedians across standup, some research has highlighted humor's potential to empower the stigmatized by facilitating connections between the audience and the comedians.[18] Indeed, comedians are not only permitted to be awkward when they address stigma, but they are often celebrated for doing so, especially when they pepper taboo topics with obscenities.[19] Hypothesized as a unique atmosphere where audiences hunger for connection with the comedian,[20] standup comedy is very much an intimate form of face-to-face communication that is intended to build emotional bridges.[21] Moreover, scholars note that the public generally finds pleasure engaging comedy to understand issues like politics in ways that traditional broadcast news and commentary do not offer.[22] One main reason is that comedy allows complex issues like politics and the economy to be more accessible to the general public, especially for those who have traditionally been denied access.

Most important are the key traits of comedy that are relevant to the reduction of stigma. Foremost, comedy has been hypothesized as a powerful social force because it can generate empathy and a sense of group belonging.[23] It appears to have a unique capacity to increase attention to pressing crises, lower resistance to persuasion, dismantle social barriers, and facilitate everyday discussion about topical issues.[24] Because of these traits, aggregate evidence has found that comedy (standup or otherwise) may be an effective way to destigmatize topics such as racism, sexism, and politics.[25] It has been linked to the reduction in stigma attached to mental illness,[26] and reduces

the "toxic effects" of bad experiences or trauma for the individual.[27] Those
exposed to comedy seem to have an increase in hope and optimism toward
addressing social problems like poverty and climate change.[28] As a result,
reductions in stigma through comedy are associated with increases in support for mental health treatment-seeking,[29] higher self-esteem,[30] increased
medical knowledge by the public,[31] and even increased odds of recovery after
surgery.[32] In their book the *Humor Code*,[33] McGraw and Warner use humor
to shed light on important health processes and to help reduce stigma. They
argue that humor is beneficial because it can relieve tension during stressful
moments, especially when both parties are experiencing the same stressor.
This is especially important for stigma research because it highlights the
importance of empathy in eliminating stigma. If a conversation does not help
to build empathy, stigma cannot be eliminated.

However, scholarships and other resources fall short when it comes to
addressing the issue of coping with stigma directly. There are still gaps that
can be better addressed with an explicit sociological framework that examines
stigma and health inequality. For example, McGraw and Warner have found
that humor can have serious consequences if it offends others, potentially
leading to violence.[34] What they don't identify is which issues are most likely
to face consequences? If conversations go awry, what are salient alternatives
that can counteract the negative consequence of stigma? Does standup lead to
behavioral changes among those who discriminate or experience discrimination—which is necessary for there to be stigma reduction? Most importantly,
people experience different stigma and thus have different conversations.
Among the participants in this book, issues they discus include, but are not
limited to, mental illness, trauma, relationships, being single mothers, racism, politics, genocide, sexual terrorism, being ordered to commit war crimes
while serving in the US military, and grieving the death of a child. Depending
on the issues, experiences, and sociodemographic backgrounds, who is the
least likely to successfully cope and reduce stigma?

DISCRIMINATION AND INEQUALITY IN COMEDY

This book explores the theory that stigma is made up of several parts, including labeling, stereotyping, cognitive separation into "us" and "them" groups,
status loss, social rejection, and discrimination. To combat stigma, it's important to empower those who are stigmatized. Throughout history, standup
comedy has been a powerful tool for marginalized individuals. Comedians,
who are often excluded from power and stigmatized, have used their talent
and humor to survive and even thrive.[35] For the pre–Civil Rights Movement
Black comedian, the chitlin circuit was typically the starting point from which

the comic attempted to move into "mainstream" venues.[36] Later in the early 1900s, although often closely aligned with the burlesque, these stages became economic refuges for other marginalized groups, including Jewish, women, and LGBTQ+ performers.[37]

Standup comedy has transformed over the decades into a platform for hard-hitting political and social satire. This shift has allowed many marginalized individuals, including Black comedians, to enter the mainstream consciousness. As a result, much of today's most popular comedy is rooted in social and political awareness, which is often described as "charged humor"; described as that which intends to incite social change, develop community, and lobby for civil rights, this type of standup purposely addresses sensitive issues including—but not limited to—racism, sexism, ableism, and heterosexism.[38] Three historical figures remain vitally important to comedy's transformation: Lenny Bruce, George Carlin, and Richard Pryor. Between 1959 and 1964, Bruce performed three times on the *Steve Allen Show*, where he bashed segregation laws and Arkansas's governor for ordering the National Guard to prevent Black students from attending a school in Little Rock, Arkansas.[39] Carlin solidified his fame as a critical social commentator with his monologue, "The Seven Words You Can Never Say on Television."[40] Around the same time, Pryor's Grammy Award–winning comedy albums tackled racially sensitive topics. Not surprisingly, Pryor has been praised as one of the "the first African-American standup comedian[s] to speak candidly and successfully to integrated audiences using the language and jokes Blacks previously only shared among themselves when they were most critical of America."[41]

These comics' ability to discuss issues like racism at the height of segregation is all the more impressive considering comedy's racist roots. At its conception, some of the most persistent racist stereotypes were born and nurtured in American comedy's early days.[42] Minstrel shows were the most popular forms of American entertainment, rooted in the pre–Civil War years.[43] They featured white performers in blackface, mocking African Americans in skits, dances, and songs.

The importance of acknowledging the racist origins of comedy is to highlight the underlying issue of inequality that persists in the field. While comedy can offer opportunities, the process remains unequal. Comedian men like Pryor, Bruce, and Carlin were known for openly challenging societal issues, whereas women comedians were often confined to portraying idealized versions of women's roles with men. Even the top comedian women of the time, such as Jean Carroll, were limited to joking about shopping, children, and serving their husbands. Phyllis Diller played the role of a ditzy homemaker whose husband didn't find her attractive. During the 1960s sexual revolution, Joan Rivers joked about her inability to find a husband, the social ideal, and her sexual promiscuity, highlighting the double standards of society: "A man can sleep around, no questions asked. But if a woman makes nineteen or twenty mistakes, she's a tramp."[44] Lucille Ball's character on *I Love Lucy* was often portrayed as an inept housewife. To demonstrate this, one writer asked if Lucy Ricardo—Lucille Ball's character—could function in the real world:[45]

> Lucy overdoses on seasickness pills, packs her passport in the luggage that's being sent ahead from Italy to France, leaves her purse with the New York train tickets inside on the platform in Los Angeles, misplaces train tickets to Florida, misses the departure of her trans-Atlantic luxury liner, becomes trapped inside a steamer trunk and gets her head stuck in a porthole, all in one episode.

It is not to suggest that these women were not challenging the stigma created in patriarchy through their performance. According to Miekewski,[46] comedians like Fanny Brice, Diller, Lily Tomlin, and Rivers use the stage to satirize femininity and build comradery between women who face those pressures. Beneath their humor was a carefully crafted messages of empowerment that, as one theorist argues, challenged hierarchical structures,[47] which is visible in those portrayals. Ball's character may have been overreaching with scheming ambition, but she was the person on the show with whom the audience could best empathize because of the pressures she struggled with at home. Likewise, Alice Kramden in *The Honeymooners* was smarter, more in control, and barely tolerant of the childish Ralph portrayed by Jackie Gleason. These and other comedian women build their comedy on a spectrum of subversive messaging worked to fight sociocultural expectations.[48] Those portrayals were not only important for social change,[49] but they provide evidence for humor's ability to eliminate stigma because it builds empathy.

However, while some women could be seen through a narrow filter, they were mostly white, feminine women. Where were the women of color at the same time? In her analysis of Black comedy, Haggins exposes the persistent problem faced by African American women when they attempted to cross over into the mainstream.[50] It would be decades after Pryor before standups like Whoopi Goldberg and Wanda Sykes could enter the mainstream because while they were navigating issues of femininity, they were also balancing archetypal constructions of Black femininity at the intersection of race and social justice.

Nevertheless, the point about inequality in comedy is valid because it highlights the constraints placed on certain voices. While comedian men could openly challenge racism or politics, comedian women had to be more subversive. Comedian men could call out politicians for being racist, but comedian women could only imply that sexism was wrong. It took decades for comedy to fully embrace feminist voices like Sarah Silverman, Margaret Cho, Ellen DeGeneres, Taylor Tomlinson, Chelsea Handler, Iliza Shlesinger, and Nikki

Glaser. DeGeneres didn't even come out as a lesbian until the 1990s, and it took another two decades for Todd Glass to come out as gay, despite having years of standup experience. Jerrod Carmichael didn't do a standup special as an openly gay Black man until a decade later. Mental illness was also stigmatized in comedy until recently, with Maria Bamford being one of the first to openly discuss her diagnosis of bipolar disorder in the late 2010s. It wasn't until another decade later that Hannah Gadsby was able to speak openly about her trauma and mental health, possibly because she was also a queer woman. Despite their immense talent, stigma silenced these voices for far too long.

I agree with scholars who argue that we are in a new golden era of comedy where there is a growing marketplace for new, diverse voices. The diversity has contributed to the industry's recent economic boom; comedy increased revenue by 16.8 percent between 2013 and 2018 (an annualized 3.1 percent). Today's late-night talk shows such as *Conan*, *Jimmy Kimmel Live!*, and *The Tonight Show with Jimmy Fallon* regularly host women and minorities. Of the eleven standup comedians Colbert hosted in 2017 on the *Late Show*, less than half were white men.[51] Looking at Netflix, arguably the current most dominant comedy platform, of the fifty-nine Netflix Original Comedy Specials in 2018, forty (≈80%) featured people of color. And even without significant comedy hosts such as IFC, FX, HBO, Comedy Central, TBS, Netflix, Amazon, and Hulu, comedians can still build a fan base through the internet and podcasting. The digital media age has been very important for democratizing these new voices and reaching audiences that are keenly interested in learning about social justice issues through comedy.[52] Many marginalized people are for the first time making it to the stage. For example, consider one research participant, Nathaniel, a comedian confined to a wheelchair because of cerebral palsy:

> This is a ripe time for people that look different, think different, struggle with different illnesses or are different genders. This is a ripe time for us to be heard. I think this is perfect timing for someone like me, someone with cerebral palsy. Ten years ago, I would have had a hell of a bad time. But I think this era is more about your personal story. This era is ripe for us.

However, several points need to be made. First, according to the Bureau of Labor Statistics, the standup comedy occupation is still almost 90 percent men. Between 2010 and 2021, the unemployment rate of standup comedians fluctuated between 23 percent (2019) and 44 percent (2021).[53] Although exact marital and parental statistics are unknown, those statistics on gender and unemployment highly suggest that standup comedy skews heavily toward single, childless men, a reality at least confirmed anecdotally by prominent comedian mothers like Ali Wong and Amy Schumer.[54] Second, the comedy world is also very segregated.[55] One study of the most prominent comedy show bookings in Chicago found that of nineteen shows, only two were both gender and race balanced. The other twelve were only men, mostly white.[56] Despite what may be seen at the top, comedy is barely diverse and not that inclusive.

Cyrus, who was part of the study, suggested that the reason for the lack of top comedian women is a simple math problem. He explained, "The truth is that there are more men doing comedy than women. And let's be honest, most people aren't good at standup. If 90% of men are bad at it and 90% of women are bad at it, then it's not surprising that there aren't more women at the top."

At first glance, Cyrus's reasoning may seem sound, but upon closer inspection, the flaws become very apparent. What he and others fail to consider is the lack of representation for women and minorities. This is where analyzing comedy through the lens of stigmatization can provide valuable insights into both persistent inequality and the stigmatization process. The consequences of stigma are often more subtle than outright discrimination. For example, in 2017, the US Labor Department investigated Google for gender discrimination and found "systemic compensation disparities against women pretty much across the entire workforce."[57] Although there were instances where Google paid women less for doing the same work, the major issue was the company's hiring practices. Women were often placed in lower-paying jobs, even if they had the same qualifications and educational backgrounds as their counterpart men. This discrimination has been supported by research, which found that women with identical credentials were less likely to be hired than men. Additionally, Black men without criminal records were less likely to be hired than white men with felony records, and mothers were often hired at lower pay than fathers.[58] Based on the stigma research, these finding are explained by stereotypes attached to each group, specifically, women are not tech savvy or more incompetent employees than men, Black men are criminals, and mothers are more committed to their family than fathers.

Although there may be some diversity in standup comedy, stigma research demonstrates that diversity does not mean equal treatment, because those top comedians are living in marginalized bodies which assume all the consequences of inequality.[59] Marginalized comedians recognize their status and often perform as outsider figures in the comedy world. As argued by James Thomas, standup should not just be thought of strictly as discursive or disruptive environment. Rather, it functions as both enablers and constrainers of social difference in race, class, gender, and heteronormativity.[60] We've already discussed how standup women are confined by sexism, forced to present "subversive" humor rather than being direct. But the constrained voices extends to all groups including racial minorities. For Black comedians, that may often lead to them purposely perpetuating potentially destructive images of Black culture as a means to ridicule stereotypes held by whites.[61] For other minorities including Latinos, that may mean portraying stereotypes that emphasize a clownish persona that is "funny looking" and not threatening.[62] These subtle difference in performance are important, because, as this book will show, they highlight stigma that creates a perpetual barrier to being fully seen.

Equally important to the stigma question are structural issues. Socioeconomic inequality is directly associated with worse behaviors, barriers, and health outcomes,[63] and prior research has painted a very unpleasant economic picture of the comedy world. As one study describes, comedy is a brutal business.[64] Big names often work for free with fame and fortune being rare. With poverty being such a norm in comedy, it is likely that the cultural conditions are not only a facilitator of dangerous situations, but those situations are going to disproportionately harm some. We can easily highlight a consistent history of sexual predation and violence that has permeated every level of comedy. Bill Cosby was accused of drugging and raping over sixty women.[65] Louis C.K. was ostracized when years of sexually predatory behavior came to public light.[66] Chris D'Elia was accused of targeting underage women for sex.[67] And Bryan Callen has been accused of rape and exchanging stage time for sexual favors.[68] When inequality, sexism, and racism persists in very visible cultural institutions like *Saturday Night Live* (SNL), which has been described as a "fratshow" atmosphere,[69] of course inequality persists in the dark back rooms where standups confront drunk and belligerent patrons.

A good way to understand how individual speech is constrained is with the Overton Window, a model that illustrates the range of political ideas tolerated by the public.[70] In order for a political policy to be successful, it must be socially acceptable first and foremost, regardless of the personal beliefs of the politician supporting it. Politicians will only support policies that fall within the "window" of social acceptability in order to gain or maintain their elected public office. The "window" includes policies that are deemed "acceptable" for discussion, while policies that lie just outside of it are considered "radical" or "unthinkable." Politicians may attempt to shift the window by nudging a topic until it becomes politically viable. The window can also shift and expand as cultural changes occur, which affects what policies politicians can endorse. For example, marijuana legalization was once intolerable, but now it is becoming more widely accepted. Similarly, gay marriage was once considered unthinkable, but now it has become the norm. As a result, we often see politicians change their positions depending on public opinion.

Like political policy, standup speech is confined by culture. Many Americans may be accustomed to political commentary throughout different aspects of comedy, but according to Jones, "political television" is relatively new phenomenon that really started to rise in the early 2000s with shows like

The Daily Show and *The Colbert Report*.[71] Jones rightfully points out that prior to this new era, there was a common cultural conception that comedy satire diminished political or social importance, which is evident with how some of those pioneering comedian men were treated and constrained. Lenny Bruce was witness to the horrible injustice—as many Americans were—of Black Americans who returned home to racist America after helping to destroy one of the most homicidal regimes in human history—Nazi Germany.[72] Pryor and Carlin—both staunch critics of the government—developed their comedy during the American counterculture movements of the 1960s and 1970s. They were witnesses to a country torn apart by the Vietnam War, the impeachment of Richard Nixon, and the assassination of civil rights leaders such as Dr. Martin Luther King.[73] A little-known fact is that Pryor spent time learning from Black intellectuals and writers in Berkeley, California. That exposure was integral to his shift away from what some described as "whitebread" comedy (in which he imitated Bill Cosby) to his raunchy and culturally captivating comedy that we have come to closely associate with him.[74]

Then there is Carlin, whose original comedy—as late as 1967—was very conventional, run of the mill. He performed clean-shaven, with short-cropped hair, and while wearing a suit and tie. But as the United States became further embroiled in the Vietnam War, the counterculture movement strengthened, and America's views shifted on race relations, sexual mores, women's rights, and traditional government authority; so did Carlin and his comedy.

Despite some scholars suggesting that comedy leans toward a liberal perspective at the highest levels,[75] we can easily observe that there are top comedians like Dave Chappelle who hold more conservative views on a host of issues including gender and sexuality. This shows that comedy can still be influenced by the discriminatory cultural norms prevalent in America. Therefore, by analyzing stigma through the prism of comedy, this book has the potential to provide valuable insights into why comedy and other institutions remain underrepresented. It will also help to shed light on why many individuals find it difficult to effectively challenge their own stigmatization.

THE STUDY

Studying stigma within standup comedy can be challenging, especially when it comes to discerning the truth behind the comedian's words—particularly if you're just hearing them as a member of the audience. Comedians are performers with personal agency who often filter their life experiences through their work. However, as Hannah Gadsby's *Nanette* illustrates, comedians may also censor or leave out certain details of their lives when performing. For years, Gadsby used humor to discuss her experiences as a queer woman while leaving out details of a violent assault. As a result, it can be difficult for audiences to know the full truth behind the stories, how the comedians feel about those experiences, and how their performances have affected their identities.

To understand those hidden details, I chose emergent research methods[76] to conduct guided, in-depth interviews. This method proved useful because although we already "know a reasonable amount about the topic—enough to identify the domain and the questions to be asked," we don't know enough to anticipate the standup comedians' responses.[77] Moreover, this method allow us to "explore new areas and discover and unravel intriguing puzzles."[78]

I began by constructing an interview questionnaire based on collective knowledge of comedy culture, and social theories on distress and coping (see appendix A for instrument). To gain entry into the comedy world, I began by attending open-mic nights at a local comedy club in the Midwest. This comedy club was a great start because of the full range of professional levels. In addition to open-mic-ers who only perform unpaid free nights, the club was also home to touring comics who were connected to comedians in other major metropolitan areas. The club also hosted weekend shows with headliners from significant urban comedy hubs such as Los Angeles, Chicago, New York, and Toronto.

At first, local comedians were reluctant to participate, but with some persistence and developing some rapport, I recruited a visiting headliner as the first participant. This headlining comic—based in Hollywood—has performed on multiple late-night talk shows on syndicated television. After her happy participation, other comedians within the club immediately started scheduling appointments. With that entry into the standup world, I was able to recruit participants using snowballing techniques whereby participants referred other colleagues. Some reached out directly while others contacted me via email, social media, their agent, or even in person after a show.

Then, I used snowball sampling techniques and recruited participants without establishing a set number of respondents; instead, I added more participants as new dimensions become apparent in interviews.[79] During the investigation, I "systematically examine[d] concepts" then sorted "them into appropriate groups" to look for further patterns. After transcribing each interview, I carefully examined responses—based on survey demographics—and then excluded future participants when those groups no longer provided new information.

The comedy community is small and tight-knit, and the methodology proved very effective in recruiting a diverse group (see Appendix B for sociodemographics and health statistics). About one-fourth of the participants are cisgender white men. But over 50 percent of the participants are women, 50 percent are a racial or ethnic minority, and almost 50 percent identify as LGBTQ+. Some of the participants have survived cancer or live with cerebral palsy or multiple sclerosis, and almost two-thirds are living with mental illness, including depression, anxiety, PTSD, alcohol dependency, bipolar disorder, and schizoaffective disorder. While thirty-eight are single, twenty-seven are married, twenty-six are cohabiting or dating, and eight are currently divorced. About a fourth are parents. Over 50 percent have a college degree or higher. Most are employed full-time even though most are living off of $30,000 annually. Finally, about one fourth are professional comedians; thirty-three years was the longest career.

The guided in-depth interviews were straightforward and narrow in scope whereby I asked very pointed questions about how they use the stage to discuss very personal and intimate details of their life. Interviews began by describing themselves as children and their relationships with their families and communities. They were asked what stresses them and how they try to manage those stressors. They were then asked to describe personal experiences—including but not limited to mental illness and trauma—that they sometimes bring to the stage. They revealed how they introduced those subjects onstage, how their life was impacted by those public conversations, their relationships with the unknown audience, and their relationship with people who may have been particularly discriminating such as family. Interviews lasted from forty-five minutes to over two hours. Participants often revealed deeply personal experiences in this study that they had not disclosed to anyone else, even if they used the story in their comedy.

While many things can derail intimate conversations, the truth is, I could not have chosen a better group of people to study. Many aspects of our conversations were fun to have, like when they reminisced about how they got started behind the mic. For instance, Lawshawn laughed about bombing his first open-mic performance while still catching the comedy "bug." When I interviewed Lawshawn over Skype, he was on a comedy tour in Hawaii. He explained to me that he wanted to perform for many years but only worked up the courage after a life-changing car crash: "About four months earlier, I flipped my truck off a bridge, and if that didn't kill me, nothing would. My first night, it was awful. It was the worst. I went up at one-thirty. I got heckled. It was probably the worst feeling ever after flipping my truck off a bridge. And I loved every minute of it."

Some participants in the study had a more serious tone, like Carson, who recently became a full-time traveling comedian headliner in major comedy clubs. He dreams of reaching a high enough professional level to stop struggling financially, saying, "To do it full-time and make a full living from doing it. I do a couple of part-time jobs to help make ends meet. So, the quick answer is no, it does not provide enough. I want to get to a point where people are coming to see me, instead of just coming to a comedy show."

All participants understood the purpose of the study before I asked any questions. When I asked them to discuss their comedy careers at the beginning of our conversations, they quickly delved into personal details without any prompting. Rebecca, for instance, shared her painful truth within the first few moments of meeting her. This openness was not unique among the comedians. They were not only interested in the study, but also excited to engage in a pointed and personal inquiry. This method was particularly illuminating because the performative nature of comedy seemed to melt away, and their eagerness to talk about the truth behind their stories emerged. What I discovered was that while many of the standup comedians had immense skills onstage to garner laughs that signaled agreement, in this interview setting, where there were no laughs, participants found themselves revealing and explaining far more details.

After identifying how comedians used the stage to manage stigma, the second part of this study aimed to understand what might have been preventing some comedians from fully taking advantage of the "open" mic. Many of these answers came from follow-up questions. For example, if a comedian identified a romantic relationship as a major stressor in their life that they had not disclosed to the audience, I would ask, "Why have you not discussed that onstage?"

But the most important revealing question was often the last one in the interview: "How does the comedy world treat you based on your gender, race, ethnicity, or LGBTQ status?" The participants would then often swell up in emotions revealing atrocious behaviors they had to endure due to their gender, race, ethnicity, marital status, and LGBTQ+ status.

In the subsequent chapters, I will be discussing the emergent themes on stigma management. I will explore the available communication strategies for managing stigma, how individuals can recognize the social constraints of a stigma, and what happens when a stigma is visible or invisible. Additionally, I will examine how individuals cope when they are dealing with multiple problems simultaneously and how these mechanisms and processes differ for different people. Finally, I will explore how individuals can gain access to the most basic resource that is key to equality and eliminating stigma: their voice.

ENDURING DILEMMAS

During the initial stages of this project, one anthropologist challenged some of the conclusions regarding the limits of comedy and criticized the theoretical framework. As a comedy scholar who has studied how this art form can empower people, their concerns were twofold. Firstly, they believed that my view on the limits of comedy was too simplistic, as individuals and entire communities have found much more freedom and liberation in comedy than my analysis suggested. Secondly, they were concerned that although the sample size was large and diverse, there may be a bias issue where only those with negative experiences were captured. They suggested that because the participants are natural performers, they may have continued to perform during our interviews, which could compromise the accuracy of the findings.

Although there are no easy answers, there are several significant responses that can clarify the purpose of this book and alleviate any concerns. Firstly, research has shown the effectiveness of comedy in empowering marginalized individuals. Anthropology, communication, and media studies have conducted important work in comedy research, leading the way in this field. In the previous section, I referenced some of these fundamental studies when relevant to my examination of stigma and inequality in standup comedy.

But ultimately, this book is focused on one simple act: stepping in front of a faceless crowd and disclosing out loud a stigma. This book is approaching standup comedy as if it is a coping mechanism and trying to understand why some can use it, and others cannot. Importantly, I am not advocating for the use of comedy to cope. And in fact, drawing on participant experiences, I argue in later chapters that relying on standup for coping purposes is a bad idea. Nevertheless, while the other anthropological and media research is critically important for laying out a historical context of comedy, this book is not trying to challenge the authority of those comedy scholars. Nor is it trying to understand the macro institution or comedy (or entertainment) as a place to spur on social change though public engagement, although I do believe that this book provides insights into how inequality is reinforced through stigma, a subject that previous comedy scholars have yet to engage. Rather, I am using medical sociological theory (i.e., the modified labeling process and fundamental causality) to analyze one unique aspect of this important performative art—communal coping. If successful, my book will use comedy to provide insights into the sociology of stigma and stigma reduction.

While other anthropological and media research is critically important for laying out a historical context of comedy, this book is not trying to challenge the authority of those comedy scholars. Nor is it trying to understand the macro institution of comedy (or entertainment) as a place to spur on social change through public engagement. However, the book does provide insights into how inequality is reinforced through stigma, a subject that previous comedy scholars have yet to engage.

Instead, the book uses medical sociological theory to analyze one unique aspect of this important performative art—communal coping. If successful, the book will use comedy to provide insights into the sociology of stigma and stigma reduction.

I can certainly understand concerns about the potential bias in qualitative data like this. It's possible that standup comedians, being highly skilled in the art of oratory, may use those skills to their advantage during interviews. Additionally, there is a significant difference between the communication experience of standup comedians and that of the general population. Comedians make a career out of testing the boundaries of social norms and conventions, and they do so frequently and in front of diverse audiences, often experiencing failure along the way. Some comedians, particularly those in larger cities, perform on multiple stages each night, repeatedly practicing the same set. There are very few "natural" conversationalists in the comedy world; most comedians reach that level through repeated practice, failure, and opportunities to learn from their mistakes.

But qualitative methods, like those used in this book, are not seeking one truth. Rather, these methods are inductive and accept "multiple perspectives of truth" that is "constantly changing."[80] This book adopts an interpretive and constructive perspective that aims to build understanding by focusing on the shared meaning within a specific cultural arena, namely standup comedy. However, it also acknowledges that each individual interprets events differently due to their unique backgrounds, cultural histories, and social and emotional resources. As the quote states, "All accounts must be interpreted in terms of the context in which they were produced . . . The goal must be to discover the best manner of interpreting whatever data we have." This means that it's important to consider the context in which information is presented and to interpret it in the most effective way possible.[81] Although comedians may be primarily spinning a yarn, careful consideration of their background beyond comedy, as well as a historical understanding of inequality in the arts which is well documented, allows those potential pitfalls to be an incredible benefit for a study with my focus. Specifically, things like their continual conversation practice provides us ample direct insights into the peril of managing stigma.

What is important is that these methods do not deny that potential of bias. Rather, it is better to create "reflections" that acknowledge positionality of all parties as people with statuses and lived experiences that can affect all aspects of the study.[82] What are those biases? What are those oppressions? And how can our backgrounds bias and benefit the study?

ACKNOWLEDGING POSITIONALITY: YOU ARE NOT ALONE

This book aims to shed light on why so many people suffer in silence. The participants in this study are living with a stigma and have a vested interest in finding a remedy. I also have a personal interest in stigma reduction due to my own experiences. When I started this research, I asked participants to reveal deeply personal and painful truths, even though I had been hiding my truth for my entire life. My voice was shackled, unable to acknowledge my painful past. As a man raised in a military family, I had been taught not to show my feelings. Speaking about them would reveal my "weakness," so for more than thirty years, I remained silent. For three decades, I was unable to acknowledge that I was a child who was physically, emotionally, and sexually abused.

How I came to speak these truths was a result of various factors, interconnected throughout this book, that began with my conversation with Rebecca. Within three minutes of our discussion, Rebecca shared with me, a cisgender, white-passing Latino man, about her assault. She confided in a stranger that she had been raped. I was speechless, but I managed to ask if she was comfortable continuing the interview. For the next fifteen minutes, she recounted vivid personal details of the violent trauma, her months of physical therapy, and her fight in the court system. She told me how the rape shattered her identity. It was only after getting on the comedy stage and telling her story that she had the epiphany that she was still the person she knew herself to be.

As she shared her story with me, I struggled to hold back tears and keep my composure. While she seemed to be doing okay, I was not. When the interview was over, I thanked her and packed up my things. As soon as I was alone, I went to my room and cried. As she spoke, memories of my own childhood trauma came flooding back—the physical, emotional, and sexual abuse I had endured. But that conversation was the first step on a difficult path toward healing and truth-telling. I eventually shared my story with my spouse, parents, and other family members. Speaking with Rebecca was a critical first step, because she showed me that it was possible to thrive and be happy despite the trauma of rape. She was an inspiration to me and countless others, demonstrating that we can take charge of our lives and overcome seemingly insurmountable obstacles.

However, open conversations are not always universally helpful as some advocates may suggest. After about a year of researching and reflecting, I decided to share my truth with my wife and parents. My wife Amanda, who was a former advocate for domestic violence victims, was the perfect ally. She kindly and attentively listened to me, hugged me, and reassured me that everything would be okay. However, my parents' response was quite different. The conversation quickly turned into shouting, crying, and blaming. In just a few days, my relationship with my parents became so toxic that I completely cut off contact with them. It would take almost two years before I spoke with them again.

My hope is that as you moved through this chapter, you began to recognize that the stigma that creates discrimination is universal even when the details of the experience seem so radically different. One goal of this book is to build empathy, a cornerstone of open and productive, communal conversations.[83] Open conversations are powerful: I can personally attest to that. It would be a disservice to hide these details when the openness of the comedians featured in this book helped me heal.

ORGANIZATION OF THIS BOOK

The subsequent chapters are divided into several general and overlapping sections. Chapter 2 delves into topics that comedians try to cope with. The purpose of this section is to understand which topics are the most taboo. In chapter 2, we explore the invisible taboos that comedians have to verbalize so that the issue is known to the audience. At one end of the spectrum, comedians revealed that family conflict is generally easier to discuss in public. More difficult to disclose are issues like mental illness, cancer, and death and dying. And virtually unspeakable are issues related to the harm of children. In a later chapter, we will see how comedians discuss each of those topics and the specific tactics used.

In chapter 3, we explore the visible stigmas that some comedians must deal with, such as gender and sexuality. We'll also examine how a comedian's background can influence how an audience perceives them. Not only are personal experiences like trauma or abuse independently distressing, but the presence of a visible stigma can also create a barrier and limit a person's ability to discuss certain issues. While some comedians may have the skills to talk about these topics, it can be difficult to connect with an audience that is distracted by their visible differences.

In the next section, we will discuss the overall coping process over three chapters. Chapter 4 begins by highlighting how comedians recognize public perceptions of taboo subjects. Before revealing a stigma, comedians go through a process to understand potential reactions. At one end of the spectrum are long, productive dialogues where the comedians lead the audience. On the opposite end, comedians may conceal their experiences or even withdraw, fleeing from public reactions that include harassment and violence.

Chapter 5 delves into the specific tactics used to eliminate stigma during conversations. While we might expect honest and detailed conversations to lead to new understanding, comedians sometimes engage in subtle conversations that leave bread crumbs, or overcompensate. These tactics include veiled conversations, existing and resisting, advocacy, and compartmentalizing problems. According to the comedians, there are many ways to be seen, even if the audience doesn't know what they're looking at.

Chapter 6 takes an intersectional approach to highlight the importance of context. The chapter focuses on the experiences of Black and Latino individuals and reveals that marginalized people have different experiences. Some found it easier to speak openly within their own communities, while others felt constrained. Factors such as gender and location played a significant role in whether comedians were able to discuss taboo topics and heal. For Latino comedians, their voice seemed to be less restricted in the southwest compared to major metropolitan areas like Los Angeles. For Black comedians, their ability to speak varied depending on location, such as New York versus the Midwest or Deep South. Gender intersected negatively for both groups.

The next section delves into the positive outcomes and barriers obtained through the coping process. Chapter 7 highlights that while some people may feel the need to hide parts of themselves or even leave comedy altogether, there are many alternatives to open conversations. Regardless of whether they find closure on specific issues, many comedians find other valuable resources through performing, such as improved self-esteem or a sense of mastery that they can apply elsewhere. Some find healing through friendships and comradery, while others recognize the boundaries of comedy and choose to compartmentalize their issues.

Chapter 8, "The Structure and Culture of Inequality," delves into larger structural and systemic problems that pile on top of comedians and make managing stigma much less likely. Comedians reveal that the comedy world provides a confluence of stressors that exacerbate problems and counter any potential gain from comedy as a coping mechanism. Due to a culture of drug and alcohol use, poor sleep habits, and poverty, successful conversations provide little overall healing for comedians. Furthermore, comedians are still embedded in a culture that actively throws up roadblocks such as segregation, harassment, violence, blame, and financial exploitation that silence voices. Chapter 9 then ties all of these roadblocks together to illustrate those missed opportunities to heal, which are disproportionately felt by women, people of color, parents, and those who are LGBTQ+.

The last chapter concludes with a discussion of the key takeaways and lessons on stigma that could be applied outside comedy. Firstly, a fundamental issue driving stigma and inequality is segregation. Empathy requires social contact, and places like comedy are highly segregated. Despite these barriers, some people were able to cultivate positive outcomes with alternative processes. Two of the most important tactics for stigma management were growing interpersonal skills and compartmentalizing problems. The chapter then discusses the stigmatizing audience, who may themselves be hiding deeply troubling issues. Finally, the book's overall purpose is highlighted, which is to understand stigma, not celebrate comedy.

NOTES

1. Bernice A. Pescosolido et al., "'A Disease Like Any Other'? A Decade of Change in Public Reactions to Schizophrenia, Depression, and Alcohol Dependence," *American Journal of Psychiatry* 167, no. 11 (2010): 1321–30, https://doi.org/10.1176 /appi.ajp.2010.09121743; Bernice A. Pescosolido, Bianca Manago, and John Monahan, "Evolving Public Views on the Likelihood of Violence from People with Mental Illness: Stigma and Its Consequences," *Health Affairs* 38, no. 10 (2019): 1735–43.

2. Joie Acosta et al., *Mental Health Stigma in the Military*, RAND Corporation (Santa Monica, California, 2014).

3. S.2938 - Bipartisan Safer Communities Act. Public Law 117–159. Sponsor: Sen. Rubio, Marco [R-FL].

4. National Alliance on Mental Illness "Annual Report 2021" (Arlington, VA: National Alliance for Mental Illness, 2022).

5. Lisa M. Schwartz and Steven Woloshin, "Medical Marketing in the United States, 1997–2016," *JAMA* 321, no. 1 (January 1, 2019): 80, https://doi.org/10.1001 /jama.2018.19320.

6. Bernice A. Pescosolido, Brea L. Perry, and Anne C. Krendl, "Empowering the Next Generation to End Stigma by Starting the Conversation: Bring Change to Mind and the College Toolbox Project," *Journal of the American Academy of Child and Adolescent Psychiatry* 59, no. 4 (2020): 519–30, https://doi.org/10.1016/j.jaac.2019 .06.016.

7. Bernice A. Pescosolido et al., "Trends in Public Stigma of Mental Illness in the US, 1996–2018," *JAMA* Network Open 4, no. 12 (December 21, 2021): e2140202, https://doi.org/10.1001/jamanetworkopen.2021.40202.

8. M. Reinhart, D. Fritze, and T. Nguyen, "The State of Mental Health in America" (Alexandria, VA: Mental Health America, October 2021).

9. Graham Thornicroft et al., "Evidence for Effective Interventions to Reduce Mental-Health-Related Stigma and Discrimination," *The Lancet* 387, no. 10023 (2016): 1123–32, https://doi.org/10.1016/S0140-6736(15)00298-6; George Schomerus et al., "Do Attitudes Towards Persons with Mental Illness Worsen During the Course of Life? An Age-Period-Cohort Analysis," *Acta Psychiatrica Scandinavica* 132, no. 5 (2015): 357–64, https://doi.org/10.1111/acps.12401.

10. Pescosolido, Perry, and Krendl, "Empowering the Next Generation to End Stigma by Starting the Conversation: Bring Change to Mind and the College Toolbox Project."

11. National Alliance on Mental Illness, "Starting the Conversation: College and Your Mental Health," National Alliance on Mental Illness (Arlington, VA: National Alliance on Mental Illness, 2016); Jeffrey Borenstein, "Stigma, Prejudice and Discrimination Against People with Mental Illness," American Psychiatric Association, 2020, https://www.psychiatry.org/patients-families/stigma-and-discrimination.

12. W.K. Kellogg Foundation. Truth, Racial Healing & Transformation. April 18, 2023. https://healourcommunities.org/.

13. Willett and Willett, *Uproarious: How Feminists and Other Subversive Comics Speak Truth.*

14. Patrice A. Oppliger and Eric Shouse, eds., *The Dark Side of Standup Comedy* (London, UK: Palgrave, 2020).

15. Judy Berman, "'Nanette' Is the Most Discussed Comedy Special in Ages. Here's What to Read About It," *New York Times*, July 13, 2018, https://www.nytimes.com/2018/07/13/arts/television/nanette-hannah-gadsby-netflix-roundup.html.

16. "Comic Jerrod Carmichael Bares His Secrets in 'Rothaniel'" (NPR, December 28, 2022).

17. Rebecca Krefting, *All Joking Aside: American Humor and Its Discontents* (Baltimore: Johns Hopkins University Press, 2014).

18. James M. Thomas, *Working to Laugh: Assembling Difference in American Standup Comedy Venues* (Lanham, MD: Lexington Books, 2015): Mizejewski, *Pretty/Funny: Women Comedians and Body Politics*; Erin L. Kelly et al., "Changing Work and Work-Family Conflict: Evidence from the Work, Family, and Health Network," *American Sociological Review* 79, no. 3 (2014): 485–516, https://doi.org/10.1177/0003122414531435; Willett and Willett, *Uproarious: How Feminists and Other Subversive Comics Speak Truth.*

19. Susan Seizer, "On the Uses of Obscenity in Live Standup Comedy," *Anthropological Quarterly* 84, no. 1 (2011): 209–34, https://doi.org/10.1353/anq.2011.0001.

20. Judy Batalion, ed., *The Laughing Stalk: Live Comedy and Its Audiences* (Anderson, SC: Parlor Press, 2011).

21. Ian Brodie, *A Vulgar Art: A New Approach to Stand-Up Comedy* (Jackson: University Press of Mississippi, 2014).

22. Jeffrey P. Jones, *Entertaining Politics: Satiric Television and Political Engagement* (Lanham, MD: Rowman & Littlefield, 2009).

23. Cynthia Willett and Julie Willett, *Uproarious: How Feminists and Other Subversive Comics Speak Truth* (Minneapolis: University of Minnesota Press, 2019).

24. Chattoo and Feldman, *A Comedian and an Activist Walk into a Bar: The Serious Role of Comedy in Social Justice.*

25. Raúl Pérez, "Learning to Make Racism Funny in the 'Color-Blind' Era: Stand-up Comedy Students, Performance Strategies, and the (Re)Production of Racist Jokes in Public," *Discourse and Society* 24, no. 4 (2013): 478–503, https://doi.org/10.1177/0957926513482066; Elise Decamp, "Humoring the Audience: Performance Strategies and Persuasion in Midwestern American Stand-up Comedy," *Humor* 28, no. 3 (2015): 449–67, https://doi.org/10.1515/humor-2015-0067.

26. Maya Twardzicki and Norman Jones, "'Have You Heard the One About . . .' Using Comedy to Tackle Mental Health-Related Stigma with UK Military Personnel?," *Journal of Public Mental Health* 16, no. 1 (2017): 9–11, https://doi.org/10.1108/JPMH-03-2016-0017.

27. Susan Seizer, "Dialogic Catharsis in Standup Comedy: Stewart Huff Plays a Bigot," *Humor* 30, no. 2 (2017): 211–37, https://doi.org/10.1515/humor-2016-0026.

28. Caty Borum Chattoo and Lauren Feldman, *A Comedian and an Activist Walk into a Bar: The Serious Role of Comedy in Social Justice* (Oakland: University of California Press, 2020).

29. Maya Twardzicki and Norman Jones, "'Have You Heard the One about . . .' Using Comedy to Tackle Mental Health-Related Stigma with UK Military

Personnel?," *Journal of Public Mental Health* 16, no. 1 (2017): 9–11, https://doi.org/10.1108/JPMH-03-2016-0017.

30. Rudnick et al., "Humour-Related Interventions for People with Mental Illness: A Randomized Controlled Pilot Study."

31. Norman Jones et al., "Modifying Attitudes to Mental Health Using Comedy as a Delivery Medium," *Social Psychiatry and Psychiatric Epidemiology* 49 (2014): 1667–76, https://doi.org/10.1007/s00127-014-0868-2.

32. Steve Wright et al., "Evaluation of a Comedy Intervention to Improve Coping and Help-Seeking for Mental Health Problems in a Women's Prison," *International Review of Psychiatry* 26, no. 4 (2014): 423–29, https://doi.org/10.3109/09540261.2014.924096.

33. Peter McGraw and Joel Warner, *The Humor Code: A Global Search for What Makes Things Funny* (New York: Simon & Schuster, 2014).

34. McGraw and Warner, *The Humor Code: A Global Search for What Makes Things Funny.*

35. Joanne R. Gilbert, *Performing Marginality: Humor, Gender, and Cultural Critique* (Detroit, MI: Wayne State University Press, 2004).

36. Bambi Haggins, *Laughing Mad: The Black Comic Persona in Post-Soul America* (New Brunswick, NJ: Rutgers University Press, 2007).

37. DeRochers, *The Comic Offense from Vaudeville to Contemporary Comedy: Larry David, Tina Fey, Stephen Colbert, and Dave Chappelle.*

38. Krefting, *All Joking Aside: American Humor and Its Discontents.*

39. Kulvir Lheal, "Lenny Bruce: 'Are There Any Niggers Here Tonight?,'" *Medium*, September 2016, https://medium.com/applaudience/lenny-bruce-are-there-any-niggers-here-tonight-71c6cf9f2a2c.

40. Scott Bomboy, "Looking Back: George Carlin and the Supreme Court," National Constitution Center, 2019, https://constitutioncenter.org/blog/a-controversial-order-leads-to-internment-camps.

41. Michael Oricchio, "Pryor Wrote the Book on Comedy and Now, a Memoir of His Tumultuous Life," *The Baltimore Sun*, May 31, 1995, https://www.nydailynews.com/bs-xpm-1995-05-31-1995151149-story.html.

42. Bethany Parker, "Probing Question: What Are the Roots of Stand-up Comedy?" (Penn State, 2008).

43. David Monod, *Vaudeville and the Making of Modern Entertainment, 1890–1925* (Chapel Hill: University of North Carolina Press, 2020); Sammond Nicholas, *Birth of an Industry: Blackface Minstrelsy and the Rise of American Animation* (Durham, NC: Duke University Press, 2015).

44. Alexis Soloski, "The (Elegant, Brazen, Brainy) Pioneering Women of Comedy," *New York Times*, November 21, 2017.

45. Anam Rana Afzal, "How Lucille Ball Fought the Patriarchy, While Lucy Ricardo (Indirectly) Contributed to Second-Wave (White) Feminism" (City University of New York, 2018).

46. Linda Mizekewski, *Pretty/Funny: Women Comedians and Body Politics* (Austin: University of Texas Press, 2014).

47. Angela Rosenthal, David Bindman, and Adrian W. B. Randolph, eds., *No Laughing Matter: Visual Humor in Ideas of Race, Nationality, and Ethnicity* (Chicago: Chicago University Press, n.d.).

48. Rick DeRochers, *The Comic Offense from Vaudeville to Contemporary Comedy: Larry David, Tina Fey, Stephen Colbert, and Dave Chappelle* (New York: Bloomsbury, 2014).

49. David S. Pedulla and Sarah Thébaud, "Can We Finish the Revolution? Gender, Work-Family Ideals, and Institutional Constraint," *American Sociological Review* 39, no. 1 (2015): 116–39, https://doi.org/10.1177/0003122414564008.

50. Haggins, *Laughing Mad: The Black Comic Persona in Post-Soul America*.

51. Jude Dry, "Stephen Colbert's Most Anti-Trump Act Is Giving Diverse Stand-Up a Platform," *Indie Wire*, August 4, 2017.

52. Chattoo and Feldman, *A Comedian and an Activist Walk into a Bar: The Serious Role of Comedy in Social Justice*.

53. Stand Up Comedian Demographics and Statistics in the Us. Zippia: The Career Expert. April 18, 2023.

54. Elizabeth A. Harris, "Amy Schumer, Ali Wong and the Rise of Pregnant Stand-Up," *New York Times*, April 19, 2019.

55. Thomas, *Working to Laugh: Assembling Difference in American Stand-Up Comedy Venues*: Jeffries, *Behind the Laughs: Community and Inequality*.

56. By Meredith Kachel and Austin Sheaffer, "What's the Deal with Standup Comedy Bookings?: Using Data to Show Discrepancies in Gender in Chicago's Stand-Up Comedy Scene," Meredith Kachel, 2017.

57. Patricia M. Smith et al., Office of Federal Contract Compliance Programs, United States Department of Labor v. Google, Inc., (January 4, 2017).

58. Shelley J. Correll, Stephen Benard, and In Paik, "Getting a Job: Is There a Motherhood Penalty?," *American Journal of Sociology* 112, no. 5 (2007): 1297–1339, https://doi.org/10.1086/511799; Devah Pager, "The Mark of a Criminal Record," *American Sociological Review* 103, no. March (2003): 937–75, https://doi.org/10.1086/374403; Natasha Quadlin, "The Mark of a Woman's Record: Gender and Academic Performance in Hiring," *American Sociological Review* 83, no. 2 (April 15, 2018): 331–60, https://doi.org/10.1177/0003122418762291.

59. Linda Mizejewski and Victoria Sturtevant, eds., *Hysterical!: Women in American Comedy* (Austin: University of Texas Press, 2017).

60. Thomas, *Working to Laugh: Assembling Difference in American Stand-Up Comedy Venues*.

61. Terrence T. Tucker, *Furiously Funny: Comic Rage from Ralph Ellison to Chris Rock* (Tallahassee: University Press of Florida, 2018).

62. Tanya Gonzalez and Eliza Rodriguez y Gibson, *Humor and Latina/o Camp in Ugly Betty: Funny Looking* (Lanham, MD: Lexington Books, 2015).

63. Bruce G. Link and Jo C. Phelan, "Social Conditions as Fundamental Causes of Disease," *Journal of Health and Social Behavior* 35, no. Extra Issue: Forty Years of Medical Sociology: The State of the Art and Directions for the Future (1995): 80–94.

64. Michael P. Jeffries, *Behind the Laughs: Community and Inequality* (Stanford, CA: Stanford University Press, 2018).

65. Carly Mallenbaum, Patrick Ryan, and Maria Puente, "A Complete List of the 60 Bill Cosby Accusers and Their Reactions to His Prison Sentence," *USA Today*, September 26, 2018.

66. Molly Redden, "Louis CK Accused by Five Women of Sexual Misconduct in New Report," *The Guardian*, November 9, 2017.

67. Amy Kaufman, "After Twitter Outcry, Five Women Detail Chris D'Elia's Alleged Sexual Improprieties," *L.A. Times*, June 20, 2020.

68. Amy Kaufman, "Actor Bryan Callen Accused of Sexual Assault, Misconduct," *L.A. Times*, July 20, 2020.

69. Nick Marx, Matt Sienkiewicz, and Ron Becker, eds., *Saturday Night Live and American TV* (Bloomington: Indiana University Press, 2013).

70. Joseph G. Lehman, "A Brief Explanation of the Overton Window," Mackinac Center, 2019, https://www.mackinac.org/OvertonWindow.

71. Jones, Entertaining Politics: Satiric Television and Political Engagement (Communication, Media, and Politics).

72. Annette McDermott, "Did World War II Launch the Civil Rights Movement?," History, 2018, https://www.history.com/news/did-world-war-ii-launch-the-civil-rights-movement.

73. Oricchio, "Pryor Wrote the Book on Comedy and Now, a Memoir of His Tumultuous Life.": The Telegraph, "Obituaries: George Carlin," *The Telegraph*, June 23, 2008.

74. Cecil Brown, *Pryor Lives!: How Richard Pryor Became Richard Pryor or Kiss My Rich, Happy Black . . . Ass! A Memoir* (CreateSpace Independent Publishing Platform, 2013).

75. Dannagal Goltwaite Young, *Irony and Outrage: The Polarized Landscape of Rage, Fear, and Laughter in the United States* (New York: Oxford University Press, 2019).

76. Rubin and Rubin, *Qualitative Interviewing: The Art of Hearing Data*.

77. Ben K. Beitin, "Interview and Sampling," in *The Sage Handbook of Interview Research: The Complexity of the Craft*, ed. David Pilgrim, Anne Rogers, and Bernice Pescosolido (Thousand Oaks, CA: Sage, 2012), 243–52, https://doi.org/10.1016/j.colsurfa.2008.07.019.

78. Herbert J. Rubin and Irene S. Rubin, "Why We Do What We Do: Philosophy of Qualitative Interviewing," in *Qualitative Interviewing: The Art of Hearing Data* (Thousand Oaks, CA: Sage, 2005), 19–38, https://doi.org/10.4135/9781452226651.n2; Herbert J. Rubin and Irene S. Rubin, *Qualitative Interviewing: The Art of Hearing Data* (Thousand Oaks, CA: Sage Publications, Inc., 2002).

79. Irving Seidman, *Interviewing as Qualitative Research: A Guide for Researchers in Education and the Social Sciences* (New York: Teachers College Press, 2006).

80. Herbert J. Rubin and Irene S. Rubin, "Why We Do What We Do: Philosophy of Qualitative Interviewing," in *Qualitative Interviewing: The Art of Hearing Data* (Thousand Oaks, CA: Sage, 2005), 19–38, https://doi.org/10.4135/9781452226651.n2.

81. Martyn Hammersley and Paul Atkinson, *Ethnography, Ethnography* (New York: Taylor & Francis, 2007), 102., https://doi.org/10.4324/9780203944769.

82. Herbert J. Rubin and Irene S. Rubin, "Research Philosophy and Qualitative Interviews," in *Qualitative Interviewing: The Art of Hearing Data* (Thousand Oaks, CA: Sage, 2012).

83. Graham Thornicroft et al., "Evidence for Effective Interventions to Reduce Mental-Health-Related Stigma and Discrimination," *The Lancet* 387, no. 10023 (2016): 1123–32, https://doi.org/10.1016/S0140-6736(15)00298-6; Sam McFarland, "Authoritarianism, Social Dominance, and Other Roots of Generalized Prejudice," *Political Psychology* 31, no. 3 (2010): 453–77, https://doi.org/10.1111/j.1467-9221.2010.00765.x; Renee F. Lyons et al., "Coping As A Communal Process," *Journal of Social and Personal Relationships1* 15, no. 5 (1998): 579–605.

Chapter 2

Invisible Stigma from Least to Most Taboo

In an ideal world, individuals should be able to openly discuss their problems when coping. However, when two people deal with what seems to be a similar issue, their personal perception of it and how their audience perceives it can be vastly different. This was the case with Vivian and Chacha, two middle-aged women who both experienced destructive relationships. Vivian, a middle-aged white woman, explained how she felt constrained from discussing her divorce in public.

> When I got divorced, some people say that is what you are going to draw upon in your comedy. But my ex was adamant that I did not talk about him in my stand-up. A few times, I even tried to talk about it. There is a lot of stuff I need to set up in the first parts of my stand-up. Having a kid and being divorced. Dating. The few times he found out that I had a joke about him, he flipped out. That's an area that I haven't been able to explore.

Vivian is unable to discuss her relationship due to an immediate threat from her ex. As a result, she masks the details of her divorce by focusing on the consequences of being single. In contrast, Chacha, a Latina woman, openly discusses her relationships and even shares some of the worst aspects of her abusive relationship with her ex.

> It was really bad. An ex stalked me. This was about ten years ago. The guy broke into my apartment. He called the phone company and told them I was dead. Called my boss. Called my husband. Told them all these lies about me. Slashed my tires. The apartment complex that I was living in actually let me leave and break my contract because they didn't want him coming around. It was a really horrifying experience because I was a single mom. I had my kids. I just pray to God that he never comes to any of my shows. That person is still out there. I haven't seen him in many years. But there is no reason for him not to be in the area.

Chacha is somewhat hesitant, saying "I still fear that he is out there, and he'll hear it," but she believes that the likelihood of violence is low, especially with the support of her current husband. Therefore, she is open to discussing her issues in public. However, Vivian is still unable to discuss her circumstances because her ex is still a part of her life. The potential negative consequences are greater for Chacha, but the likelihood of harm occurring is much higher for Vivian. Most importantly, they demonstrate that speaking truth to power is an unequal process. Some subjects may be more difficult than others to openly discuss, depending on the individual and the social situation. Critically, Chacha and Vivian show that taboos can exist on a spectrum of discrimination. The more severe the expected reaction, the more extreme the coping mechanism, and the less likely a person will be able to be fully seen. Before we can address these coping mechanisms, we must first identify and categorize the issues that are causing distress. Therefore, in this first chapter, we will identify and categorize those issues that are typically the most taboo for individuals seeking closure.

INVISIBLE FAMILY CONFLICTS

The least stigmatized topic that comedians could discuss onstage is family conflict. Although some issues like child abuse were extremely taboo, as I will discuss later in the chapter, family issues tended to elicit a wide range of expected public reactions. Conflicts with parents, for example, were often personally stressful but only moderately taboo to the audience. Comedians were generally comfortable discussing those relationships, although they sometimes omitted details. For instance, a young man called Zachary used the comedy stage to analyze his parents' expectations in a middle-class family.

> I was raised in a suburban household, so there was a lot of pressure for me to succeed. There were a lot of avenues for me to succeed, and I just didn't take any of them. My dad was at one of my shows, and it was pretty stressful because I just dropped out of college. I told him this is what I want to do, and he said, well, let's see if you have what it takes. To show my dad that I don't want to go back to school, I want to do this [comedy]. And it's like, if it doesn't go well, he'll probably rag on me for dropping out. I can tell now that he's still worried about what a flimsy career to go after. It's not like a, set in stone, paycheck every two weeks [kind of job]. I can tell he is disappointed that I'm not doing what he thought I would do, but he's happy that I am doing something.

On the other hand, Alejandra often uses comedy to cope with her mother's behavior following the death of her father.

She wasn't there. She took care of me financially, but she wasn't there. I've always been really hurt about that. I did a show where the theme was "love will tear us apart." So, I told a story about how my mom would always hurt my feelings. One time for my birthday, we were getting waffles, and she said: "Would you speed this up." After my dad died, we stopped having birthday parties for all of us [her and her siblings]. She finally took me out for my birthday and told me to speed it up. She told me she had an A.A. meeting, but I know that meant she was meeting a guy. I didn't see my mom all week. It had been an hour of us eating, and I start crying heavily. This lady comes over and is checking on me. And my mom says, "No, she fine, she's worked up." And I remember being so hurt that my mom treated me like I was not important.

Both comedians are willing to speak publicly about their parental relationships because it's not a taboo subject for their audiences. Zachary feels comfortable expressing his thoughts and can connect well with people of all ages, including his parents. He says, "I was always a little scared of my parents. And onstage, I can just say whatever I want. There are not all these pressures from them."

Similarly, Alejandra is comfortable discussing these topics publicly, but she expects pushbacks. She often avoids discussing the most painful details, such as the time her mother missed her wedding dress fitting. This is a pain that she is still working through because she has yet to find humor in it. Recently, she was able to discuss this pain with her husband, and the moment was excruciating; she broke down, sobbing.

The comedy stage offers a platform to openly discuss experiences that many people have either lived through or witnessed. This allows these issues to be seen and discussed in an open and honest manner. As we continue to progress, however, it's important to note that other topics may remain taboo and become even harder to discuss. Nonetheless, comedy remains a powerful tool to shed light on hidden topics and start important conversations.

PARENTS AND RELIGION

Like many young people, some of the participants revealed that their perspective on religion had caused conflict with their parents in their personal lives. The amount of turmoil that these issues brought to a comedian's life varied radically. For instance, Ross, a thirty-nine-year-old white man who grew up as the son of a pastor in the Midwest, is a deeply religious person shaped by his relationship with his parents, which has grown and changed over the years. He said, "I've been thinking about religion my whole life. When I was a kid, I used to read a proverb after dinner every day. I had to read a psalm and write about it. I had to read and write before dinner so that I could share it after dinner." He continued by explaining how his relationship with his family had changed over the years, relying on different parents at different ages. Despite his parents being devout Christians, they nurtured his curiosity around religion, embracing those conversations.

> My relationship with my dad has been the most impactful in my life. Both positive and negative. I'm very close to him. He definitely has influenced my beliefs, my worldviews, my religious thought. I was closer with my mom when I was younger, but grew closer with him after college. I've definitely talked about religious things in a non-comedic sense with him for years. A lot of my connection with my father over the years came through those conversations.

Although Ross holds different views from his family, his relationship with them remains strong, which has enabled him to voice his opinions more freely. He expresses his thoughts on religion during his comedy performances, and his family is willing to listen, even though they know that others in the community may be offended. Ross says, "I did a tour a couple of years ago, and my family came out and heard it all. I also released an album, and they've heard that material too. My dad and mom have listened to it, and my older sister is very supportive. When my album came out, my dad asked me if I was okay with potentially offending anyone with the content, but he was still supportive."

Contrast Ross with Dylan, a millennial Indian American. His family members are devout, practicing Sikhs. They hold a conservative religious perspective that creates a lot of conflicts between him and the family, particularly his father:

> In India, if you are born into a family with a religion, you are that religion. They were very strict when I grew up. I had to visit the temple every Sunday. I had to wear a turban. I'll give you an example: online there are flyers for my comedy show. A Sikh is supposed to include their middle name that I dropped. My dad gets mad. But it's not only in comedy. Let's say at work if I don't include that middle name; he gets mad. I don't have it on my resident's card, [if it] doesn't have that middle name, he gets mad. He gets bothered by these simple things.

Despite the religious turmoil in his family, discussing religion in comedy was not considered taboo. Many comedians, like George Carlin, who discuss religion onstage, even in a critical manner, are well-received. Even conservative audiences are willing to discuss religion, albeit within certain limits, as demonstrated by Ross. As a liberal and religious person from a more conservative background, Ross understands these multiple boundaries and has been successful in navigating the subject matter, regardless of the audience.

When I first started talking about religion onstage, it was scarier to talk about that because I thought, am I going to be viewed differently by other comedians? Are they going to be less accepting of me as a comedian? Are they going to think I'm stupid or an idiot for having beliefs? Audiences, how are they going to relate to this? Christian audiences, are they going to be upset by this? The danger was that I was going to upset everybody. Christian, atheist, everyone in between. But I don't really have that problem.

Similarly, Dylan focuses heavily on religion, drawing from his Sikh faith. He enjoys discussing it with the audience, believing that they appreciate the topic because he is simply pointing out "obvious" flaws in religion:

Right now, about 40 percent of my comedy would be about my religion. It's not like I am trying to convert anyone, and I'm not a very religious person. I want to share the information and make fun of what can be made fun of. I am just making fun of the facts that religion presents. I'm not making stuff up; I'm talking about the facts. I am offering them in a way so you can see how ridiculous they are. For instance, you don't have the ability to change religion. The religion is about who you were born, not what you believe. That's my problem with it.

Despite being part of a stricter religious community, Dylan is happy to openly discuss religion, and has found a great deal of acceptance. He has even shared his ideas with members of his Sikh temple, testing and refining his beliefs through discussion and debate:

I had people from the temple, three dudes a couple of months back. I actually changed my set to only talk about religion. My wife sent me a text during my set that said, "They're not going to laugh at this. You are inviting trouble." In the end, they thought it was hilarious; well, two of those three enjoyed it. The other one was on edge. The other two were sending me text making fun of the set, callbacks to my set.

The only significant difference between Shane and Dylan is that Dylan expects a slightly angrier response from his family. In fact, he typically avoids the conversation that he desperately wants to have. "Maybe as a kid, questions here and there, but I probably got shut down from them, 'No, this is what we do.' Every now and then, if things are brought up, I'd portray my views, but it does not go well," Dylan explains. Despite his good intentions, Dylan's family and community are unwilling to listen to him. "The things, the flaws that I put forth, I just want them to hear it and think that, okay, that's logical enough, that's scientific enough, and that part of the religion doesn't make sense. But at the same time, I know that they would not listen. I don't want to trouble them for no reason."

Due to his family dynamics outside of comedy, Dylan is more aware of his audience and who is listening. As a precaution, he has never posted any videos online to ensure that his parents do not discover his ideas. This task is challenging since Dylan has been named the funniest comic in his southwestern city.

Dylan and Ross show that a person's ability to speak is influenced by their cultural background, even if they appear to be protected from it. Although the comedy community does not create many obstacles for those who want to discuss religion, external relationships can have an impact. Ross has a close relationship with his family, who enjoy religious conversations, so he can speak freely in public. In contrast, Dylan is careful not to let his comedy reach his family because they will not be pleased. In other words, he cannot say anything he wants, even if it is amusing.

ROMANTIC RELATIONSHIPS.

Romantic relationships vary in their level of public acceptance. Gabby, for example, not only feels comfortable discussing her dating life and sexual experiences onstage, but also with anyone in her personal life. She has even talked openly about sexual behaviors with her mother, in addition to her friends:

> My comedy is dirty and referential. I talk about ex-boyfriends and dates. I shared a whole bunch of text messages and a letter I shared with my ex. There were things that came up for me while I was sharing it, but for the most part, I dealt with it. My first joke right out of the gate is about masturbating to a .gif on Tumblr. I talk about it all the time. My sisters. My mom. My friends. I told a whole group of friends on the way to a concert about this one account they needed to get on Tumblr so they could masturbate.

Although Gabby's comedy can be obscene and irreverent at times, she is not describing anything particularly triggering, at least not compared to other women on the opposite end of the spectrum, like Judith, who discussed a very troubling and traumatic relationship with an ex-partner:

> I had a breakup. I was living with somebody. We had been living together for almost six years. He had told me, not quite three weeks before he left, that he thought it was okay that we start getting pregnant. Then he left me in a text message breaking up. It was the first joke I ever wrote. I still tell it sometimes. It's quite cathartic. I'm glad he did it now, for many reasons, but it was still a very traumatic experience that kind of shaped the fact that I'm even onstage.

Both Gabby and Judith are very open about their experiences, sharing explicit details of their sexual encounters and painful breakups. Gabby, who is mostly a content comedian, doesn't find her relationship issues painful at all. On the other hand, Judith found her experiences distressing, but with the help of health services and her family's support, she was able to find closure before taking the stage. She says, "My family rallied behind me." Like many others, relationships eventually become material for their comedy sets. In both cases, their family's acceptance played a significant role in their ability to be seen. It was only after their families accepted them that they were able to overcome self-discrimination.

PARENTHOOD

Parenthood was another moderately taboo subject on average. Many comedians did not expect to face public backlash for discussing it, including interview participant Mika, an Asian woman in her mid-thirties. Her most recent stand-up routine focuses on her pregnancy and the gender of her baby:

> Lately, I talk about being a mom or being a pregnant person. Right now, it's less about my experience as being pregnant, and more about my experience of other people wanting to know stuff about gender with my baby. We didn't find out the gender of our child on purpose. The reason we decided to not know about gender was because your genitals do not determine it. And we knew that if we found out one way or the other it would change people's expectations of the baby. Gifts would be all blue or all pink. It is so interesting to me that so many people have to know the gender. That is the first question they ask when they saw that I was pregnant. Is it a boy or a girl? It's weird that everyone has to know the gender in the context of a baby. How silly is that? My baby is not doing anything gendered, particularly in utero. Why is this need-to-know information?

One reason why discussing pregnancy and parenthood may not be taboo is the region where one lives. As Mika explains, she lives in a progressive community where these topics are openly discussed. After giving birth to her child, she continued the conversation by advocating for gender non-conforming individuals in the LGBTQ+ community. Mika believes that her perspective as a cis-gendered woman can help highlight the absurdity of gender norms and gain support from the LGBT community. In general, Mika has not faced much resistance when discussing pregnancy and parenthood, which is not surprising given that her circumstances are typical in liberal communities.

Most importantly, Mika is a millennial professional in a supportive marriage. If any of those factors were taken away or if she lived in a conservative community, motherhood would be stigmatized for her. On the other hand,

Bianca is a middle-aged single mom and devout Christian who became pregnant as a teen and has faced stigma as a single, Latina mother:

> I talk about being a single mom and getting pregnant in my teens. I make fun of being pregnant in my teens. Sometimes that makes people uncomfortable and judge me. I'm a Latina, so I always throw that in there to talk about the clichés. But I'm not ashamed of it. I have this joke where I talk about how I was literally breastfeeding in high school, which is how I got pregnant. I love that joke.

Bianca enjoys discussing her experiences and performing for fellow Christians, but unfortunately, the community can be unaccepting and judgmental. Teen pregnancy is too taboo for Christian audiences, which makes it difficult for Bianca to share her message. As a result, she no longer performs her comedy in front of that audience, even though she wants to advocate for young Christian women who may find themselves in similar situations.

> I used to do churches all the time a long time ago, when I had thirty minutes that were totally "clean." But my life is not clean; no one's life is pure. So, if they think that being a Christian means you can't talk about being pregnant, and young, and having a drug-addicted parent, all the abuse, the things that we go through. There are Christians that go through the exact same things. Some are hooked on pornography. That are doing drugs or are cheating on their spouse. And no one talks about it. It's like, put on a smile and praise Jesus. I'm not that kind of Christian, and I don't think God gave me this gift to be that kind of Christian. Jesus wasn't. He called people out all the time.

Both Mika and Bianca are able to openly discuss their experiences as mothers, but the audience they are speaking to plays a significant role in determining their approach. Mika is often praised for discussing gender-related topics, but this is typically within a liberal and LGBTQ+ friendly community. On the other hand, Bianca faces challenges discussing her experiences as a mother in front of a Christian audience and has even been disinvited from speaking engagements. Despite the fact that her work could help destigmatize and liberate other teen mothers within these communities, she endures pushback. This may be due, in part, to her gender, as compared to Dylan and Ross who are able to engage with their religious communities. It's possible that Bianca's community may be more hesitant to hear a woman speak, particularly if her message implies that single motherhood is not inherently sinful and could be fruitful with support from the church.

FAMILY VIOLENCE

The level of violence in family issues consistently made it harder to discuss them openly. Comedians often chose to hide these topics from the world. For instance, Marvin jokes about his mom's relationship with his ex-girlfriend, saying, "I haven't talked to my ex-girlfriend in months, and she and my mom have a Snapchat streak." Despite their past relationship, Marvin's mom and ex-girlfriend remain friends.

However, there is also Leonel, who was introduced in an earlier chapter. He was in an abusive relationship, but only recently revealed the truth about his victimhood. Leonel expressed his concerns about how others might perceive him, saying, "I don't know how they'll perceive me, whether they'll judge me negatively. As a man, you can't talk about that. I really didn't start talking about my personal life until maybe in the last three years. There was a little bit of me in it, but it was more observational."

While Marvin and Leonel were talking, it became apparent that Marvin's experience was much less taboo, albeit a little embarrassing, as his mom stole his girlfriend. Nevertheless, he has openly discussed it onstage since the beginning. In contrast, Leonel took much longer to open up about his experiences due to the pain and suffering involved.

For others, family events are so traumatic, comedians are virtually paralyzed onstage. Jada, a twenty-nine-year-old Black woman, is one of those people who experiences social paralysis due to her family history. She suffers from a significant illness that requires her to undergo dialysis three times a week. This has led her to develop a chronic fear of death, which stems directly from her father's traumatic death: "The way my dad died was one of my worst fears. He had a massive heart attack and was dead for three days before they found him. My worst fear would be to die, and nobody would know." This fear even affects her relationships with friends and family. "If I have friends that I haven't talked to in three days, I'm calling them, and they are not answering. By the third day, I'm freaking out."

Jada grew up without her father, which is still a painful experience for her. To cope with his death, she made a joke about cremation. However, she recently learned some tragic information about her father, which sheds new light on his character. This has inspired her to share some of those stories onstage:

He was an orphan at the age of six. He had three brothers; one was adopted and taken away to Dallas. These white people adopted him and his other brother. And they had to work. You got up in the morning, and you worked. You went to school, and you worked. You ate, and you went to sleep. By the time they were teenagers, they were on their own. They didn't have stable parents, and it showed. I wish I had known while he was still alive. And I wish I had talked with him then; too late now. People treated my dad badly. No matter what kind of person my dad was, he always wanted to help people. People were supposed to do right by him, and they didn't.

Jada has a joke in her back pocket, but she currently deems it too taboo to attempt onstage. Similarly, Bianca, who we met a moment ago, falls into the same category. Discussing the abuse she endured at the hands of her father is too traumatic for her to do publicly:

> My dad was very physically abusive, and he drank to medicate. Back then, people didn't really understand depression. He's never been diagnosed, but it was always pretty violent in my house. I had three brothers, and I was the only girl. My two older brothers dealt with it by leaving the house and/or doing drugs or whatever else. They would always be gone. I was the girl, and I had a little brother, and I could never leave because I had to take care of my little brother. And in a Latino family, we [the women] do the dishes; we do the laundry, we take care of the other kids, I have always been the mom. My mom is amazing; she would throw herself in front of my father. She's always been protective in that way, but I've always had to protect her because she was always so emotional. My mom divorced my father because of me. I told her that if she didn't leave him, I was going to kill myself. And I meant it because I was so depressed, I just didn't want to live in that sort of house and abuse. And my dad hated the fact that I was a girl but loved that he had a slave. And I could see the pain she was in. He almost killed her several times.

Thanks to her spirituality and decades of quiet reflection, Bianca has achieved closure regarding the abuse. However, she has not been able to talk publicly about it successfully, and she may never find the words for the comedy stage. "I've tried to talk about my dad onstage for probably the last ten years. I have been doing comedy for about nineteen years. It's this Jenga of what do I tell the audience, and I still don't know," she said. Despite her skills, the conversation is driven by the crowd. "The audience feels disrespected, and they feel sorry for you."

DEATH AND HARM TO CHILDREN: ALMOST ALWAYS TABOO

Some comedians have tackled the difficult topic of death onstage, which is no easy task. However, the audience's reaction seems to be most influenced by who is affected by the tragedy, whether it be children or adults. For example, Diego, a Latino in his mid-thirties, frequently travels between the United

States and Puerto Rico to visit his family. During a recent trip, his sister passed away suddenly, a traumatic event that has deeply affected his family. Diego shared, "A few days before this past Christmas, my sister passed away from a heart attack. I was the one who took her to the hospital and spent her last night with her. We spent it together. It was difficult. I only spent two weeks in Puerto Rico, and 98 percent of that time was spent dealing with what had happened. It was like a nuclear bomb on my happiness."

Although discussing his sister's death on the comedy stage was difficult for Diego, he was successful. The audience was receptive, and Diego believes that the stage was the right place to honor his sister who he believes would have been supportive.

> I came back to Chicago and hosted my mic. There were about twenty to twenty-five people there. I talked about what happened. I wrote out jokes, and I got people to hear my story and hear how I felt and got the release of the tensions. I had gone through something, and they [fellow comedians] didn't know how to talk to me about it or talk about it themselves. I felt that my sister would have wanted me to say something. She wouldn't have been the one to hold back or bite her tongue. If this is what I want to do, then go ahead. I did, and it got laughs. It got a lot of laughs, and it was very funny. They loved it. And for a split second, it helped me forget.

But there is Nyah, a middle-aged Black woman who lost her baby boy. She has had no success in bringing her story to the comedy world. She silently grieves and fears that the audience will respond poorly:

> My firstborn passed away in 2002. He contracted meningitis. He was eleven. My deceased son is definitely a topic that I can't even begin to approach. I want to because I have seen others do it. It wasn't a bereaved parent; it was a bereaved daughter. I've seen comics who have managed. Some comics knock the absurdity of the way society looks at death. It can be done, but I'm nowhere near being able to approach that subject.

Similarly, Carmen, a forty-four-year-old Latina, refuses to use humor when discussing the sexual trauma she endured as a child, which she blames entirely on her mother:

> I had one life with my mom, and I had one life with my grandparents. They were very polar opposites. During the summer and Christmas break, I would live with my grandparents. We went to church and would have priests over for dinner. We'd watch Mr. Rogers. We'd watch the Monkees. It was a very suburban Los Angeles. We roller-skated. We did Christmas caroling. In that section of my life, oh my gosh, I loved it. It was very structured. It was very solid. But in the school

year, I was with my mom. And my mom was single and had two other children. And it left me open to a lot of situations that I could have done without.

Carmen explained that while some personal issues like being married multiple times and being overweight are easy to joke about, she cannot find humor in child abuse. She said, "I can't find the funny in being unloved, in being hurt, in being a hurt child."

Some comedians can navigate real-world suffering onstage, but it becomes almost unmanageable when it comes to children being harmed. If an adult was harmed and the jokes are well-crafted, comedians like Diego can elicit a lot of public support. However, it's possible that Diego got a pass because he's a young man; gender and ethnic differences will be discussed in a later chapter. Regardless, if harm occurred to a child, jokes are unthinkable, as with Nyah, Carmen, and even Bianca, who has been unable to discuss the abuse she suffered at her father's hands. Regardless of the type of harm—violence or death—harm to children is almost always a taboo subject for audiences. Jokes about it are rarely funny, and comedians cannot say whatever they please, no matter how skilled they are.

Physical and Mental Illness:
Sometimes a Little Taboo, Sometimes Always Taboo

The last experiences to highlight are illnesses with a clear distinction between physical and mental health. Physical ailments were only moderately taboo, and comedians could navigate those discussions onstage as long as they appeared healthy. Let's hear from Pallavi, an Indian American who survived cancer. One of the struggles Pallavi faced during that time was the emotional burden she felt through her family. Like many families, Pallavi's family did not communicate about their emotions. Due to the lack of connection, Pallavi felt as if she had to hold it together for her family, which was a tremendous burden for someone fighting for her life:

> I had colitis and cancer. In my family, and with other people, my mom didn't really want to talk about it with anybody. It was frustrating because I want people to know what I am going through. I had to be the strong one because they [her family] were nervous and anxious and scared. I didn't have any conversations about what I was feeling or what they were feeling. It was all surface-level stuff. We're not the kind of family that discusses emotions too much. I don't know how that would have turned out. I just needed to get everyone through that time.

To cope with her cancer treatment, Pallavi turned to comedy. She would take the stage and share intimate details of her experience, using humor as a way to get through it. Her audience was receptive and supportive of her vulnerability.

> My set for about two years was talking about this. It [the comedy] helped me find my bearings and process everything that was happening. . . . I had mixed emotions. When I started it, I could understand what was happening based on the audience's reactions, because they were horrified. And I was like, okay; they are horrified too, this is a legitimate thing that is happening in my life. I met this comedian who had breast cancer. I had my colon removed, and I now have a colostomy bag. I talked about that onstage. After the show, she came up to me and told me she had skin from her stomach removed and reconstructed into a breast. I think my performance fostered a sense of empowerment and not victimhood. You don't need to feel sorry for people who have gone through this. You don't need to treat them with pity; we've been through a lot, but we are still doing cool things. We are strong and doing cool stuff.

Like Pallavi, Colleen happily speaks to the audience about surviving cancer and living with multiple sclerosis. In fact, she proudly displays her health status to the world, saying, "I wear MS, cancer, and gay shirts at all times. That's pretty much all I wear. That's why I have pink hair and a survivor tattoo. I always wear my ribbons, 'fuck cancer' on this side, and 'I'm strong' on the other side." Colleen was by far the warmest and most bubbly person who participated in the study. Her love of life has allowed her to cultivate a vast and supportive network:

> I'm very blessed. If I put a shout out right now, I'd have ten friends in my doorway. And most comedians don't have that, and it makes me sad. I was a salesperson all my life. And one of the biggest things they teach you in sales is "They don't care how much you know until they know how much you care." And I think that translates to comedy a little bit. I'm not just spitting stupid jokes out. I talk about my real life. And I think others can see that it matters to me and it's mine and its real. And that's why I connect with the audience so much. A lot of people are grateful that I talk about these issues. I met a guy who was getting chemo for his brain cancer, big guy. He played football for Purdue. And we got to be friends. And he posted a picture of himself at the chemo center and said: "I didn't know chemo could be fun." That's how I am everywhere I go, whether it is onstage or in person.

Personal presentation is crucial for both Pallavi and Colleen when discussing physical health. They need to present themselves as strong, indicating they are overcoming their illnesses. Colleen's infectious energy onstage and in real life creates a receptive audience. She comes across as someone who has triumphed over cancer and is content while living with MS, happy with whatever the future may hold. As for Pallavi, she was in pain at the time but managed to conceal it. When she stepped onstage, the audience had no idea how much she was enduring.

Now, let's compare Pallavi and Colleen to individuals who live with mental illness. These conversations were often much more difficult to have openly with the audience, and positive reception was a struggle, as demonstrated by Oliver, who talks about very serious issues. First, he discusses his own depression: "I have jokes about my depression and how I used to have suicidal thoughts. I have varying levels of depression every day." Second, Oliver tries to use comedy to bring awareness to suicide because of his father:

> My dad was sick for about a year, and then he took his own life. He had a stroke in December of 2008. He had brain surgery and a plate put in. Then he had four more strokes in the course of a year. He developed something called central nervous pain syndrome, which essentially made one side of his body feel like it was on fire. It was burning all the time. It was a massive, burning sensation. He described it as molten needles pricking every inch of his body all day. And there is no treatment. He lived that way as long as he could until could not do it anymore. No life should be only pain.

Although Oliver is passionate and will continue discussing these subjects because he wants to empower himself and others, audiences are generally uncomfortable. Oliver has not found success discussing these topics onstage. On many occasions, he has stopped midway through his set because of the crowd's shock. "To them, it was bad," he said.

Comedy is not typically an accepting place to discuss mental illness, and those who have found success often do so in "hybrid" formats where they are hired as health advocates first and comedians second. Yazmin, an Indian American who lives with schizoaffective disorder, highlights the difference between pure comedy stages and hybrid locations. On pure comedy stages, Yazmin can't use certain words because she knows they will make the audience uncomfortable. She explains, "I do have some dark bits where I talk about suicide, but it's a very hit or miss bit. It can make people very uncomfortable. Sometimes I feel a little self-conscious because I don't know how the audience will receive it because schizoaffective is a terrifying word. It can make people nervous."

To achieve success, Pallavi needs to modify her language. As she described, "sometimes I just say bipolar." Alternatively, she avoids discussing the topic directly by shifting the focus to another issue (veiling), such as arranged marriages in the Indian community. She uses comedy to keep the tone light and does not delve into many details about mental illness. Instead, she talks about how her mental illness makes things complicated, such as arranged marriages. Pallavi's mother wants to arrange her marriage, but she doesn't want to disclose her mental illness to the potential partner.

The level of stigma attached to mental illness is most evident in the reactions of comedians who live with these issues. Some are passionate and won't stop talking because they believe in advocacy, like Yazmin and Oliver. Yazmin explicitly entered the business to do charged comedy, as she describes, "I wanted to combat the stigma of mental illness through comedic means." Similarly, Oliver wants to give a voice to those who are suffering.

> I talk about it in my comedy a lot because suicide and mental illness are things that are not talked about enough in public. People should have the right to die with dignity if they no longer feel like they can live. The greatest failure of a society is that we provide no other outlet than you better have a fucking gun. My dad died in his car across the street from the sheriff's department so they would get there quickly. That's horrifying when he could have been surrounded by his friends and family.

Some people are willing to take the risk of discussing personal issues onstage, while others find those conversations completely inappropriate. Sophia, who lives with generalized anxiety and has experienced clinical depression, falls into the latter category. She does not want to talk about these issues onstage:

> It's not funny. I am very open about my mental process and issues. And I really like to talk about feelings, but that is really serious stuff to me. There are so many memes online that are like, "LOL, I want to die." Don't we all [mockingly]. I think we should not make a joke about it. People think they can only make mental illness relatable if they can laugh about it, and I disagree. In stand-up, you have to sell it. You have to make the audience think that I believe it is funny and that I am going to sell this joke to you to make you laugh. But if I don't believe it, how is anybody else going to believe it?

Unlike those who believe that comedy can be liberating, Sophia is adamant that the comedy stage does a disservice to her and everyone else who lives with mental illness. The rest of the book explores whether advocates like Oliver are correct, or if comedy is, in fact, harmful as Sophia believes. We will see that both perspectives are valid, but it ultimately depends on multiple other variables that are related to socio-cultural conditions.

RECOGNIZING OUR STIGMA

Despite the promise of an open space like that in comedy, comedians did not feel free to discuss all their stigmas equally. Different levels of stigma persist with the most taboo issues being those experiences that involve the most real-world suffering. Physical illness could sometimes be discussed on the stage if the person appeared to be thriving, while mental illness was always too taboo. It is likely that there are some diseases that people may perceive as "winnable," while other issues are viewed as a perpetual struggle. Specifically, because a physical illness—like cancer—can be "conquered" as described by Pallavi, the public is more willing to celebrate that victory. On the other hand, because mental illness is an ongoing struggle, the stigmatizing public may not perceive it as ever being won, and the conversation is avoided.

The reasons why topics related to real-world harm are considered taboo require further analysis. It is probable that the use of comedy as a platform is the main reason. Despite the skillful crafting of arguments by comedians, humor is a fundamental aspect of this genre. When it comes to harm to children, it involves the combination of the concepts of "harm" and "innocence" of a child, which most people do not find humorous. In all the circumstances described by the comedians, none of them used jokes to attack the children who were harmed, but the stigma attached to violence and harm to children is still present. Then again, Louis CK made people laugh at gun violence in schools while Dave Chappelle got the audience to laugh at child sexual assault, so clearly it is possible in some situations.

However, categorizing invisible stigmas can be challenging because many stigmas are not even visible to the victims themselves. Some participants, when describing traumatic experiences, would often fail to recognize the issue was affecting their life. For example, Claire mentioned that she didn't have a great relationship with her family, but when asked why she didn't talk about it onstage, she replied, "I don't know. I guess I'm just trying to move on."

Unlike Claire, others are much more aware of these stigmas, including Hiromi, who has struggled with mental illness and body image issues. Much of her comedy centers around body politics and weight stigma, which stem from her early childhood experiences. Hiromi told me that she was diagnosed with depression at a young age, saying, "I suffered from depression when I was eleven to maybe fifteen. I was medicated." Importantly, she links her mental illness to the stigma fostered by her parents' behaviors and beliefs in idealized views of bodies. "My family is very thin. My dad is a personal trainer. I named my mom [in my show] as someone harmful to my self-appreciation of beauty," she says. Hiromi continues, "I've talked to my dad a little about weight stigma because they are still doing it. That continues to this day; they still want me to lose weight. It's like, what do you think that would fix right now?"

Like Hiromi, others including myself also struggle with body image issues. My struggles also stemmed from my parents' often unhealthy messaging, but were further fueled by our military community. My dad was a marathon runner and weight trainer, while my brother was a cross-country runner and high jumper in high school. My mother ran one marathon and was an active gym user. I, on the other hand, was the fat kid in "husky" size pants who was bullied by my brother and sometimes beaten while being body shamed. The first time I realized I was fat was when my father grabbed my belly just before dinner in the kitchen and gleefully proclaimed that I looked like I had finally lost weight. As a first-grader in T-ball, that was probably true.

Unlike Hiromi, I had never considered how my past experiences had impacted my sense of self and mental health. It wasn't until our conversation that I remembered these events and recognized their traumatic effects. Hiromi spoke about instances of purging as a child, which made me think about my own experiences playing football in middle school. A few of us husky kids were forced to strip down to our underwear before games to be weighed in front of the coach and referee. If we were over the weight limit, the coach would encourage us to go to the bathroom and do whatever it took to get on the field, including throwing up, urinating to dehydration, or trying to defecate. This was all done to embarrass us, as the little league couldn't prevent a paid customer from participating.

I feel fortunate to have connected with Hiromi and to see myself in her. I especially connected with her when she described how reliving painful experiences left her emotionally exhausted: "Sometimes rehearsing the material is so emotionally draining that I would have to sleep for twelve hours afterward." She continued, "It's hard to hear, and it's hard to think about myself suffering when I was a little baby." I know that feeling of being so low that I couldn't get out of bed.

Unlike her and many others who actively confront stigma, some of us have pushed our experiences aside, either purposely or subconsciously. Stigma conditions people into silence, which keeps everyone quiet in a way that many cannot even recognize that there is a problem. I can't predict how people will react to stigmatized issues because I may not have recognized that my experience is a major cause of harm in the first place, which is why I've never mentioned it. While the study presented evidence that some stigmas are more taboo than others, there are likely many other stigmatized traumas comedians that I interviewed do not even recognize within themselves.

Chapter 3

Visible Stigmas that Define What People See

In the last chapter, we explored various experiences that comedians have found troubling and which issues they find most taboo to discuss onstage. But, these stigmas never occur in a vacuum. People are experiencing multiple invisible stigmas, and the moment a person steps onstage, the audience immediately reacts to the physical body they see. How the audience perceives the comedians also matters. Consider Nathaniel, a man who lives with cerebral palsy and is one of the most brilliant people I have ever met. He describes how his comedy centers on his disability, which he enjoys discussing with the audience: "My comedy is self- and socially deprecating. I use a lot of satire. I like to be critical of society, especially of how society treats people with disabilities. And it's personal. I love it [talking about my disability]. I love shoving it in their face. I love being conscious of my disability and using my disability."

But disability is not the only experience. Nathaniel talks about other important topics, but unfortunately, the audience only sees his stigma. The moment he enters the room in his wheelchair, everyone can see it. He says, "I can always feel tension when people don't know me. They are like, oh shit, are we going to give this guy laughs to make him feel better?" Although the stage has been liberating for his sense of identity, there are significant constraints. Nathaniel later explains how he purposely manages what he says because of the stigma. "Do you know how many people think I am seven years old? And I can't blow up in their face, or I'm a psychopath. You're like the crazy cripple person."

Like Nathaniel, we all face stigmas or characteristics that cause others to treat us differently. Some of these traits might result in minor reactions, while others can have a significant impact on our lives. The most influential type of status is the master status, which defines a person's identity and takes precedence over all other statuses they hold.[1] To understand the concept of a

51

master status, we can look to the Oval Office. In his analysis of race within the Obama presidency, Dr. Michael Eric Dyson noted that Barack Obama could never escape his race.[2] He was politically paralyzed by unrepentant racism that was present in many of the political attacks he faced, and personally paralyzed by his desire to avoid discussing race and then being labeled. When Obama was elected, he became the "Black" president. In contrast, every other person who had held that office was simply referred to as the president, without any racial labels. This demonstrates how a master status can impact a person's life and shape the way others perceive them.

A master status can be a visible stigma that not only causes explicit discrimination, but also affects every other aspect of our lives. For instance, Nathaniel talks about sex and relationships in his comedy and says, "That's the main issue I struggle with. I have difficulties maintaining romantic relationships because of my disability." Although relationship strain is something that could affect anyone, Nathaniel frames it around cerebral palsy. He explains, "It's important for other people to know the stigma attached to disability and relationships."

Although Nathaniel enjoys discussing romantic relationships, he cannot avoid the topic of his disability. While others can talk about dating without their able bodies being linked to the discussion, Nathaniel must address his disability for the audience. His options are limited: he can discuss the elephant in the room to make others feel comfortable, or he can avoid the subject and risk making others more uncomfortable, which would harm the conversation and his relationship with the audience.

Like Nathaniel, who lives with a significant disability, many comedians have expressed that audiences view them not just as comedians, but as a combination of identities. Despite their efforts to present themselves in different ways, these comedians are often defined by specific statuses onstage. Unfortunately, these statuses can also be the source of pain and inequality in their lives both on- and offstage. This chapter will explore some of the most defining statuses, starting with gender. How do comedians navigate these visible stigmas onstage? How do these stigmas limit their ability to be seen and their ability to cope with other challenges?

NAVIGATING GENDER IN PUBLIC

Comedian women often centered their performances around gender, which was a prominent and ever-present topic in almost any issue they discussed. While they explicitly addressed sexism onstage, it was often intertwined with other subjects. For example, Claire uses comedy to explore marriage and dating, both of which are unique experiences for women. She shares a humorous anecdote about having her tarot cards read: "She said I was getting married to someone that I already knew, which makes for a lot of awkward interactions with my friends and acquaintances. It's ridiculous to know that you are getting married in two years. But marriage is something that is always on the mind of a middle-aged woman." Claire also jokes about a time when a potential hookup, which she was eagerly looking forward to, made things awkward:

> I tell a joke about going home with a guy I met at a bar, and it was going well. And then suddenly, he got nervous for me. I think it was hitting him how vulnerable women are when they make that choice to go home with someone. That's true, but the fact that he was asking made me think, "Are you going to murder me? It's just you and I in this room."

While gender intersects with all of their experiences, it also confines their speech. Claire provides us with examples of how gender limits one's capacity. For instance, she talks about catcalling: "I tell people I met my best friend through a catcall, which is not true. I didn't make a friend. But someone did shout, 'damn girl, you're fine; can I call you later?' I joke about walking up and down the street to get my confidence back up, that it's a workout for me."

Although sexual harassment is distressing, Claire generally refrains from discussing the issue and tries to make light of it. However, she admits that "as a woman, the stuff that I get upset about in relationships is perceived by others as petty. I don't want to be perceived as a woman who is just bitching about men all the time." While she wants to address the issue, she is aware of the gendered stigma that the audience might have. Thus, Claire often avoids discussing sexism altogether.

Earlier, we met Hiromi, who discussed significant issues including weight and mental health. Like Claire, she also manages her words depending on the location. She knows not to use specific labels that may trigger fragile audiences and invoke animosity. Hiromi said, "I try to depoliticize my language as much as possible so that as many people can join me. Sometimes I say feminist. I did say feminist in my set last night. But if I weren't in this town, maybe if I were in a more conservative city, I would say that 'this thing is not kind to women' instead of saying feminist."

And importantly, many of the issues discussed are gender-neutral and affect both men and women, such as divorce, which Jasmine tries to address. However, despite the universal nature of these traumas, she describes being unfairly judged because of her gender. This is a particularly important issue for her as a standup comedian. Specifically, if she talks about her divorce, she fears being pigeonholed and losing opportunities, which would harm her career:

I don't want to be the divorcee, female comic. It's not how I want to define myself in the comic world. Standup is already vulnerable enough, and I don't want to be that kind of comic. There's a lot more stigma on women. When people find out about it, it's like, "Well, you failed." I want to be as true to myself, but I feel like a lot of the time, female comics can get stuck in this trap of themes and identities that are placed on us onstage. Men don't have to avoid [a trope]. At an open mic, all men can talk about the same thing, but if I talk about sex, there are audible groans.

To be sure, men were not immune to sexism, but they often failed to recognize how gender impacted their lives and ability to speak publicly. The stigma of feeling emasculated was typically attached to other experiences for men. Consider Doug, a white man in his fifties who grew up very close to his family and mother. Like many children, he experienced bullying and never quite fit in, despite being a lovely individual who treats everyone with respect. As an adult, he briefly worked as a corrections officer, where he again felt like he didn't belong. While he got along well with inmates, he faced conflict from other officers who criticized him for being too nice. Doug explained, "The inmates loved me because I was very mild-mannered. I wasn't mean like the other officers. I tried not to be an asshole, but I didn't have the personality for the job. The other officers would get on me because I was too nice."

Like anyone who has ever worked, Doug made a mistake on the job. But his mistake was pretty bad. "I lost my gun," he told me with his hands over his face. "The gun ended up in the hands of a gang banger. I could have gotten somebody killed." However, because he was not tough on the inmates and was actually pretty well-liked by them, the other officers did not support him. "The other officers treated me terribly. They were all very nasty about it. None of them were my friends." Worse, despite the fact that no one was harmed, he described how these same officers were quick to support others who were outright malicious to inmates.

Compared to Doug, there is Benicio, a Latino man who is very close with several family members who live with disabilities. "I am very sensitive to them," he said. Accordingly, he befriended many kids with disabilities at his school, spending time with them at lunch. "When I was younger, I would sit with them at lunch. We'd play with Pokémon cards and other things. And we were just kids into that stuff." Because of this familiarity, he spent much of his time in school hanging out with and supporting students with disabilities. And like young, immature kids, they would tease each other. "We'd make jokes about each other. They [his friends who live with disabilities] would tease me for having messed-up teeth, and I'd hit them back for their stuff. They'd get me, and I'd get them back. It was cool." Benicio has a lot of compassion for his friends and family with disabilities. He cares for them and tries to be inclusive, even doling out friendly ribbing that they are more than happy to reciprocate.

However, those who are not part of Benicio's group of friends immediately perceive him as a bigot and unsympathetic to those who welcome his jokes. Even though his friends with disabilities have defended him, Benicio is still upset about how outsiders perceive him. "I'm not an asshole," he says. "It bothers me when people think I'm mean because I'm not mean. I feel horrible that when I was younger, I may have hurt people. I'm embarrassed that I have said things to my friends that I didn't realize. I don't want to hurt anyone, and I don't want people to think I'm cruel."

Both Doug and Benicio struggle with masculinity in different ways, unaware of how it affects them. Doug perceives masculinity as a stigma that manifests as being too nice and incompetent in the workplace, as society expects men to excel in hyper-aggression. Meanwhile, Benicio is coming to terms with the fact that when he behaves like a stereotypical masculine man, he is perceived as inconsiderate of those he cares for deeply.

The main difference between these men and women is that men didn't understand how masculinity norms affected their stage presence, while women were fully aware of sexism. They not only had to manage the stress of sexism in their lives, but they also knew how it affected how the world perceived them. As a result, many women intentionally changed their behavior. As Fernanda explained, "Men are allowed to be bitter, mean, and rude to the audience. They can also be handsome when they do it. They can also be smart when they do it. Think about someone like Daniel Tosh. He's a good-looking guy. He's not disgusting." However, women are not allowed to be both. She continued:

> Female comedians have to dumb down or wear a cloak. So, like Amy Schumer, she's an incredible satirist, but she puts on a persona of being a mildly attractive, slutty fat girl. Which is so funny; if you read her stuff, that's not her. But she can only get away with the stuff that she says because she has that cloak on. With Sarah Silverman, she plays up this air of naivete a little bit. She'll [imitating an airy, ditzy voice] "I'm going to talk like this but also say like really weird things that are vulgar."

Most importantly, Fernanda points out that men can be their true selves without fear of ridicule, saying, "Men just wear a suit and look nice and be a dickhead." On the other hand, women are never fully seen. "I have to take something away to be allowed to be who I am every fucking day. And they can mock women all day. When we say something about men, we're shot down." Fernanda continues, "For example, there is this stereotype that women are very dramatic, so my set is about how men are actually more dramatic than women. When I was done, the host said, 'All right, that's Fernanda with how stupid men are.' I never said that!"

QUEERNESS AND GENDER: INEQUALITY ACROSS LGBTQ+ STATUS

Queerness was a master status that impacted every aspect of a comedian's life, both on- and offstage. For example, consider Blake, a young college student who grew up in a typical middle-class Jewish family:

> I was a boy's boy. I loved sports. I love dork stuff. I was studious. I was a little anxious. I was very liked by others. I was just another boy. My family is very nice, very supportive. I'm an only child growing up in a Jewish household. I went to Hebrew school. I had a bar mitzvah. I had a lot of friends; we played sports and video games. I was as stereotypical middle class as you could be. My parents were literally by my side no matter what. We would eat dinner together. Watch TV together. My dad was the kind of guy who would play catch with me. My mom was always at my school. She would take me to the mall. My parents were the kind of people that were always loving.

Although these are normal childhood experiences for many, society frames them differently for a transgender woman. For Blake, all of these experiences are filtered through the lens of being a transgender woman. Even though girls play video games and sports, have bar mitzvahs, and attend Hebrew schools, Blake is still labeled as a trans woman. Therefore, she centers all of her comedy around that stigma, and is forced to address her status even though it has little to do with the actual comedy she presents. As Blake describes, "my jokes are trans-oriented."

Lesbian women also feel the need to address the stigma of their sexual identity onstage. They can feel confined by their status, even if they don't fit the stereotypical lesbian mold. For instance, Lydia, a thirty-three-year-old woman, is very feminine and acknowledges that her sexuality is unknown until she verbalizes it. "I look straight," she says. Despite her sexual identity being invisible, and all of her relationship experiences being things other women could have, her orientation inevitably remains the center of her comedy. "I'm not going to hide my sexuality," Lydia says. "My standup is really in your face. It is unapologetically queer." Like other LGBTQ+ comedians in this book and elsewhere, Lydia's queer comedy stems from her childhood experiences. In her case, she grew up in a devout Catholic family:

> The lack of sexual education that I learned in Catholic school, which was traumatic for me and my sexual orientation. Coming out as queer meant I only

knew negative things, or nothing at all. I didn't even know what could get you pregnant at eighteen. And that terrifying lack of information and misinformation shapes a lot of my comedy. It is so important to talk about how kids are so impressionable. I've never used the word trauma, but it's very fitting. I think oppressive religious upbringing is terrible for anyone, but to take anyone's ability to sexually figure out who they are because of what they are told. I was told when I came out that I was going straight to hell, and I went back in the closet for years. In the fifth grade, I told my mom that I thought I was a leper. I was convinced because in the bible it said that sinners are lepers. And I was a sinner [for being lesbian], so I must have leprosy.

Similarly, gay participants also believed that addressing their status was essential for their comedy to succeed. They considered it an integral part of their material. For instance, Cam enjoys discussing the topic of straight women invading gay bars:

There is so much of a conversation about whether straight people should be allowed in gay bars. What should the etiquette be when they are there? A lot of straight women will come into gay bars, and when they are with their gay friend, they suddenly want to play matchmaker. At the end of the day, I do agree that it's not their space, so to go in there and act like a fucking fool is disrespectful toward us.

Like Cam, Ethan discusses his bisexuality in his comedy routine, which is a part of his identity that he discovered during his young adulthood. "I felt very rebellious about it," he explains. "Sometimes I questioned whether I was really bisexual because I didn't have sex until I was twenty-one, but I knew I was bisexual when I was eighteen." Ethan explains how he has to handle certain topics because he is a cisgender man. "Sometimes I forget to mention that I'm bisexual. I'll start talking about having sex with guys, and people will get confused. I have this one bit where my mom's boyfriend downloads Grindr, and I say I'm having sex with my mom's new Grindr boyfriend."

But where Ethan stands out from other LGBTQ+ comedians in that he has experienced actual threats of violence while performing standup comedy. Although all the LGBTQ+ comedians describe feeling unwelcome in the comedy scene due to their identity, Ethan's experiences are more extreme. He shares, "There are times when I won't do my jokes because people think it's a gimmick. I'm the bi-guy. Or people in my hometown are like, 'We need to kill this guy.' I did a show and someone, whose face I didn't see, which is equally terrifying, said, 'I hope you get lynched.' That was a nightmare."

One major difference between gay men and other members of the LGBTQ+ community is that while every LGBTQ+ comedian describes their sexual identity as a salient part of their identity, there are major differences between women and men. Gender significantly moderates LGBTQ+ identity, and gay men have a different relationship with the audience compared to women and transgender comedians. Women and transgender comedians consistently try to reach the audience through their performance to bridge the gap and dispel stigma. They make a consistent effort to build relationships and empathy with the audience. For example, Lydia expressed concern that her comedy may be misinterpreted by the audience, which could affect others in the LGBTQ+ community:

> I feel a responsibility to try to make sure that I am educating people while I tell jokes. I don't think men, and straight men specifically feel that pressure. They feel that opposite, that they can say anything. But for me, the pressure is if I fuck this up, they [the audience] are going to hate gay people. Then, I'm doing the LGBTQ+ community a disservice.

Similarly, Holly, a trans woman, is confined to a certain self-presentation as a trans-woman. She wishes she didn't have to disarm the audience, but like Lydia, she recognizes that her mere presence is distracting. To be fully seen, she has to alleviate the tension if she wants a positive connection with those strangers: "It's limiting because when I am performing in front of a broader audience, an audience dominated by cis-gendered heterosexual people, at some level, I have to start every performance by saying I am trans." While she can make those jokes, the constant public assurance is wearing thin on her:

> I have to find a way to make that announcement funny. How many ways can I make that announcement funny? I have two to three openers that I have been using for six years. I'm so bored with it and fed up with doing. But if I don't say that I am trans as the first thing that I talk about, that audience is so reserved because they are trying to figure something out. They get so distracted by trying to figure me out that they are just not present and listening to the material.

Like Holly, Blake also spends time building empathy with the audience because of her trans identity. "I try to make things relatable and bridge the gap between trans people and cis people," she explains. "It's basically all my material. I try to talk about my experiences and how they aren't different. They aren't weird. We're typical human beings."

Now, let's compare Blake, Lydia, and Holly to Cam, whom we met a moment ago. While the women feel very restricted onstage and are willing to make those concessions, Cam is entirely apathetic to the audience's feelings. He says, "Do I feel restricted? Not really. I don't give a shit." He is entirely comfortable with creating a wedge, even if it means losing opportunities. For instance, when he put out his first standup comedy album, he produced it himself. Cam felt that it was material he was comfortable with, and if no one wanted to put it out because it had two gay jokes on it, he didn't care. He said, "I'm still going to put it out."

Like Cam, Ethan remains antagonistic toward his audience, regardless of threats of violence. He couldn't care less about how the audience reacts:

> When it happens in my hometown, I feel very rebellious because this was the hometown that rejected me and my sexuality. It rejected a lot of things about me. When it happens, all I can think is fuck these people. Who cares? I'm going to make fun of this town. If you are trying to be everyone's friend, then you are not really you, and I think you need to accept the fact that you do rebel.

Being LGBTQ+ can be very limiting onstage due to a clear division in how men, women, and trans women interact with the audience. However, we must be clear about the root cause. It may seem like gender is the determining factor; men like Ethan and Cam may be more comfortable provoking indignation and thus more liberated onstage. As Ethan puts it, "there are some people that you want to take a bat to." On the other hand, trans and lesbian comedians like Blake, Lydia, and Holly appear to be more constrained, often carefully cultivating their image and relationship with the audience. This difference may lead some to believe that the solution is to be more assertive: if these women stop caring, they will be able to challenge the audience and achieve greater liberation.

However, the issue is not with choice, but with reality. The reality is that trans women and women in general face the real possibility of violence, which limits their freedom. When comedians perform onstage, they are unaware of who is in the audience. They understand the potential harm that could come to them and others if they provoke the audience, and as a result, they are not fully expressing themselves.

THE GAY MASCULINITY PASS

Gay men, on average, experience more social acceptance than their counterpart women, but they are not completely immune to discrimination. Chaz, for example, acknowledges that he is undeniably gay, but as a white man, he believes that strangers automatically view him as legitimate, a legitimacy that he believes many of his colleagues have to struggle for:

> I think being a white male is one of the easiest things you can be. I don't believe it personally possible to disentangle those things. I can't avoid being a gay man. I'm sure being a cis man affects me. But people ask fewer questions about me and my legitimacy. I think that's a huge issue for people who don't look like the typical straight white dude. My friends who do comedy who are women, trans,

people of color, they have to legitimize themselves a lot. If I'm on a lineup, people are going to assume that I am funny. I don't think people question my legitimacy the way they would question other people. There is less to prove.

One potential problem is how he presents himself. Chaz acknowledges that, despite having certain advantages, his identity as a gay man can create difficulties:

Literally, no one would mistake me for straight. Without talking to me or knowing me, they would still pick me. I haven't had the experience of someone saying, "You're pretty funny for a gay dude." I've had the experience of "Wow, I didn't know about your experience, and you were pretty funny." To me, those are two different things.

Chaz highlights that masculinity was a significant factor in defining gay men, and that displaying masculinity was crucial for acceptance in society. Gay men who were more masculine in appearance had an easier time in public. Lance, who was interviewed, exemplifies this both on- and offstage. As a white man who presented himself as very masculine, he could not recall any blatant discrimination against him for being gay. Although Lance had some difficulty revealing his sexual orientation to his parents, they ultimately supported him and even told him they had known for years. Lance was openly gay in the Boy Scouts, even though homosexuality was strictly prohibited at the time:

Boy Scouts was a huge part of my life for a very long time. I made Eagle [the highest rank]. I worked at a summer camp in New Mexico for a summer. I worked at a local camp for five years. I was involved in Order of the Arrow. I came to our town in 2002, and I was the operations manager for the local chapter. The people that I was friends within Boy Scouts all thought it was a dumb policy. I came out to people when I was in a Boy Scout camp, and I never got any backlash. They did not give a shit.

Lance, as a comedian, has faced little resistance when discussing his sexuality. He has even received support from some rural and conservative audiences. By talking about his career in mixed martial arts (MMA) and his ability to professionally defeat opponents, his masculinity helps to counteract some of the negative stereotypes associated with being gay:

I went on tour with other comedians, and we were down in Alabama. We did a show in some backwater place, exactly where you would think. And you bring up the gay thing. And someone in the audience would be like "Aww shit." It's never been a bad reaction. But I don't read as gay particularly. I feel like my gay presence does not threaten people. I also talk about how I was in a cage fight, so people come up to me and talk about that. I think they feel, well, he's gay, but I could kick their ass. In our town, when I say I'm gay, I get applause. It's like, why are you clapping? When I go to Alabama, they are not going to clap, but they are not going to throw something at me.

Lance's argument that "No one really hates gay people anymore" is vastly different from the experiences of other gay men due to his hypermasculinity. This is particularly evident when we compare his experience to that of Ethan, who has reported experiencing violence and threats, and Cam, who was advised by his parents to hide his sexuality from his grandparents. Cam explains, "My mom would give us these jokey pep talks, 'Remember, don't tell her you're gay; just let her die.'"

But despite the fact that some white, gay men may face fewer barriers, stigma still persists. It is important to recognize that marginalized individuals, particularly those who only see one's gender or race, can make gay white men feel marginalized. Here are Cam's thoughts:

When I am hanging out with other marginalized people, other queer people, or people of color, who are struggling with typical straight white males who abuse them, I relate to them more. But sometimes it feels like, "You may be gay, but at the end of the day, you are still a white man. You have an advantage." There is a disconnect between other marginalized people and me, and it does afford me degrees of privilege, and I do recognize and respect that. But at the same time, when I am hanging out with the straight white males, I'm still a gay guy. Even though we may have a couple of things in common, there is a gap there. It feels like I'm between two communities.

Cis-presenting, gay white men may be accepted to varying degrees, but their relationship with the world is vastly different from others. White masculinity affords them certain privileges, such as the ability to disregard their audience. Conversely, lesbian women and trans comedians are acutely aware of their status, how they present their topics, and how those conversations might impact other queer individuals. Ironically, some of these lesbian and trans women live in the same community as Lance, who believes that gay hatred is no longer an issue. However, Treyvaughn, who was ostracized by the Black community for being gay, would disagree. His speech is constrained, a result of the immediate harm inflicted by straight Black male comedians. Therefore, when Lance argues that gay people are no longer hated, his statement may only apply to a small group of nonthreatening white, middle-class men in America.

NAVIGATING EVERYTHING AT ONCE:
PARENTHOOD, GENDER AND RACE

The ability to speak onstage is shaped by a variety of experiences, including family issues, trauma, race, and gender. Each of these factors carries its own weight, making it challenging to navigate the path to freedom of expression. While it's crucial to separate these social categories and experiences to identify their independent effects, looking at them independently has limitations. Binary perspectives often fail to account for life's intricacies.[3] People are never defined by just one status or coping with only one stigma at a time. Instead of considering them separately, we must view them as a whole. As per Dickenson,[4] age, race, ethnicity, and class all play a significant role in the creation and reception of humor and must be understood in relation to gender.

Parenthood is a topic that perfectly demonstrates complexity like no other. Although all parents universally experience stress, each parent experiences it differently based on their gender. It's not surprising that mothers often feel particularly restricted. For example, in her set, Molly talks about parenthood but avoids including too much parental material and often avoids the label of motherhood altogether:

> For women, it's a very fine line of whether you are going to be branded as a "mom" comic or just a comic. So, I talk about it, but it's not my main thrust. My whole person is not that I am just a mother. I am a mother, but I am also a lot of other things, so I want to be able to talk about those other things. With audiences, once you are a mom, you are a mom in their eyes. I don't think men have the same pressure. Men don't get pigeonholed in the same way. When I got pregnant, a lot of bookers told me, "Don't just talk about your kid. Don't become a mom comic." And it's not an outright restriction; it's just more of a "no one wants to hear you talk about lady stuff." And being a parent is not just lady stuff. I had a lot of people ask if I was going to keep doing comedy after I got pregnant. I don't think anybody has ever asked a man that when they have a kid.

The comedian women in the study believed that discussing motherhood onstage was more taboo than talking about other controversial topics like sex. They feared that mentioning motherhood would stereotype them and limit their style of comedy. Additionally, they felt pressure to conform to societal expectations of marriage, even if they didn't want to. For example, Meghan, a white woman in her late twenties, shared her experience of being constantly asked about her plans to get married by her friends, despite not having any intention of doing so. This highlights the societal pressure placed on women to conform to traditional gender roles, which can be limiting and frustrating. Meghan uses comedy to address a range of issues, including her disdain for the wedding industry and the expectations placed on women regarding marriage and childbirth. These are issues that bother her a great deal. "I just want to scream at people that it's fine," she says. "We don't want children, and that's fine with me. There's a stigma that we won't be as happy until we're engaged. But we [Meghan and her partner] are fine."

Most importantly, Meghan understands that being happily unmarried is taboo and often leads to heated conversations. However, she also notes that men do not face the same scrutiny. Her partner is never questioned or shamed in a passive-aggressive manner. As Meghan puts it, "He doesn't get as much pressure as a man. I doubt he hears from his grandmother, 'That's just a whole different type of love that you'll never know.'"

Compared to women, men are more willing to openly discuss parenthood, as demonstrated by Jeremy, a middle-aged white man. During our conversation, he quickly pointed out that in comedy, "Many of the things I talk about are things that affect me as a dad. You talk about what you know, and when you have kids, they just take up so much more of your time. I'm turning into Bill Cosby, pre-rape. I am talking about the funny things these kids say." Jeremy explained that his jokes are based on real experiences, but are generally lighthearted and stress-free. For example, he told me about a time when he compared his children to others:

> Sometimes you see your kid doing something so fucking dumb. I'm never going to be able to retire because my kid is an idiot. My kid had this playdate with this boy who spoke Portuguese and English and he's four. And he was doing math on this chalkboard, pretty good math. I'm watching this other kid speak both languages while doing math, and I turn to my kid. My daughter was fucking up the easiest puzzle ever made. It was four pieces of a duck, and she started to put it in backward and started to eat a piece. She had her hand in her butt.

Compared to the mothers who found these mild and playful subjects too taboo, Jeremy finds himself welcome to any audience. "I do a fair number of clubs," he describes, "but I can also do corporate stuff and family events. I can work in those scenarios." Moreover, his comedy around family life has only increased: "Now, I talk more about my family than I used to, just like so many others."

Jeremy's experience with parenthood was typical for most white-passing fathers. They could talk about it without fear of consequences to their careers, which was a stark contrast to mothers, especially those of color. However, discussing parenthood became even more complicated when race was added to the equation. For Black men like Demarcus, fatherhood was very taboo for him and the audience. Demarcus uses the stage to discuss Back fatherhood from a social justice perspective. He wants to be a responsible role model for the Black community, particularly for other Black men who may be headed down the wrong path. Demarcus dabbles in many art forms, and part of his mission is not just to tell, but to show how to be a good father by actively involving his children in as many activities as possible:

> I try to incorporate my kids into whatever I am doing, first and foremost. Because of the nature of my job, I can bring my kids with me to a lot of things. I can bring them to readings and shoots and studio sessions, and workshops, and shows. They'll get to see me perform, and they get to know the environment that I work in.

Moreover, Demarcus makes a special effort to support his children's interests. "My oldest daughter is nine, and she enjoys creating comic books and YouTube videos," he explains. "My seven-year-old is interested in coding games like Minecraft. I am always involved in their world and whatever projects they enjoy doing."

Like Demarcus, who is very aware of how race affects his fatherhood, Candice spent considerable time talking about her race and parenthood. She recognizes her Blackness as a mother and how she is viewed onstage. Candice comes from a mixed-race family—her father is Black, and her mother is white—and she physically presents as a Black woman. As a proud and accomplished Black woman, it has been distressing navigating how to raise her interracial child who physically presents as whiter than her. Specifically, Candice struggles with whether her child will be able to embrace her Blackness, how her daughter will be received within the Black community, and how she can help her daughter navigate her mixed-racial identity that will be lived differently than hers:

> If my daughter is white looking and I'm Black looking, are people going to even think we are related? What am I going to teach her, and what's that going to look like for me? I thought she would have the same racial identity that I have. And I thought that I could navigate it; I could help her understand what it means to be Black and white—mixed—but still identify with Black culture. But since she doesn't even look like I do, I think she might experience an uphill battle of seeing herself that way and convincing others if she does identity as Black. I am so worried because I experienced it as a child. I was raised by a white mom, and I was challenged about not being in touch with my Blackness. And as an adult, I still feel insecure about it. At the onset, I thought I would map out the things that were hard for me and make it easier for her, but I can't. She's not going to grow up in the same era, and she's not going to have the same understanding that I do.

Candice is distressed by various issues that may be relatable to white parents. However, she is also struggling with her racial identity and how she portrays herself as a Black woman and mother to her interracial child. These topics are often considered taboo, especially when she tries to discuss them with a standup audience. This affects her stage presence, voice, and ultimately how honest she can be with her audience:

> I feel a little exposed. I worry that people will judge me and think that If I'm talking about the fact that my daughter came out much lighter than me and didn't look like me, I'm afraid that people are going to think, "You're ashamed of your daughter because you are ashamed of the whiteness." I'm picturing white people going, "There's nothing wrong with being white." And I'm picturing Black people saying, "You brought this on yourself." No one in the audience ever says that, but it is my worry. I'm trying to make something funny, and if it's not funny yet, people are going to read it wrong. And they don't know that I feel weird talking about it either.

Candice's experience as a mother provides a clear example of the challenges that arise when dealing with intersecting stigmas, especially when considering her husband Ross, who was also interviewed. Throughout the interview, Candice discussed the constant struggles she faces as a Black mother with a child of a visibly different race, which complicates her relationship with the audience. However, Ross did not mention the race of their child as a stressor during the interview. This is not to say that Ross is unconcerned about his wife's worries. Candice stated that they have had conversations about this issue, and Ross is genuinely troubled by her distress. But Candice also recognized that while her husband sympathizes with her turmoil, he cannot fully understand it as a white man. As she describes, "My husband, who can only speak from a white experience, says things like, 'Well, if she identifies as white, we should probably support her.' For me, that feels like an erasure of Black culture. To me, that would be devastating. Something he can't even understand."

The difficulty of being seen is compounded when it intersects with other variables beyond gender and race, such as mental illness. For instance, Trina is the mother of an adult son who lives with schizophrenia, and she recognizes that people perceive him as dangerous due to his identity as a young Black man and his mental illness:

> It's a huge fear. Something as simple as him wanting to get out and take a walk. I have to make sure that he has something on him that says, "I have a mental illness." Even when he's at my parents' house, and something happens, I have to make sure that the right police officers are called. You can't just call any police officer. You have to call a certain kind of police officer. And my trust with the police officer, because of the situation of who my son is, that trust is nonexistent. I have to be aware of these things. If he takes a walk and is gone too long, I am

panicking. Nothing has ever happened, thank God. I have to worry about him because he's Black. And then on top of that, I have to worry about him because he has a mental illness. The officer who comes up or the neighbor that sees him walking down the street talking to himself; they don't know. All they know is a strange Black man in the neighborhood is talking to himself. That's very scary.

Additionally, Trina is highly conscious of her community's background. She is not only concerned about racism beyond her neighborhood but also about the Black community that harbors many stereotypes regarding mental illness. Trina's comedy is a battle for her son's life:

> Every comedian has their thing, and mine is mental illness in the Black community. That hits home for me. I'm there to make you laugh. But when I get to that mental illness part, I'm there to get you information that you need to know. In the Black community, it is so stigmatized. You don't seek help. If you do, then you are weak. I'm trying to stamp that out because our people need treatment. They need help. I want people not to be afraid to get help or to say I'm hurting here. I'm suffering. Let me talk to you or let me get help. Show me which way to go.

Trina is navigating the challenges of parenthood, race, and even gender. She is acutely aware of the community she comes from and the racism that extends beyond her neighborhood. Additionally, Trina is concerned about the many stereotypes attached to mental illness within the Black community. Despite her eagerness to discuss the topic, she understands that it can be offensive. "It's challenging because I don't want to cross any lines," she explains. "I don't want to offend the person with the illness or the people around them. I understand it well; I would be upset if someone said something about my son." Speaking openly onstage is a delicate matter for Trina and can potentially be harmful. With so many issues to navigate, Trina finds it easier to remain silent.

STIGMA HARMS EVERYONE, EVEN THOSE WITH PRIVILEGES

According to Krefting,[5] comedy functions as a "modern-day minstrelsy" in which comedians play with stereotypes and struggle with the fear of exploiting them for laughs. Gender and LGBTQ+ identities, which are widely recognized as master statuses in the United States, were unavoidable for the comedians in this study as they constantly navigated these stereotypes. Lydia noted that when it comes to women, "Our vaginas are always the punch line." Although I only briefly touched on race and ethnicity in relation to parenthood, they operate similarly in how they limit comedians' ability to be seen. (Rest assured, we will delve into race and ethnicity in greater detail in later chapters.) These statuses not only define how the world views them, but also directly limit their ability to resist stigma and speak out.

From an evidential standpoint, none of these findings come as a surprise. Krefting argues that the audience's reception of a comedian is largely informed by cultural capital, rather than innate biological or psychological traits. Those bodies that hold the most importance in a national imagination are culturally positioned to have the highest social capital and are therefore regarded as the highest relative to any task they undertake. There are potentially thousands of publications that demonstrate how society is structured around men and white masculinity in our social world.[6] White, cisgender men are the default in our social consciousness and culture, and those outside of this frame, such as women and minorities, are the exception and are less likely to be accepted or are harmed by the frame.[7] For instance, feminine roles, although equally important to society's functioning (such as motherhood and nursing), are met with hostility and low compensation. This is evidenced by women writers who often feel a more significant microscope focused on their bodies and work, are criticized more harshly, and are often tokenized.[8] In the same process, because male bodies are often the reference in medical research, women are more likely to be harmed by medicine. Until recently, the U.S. National Institutes of Health did not require the inclusion of female subjects in research. In one telling example, doctors are almost exclusively trained in male heart attack symptoms, even though women have significantly different symptoms. Due to this gendered training, women are more likely to be misdiagnosed and die from heart attacks and other cardiovascular diseases.[9]

It's important to note that while masculinity can stifle discussions about trauma, it doesn't provide immunity from it. Men, including white men, are not exempt from struggles and trauma. Hegemonic masculinity can have negative consequences for anyone who doesn't fit the mold of a white, cisgender, heterosexual man, but it's also important to recognize that men experience unique pressures based on societal expectations of manhood.[10] These expectations include being violent or aggressive, emotionally distant, stoic, courageous, risk-taking, competitive, and sexually dominant.[11] As a result of these pressures, men have higher rates of problem drinking, gun violence, and mortality and morbidity risk from accidents.[12] The military, a hypermasculine environment, is a prime example of how these expectations can lead to devastatingly high rates of rape, problem drinking, and low rates of emotional care related to trauma, ultimately resulting in higher rates of suicide and mental illness.[13] While women experience sexual trauma more often than men,[14] men are still impacted in destructive ways and are more likely to hide their trauma due to societal stigma.[15] Military men who experience sexual trauma may even lie and say their PTSD is related to war.[16] Toxic masculinity partially explains why men use fewer medical resources, die younger, and are more likely to be school shooters. It also may explain why some male comedians exhibit antagonistic behavior toward their audience, while women and minorities feel the need to be more deferential.

Societal messaging plays a role in explaining why Rebecca felt comfortable sharing her trauma onstage, particularly at the intersection of invisible and visible stigma. The positive messaging was both implicit and explicit. Rebecca lived in a liberal culture where issues of gender and violence were openly discussed in various settings, including the arts. Additionally, her fellow comedians encouraged her to discuss the event onstage, providing unquestioning support. The club owner even helped Rebecca with the setup and pacing of her set.

Comparing Rebecca's experience to mine, I kept my sexual trauma a secret for over thirty years. This was due to consistent messaging that I heard in the various communities I lived in, which was reinforced by my parents. The military culture that I grew up in, which hasn't changed much, is incredibly unhealthy. It consistently marginalizes sexual violence and revictimizes those who have been harmed. This culture helped foster some of my parents' prejudice, particularly my father's. When I was a child, my father, like most of his peers in the military, was proud to disparage those who wanted to remove "don't ask, don't tell," comfortable with calling colleagues "dykes" and "faggots." He was someone who had proclaimed that women were too weak to be in the military, and my mother wouldn't challenge the idea to his face, although she would tell me later, that she disagreed. Stories of rape, sometimes gang rape, frequented our military community, as they do today. Although sympathetic to the victim, my parents, like many others in the military, would question why the victim put themselves in that situation.

Since my father's retirement from the marine corps, my parents—particularly my father—have made significant progress. They support LGBTQ+ rights, women in the military, and the elimination of sexual violence in communities. I have heard them criticize family members who make insensitive comments about LGBTQ+ individuals. I have even witnessed my father directly challenge service members and veterans who defend a toxic military culture. Although my parents may reflect on their past opinions with remorse, the damage has already been done. Decades of negative socialization kept me silent for years.

NOTES

1. James M. Henslin, *Essentials of Sociology: A Down-to-Earth Approach* (New York: Pearson, 2019).

2. Michael Eric Dyson, "Whose President Was He?," *Politico*, The Obama Issue (2016): 1–5.

3. R. W. Connell and James W. Messerschmidt, "Hegemonic Masculinity: Rethinking the Concept," *Gender and Society* 19, no. 6 (2005): 829–59, https://doi.org/10.1177/0891243205278639.

4. Peter Dickenson et al., eds., *Women and Comedy: History, Theory, Practice* (Vancouver, BC: Fairleigh Dickinson University Press, 2017).

5. Krefting, *All Joking Aside: American Humor and Its Discontents.*

6. April H. Bailey, Marianne LaFrance, and John F. Dovidio, "Is Man the Measure of All Things? A Social Cognitive Account of Androcentrism," *Personality and Social Psychology Review* 23, no. 4 (2019): 307–31, https://doi.org/10.1177/1088868318782848.

7. Sandra Lipsitz Bem, *The Lenses of Gender: Transforming the Debate on Sexual Inequality* (New Haven, Connecticut: Yale University Press, 1993): Ronald Levant et al., "The Femininity Ideology Scale: Factor Structure, Reliability, Convergent and Discriminant Validity, and Social Contextual Variation," *Sex Roles* 57, no. 5–6 (2007): 373–83, https://doi.org/10.1007/s11199-007-9258-5: Charlotte Perkins Gilman, *The Man-Made World, or, Our Androcentric Culture* (New York: Charlton Company, 1911).

8. Brett Mills and Sarah Ralph, "'I Think Women Are Possibly Judged More Harshly with Comedy': Women and British Television Comedy Production," *Critical Studies in Television: The International Journal of Television Studies* 10, no. 2 (2015): 102–17, https://doi.org/10.7227/cst.10.2.8.

9. Nancy N. Maserejian et al., "Disparities in Physicians' Interpretations of Heart Disease Symptoms by Patient Gender: Results of a Video Vignette Factorial Experiment," *Journal of Women's Health* 18, no. 10 (2009): 1661–67, https://doi.org/10.1089/jwh.2008.1007.

10. Bem, *The Lenses of Gender: Transforming the Debate on Sexual Inequality*: Connell and Messerschmidt, "Hegemonic Masculinity: Rethinking the Concept."

11. Bailey, LaFrance, and Dovidio, "Is Man the Measure of All Things? A Social Cognitive Account of Androcentrism."; Connell and Messerschmidt, "Hegemonic Masculinity: Rethinking the Concept"; Carol O'Brien, Jessica Keith, and Lisa Shoemaker, "Don't Tell: Military Culture and Male Rape," *Psychological Services* 12, no. 4 (2015): 357–65; Michael Kimmel, "Men, Masculinity, and the Rape Culture," in *Transforming a Rape Culture*, ed. Emilie Buchwald, Pamela R. Fletcher, and Martha Roth (Minneapolis: Milkweed Editions, 2005), 139–57; C. J. Pascoe, "'Dude, You're a Fag': Adolescent Masculinity and the Fag Discourse," *Sexualities* 8, no. 3 (2005): 329–46, https://doi.org/10.1177/1363460705053337.

12. Sarah Rosenfield, "Triple Jeopardy? Mental Health at the Intersection of Gender, Race, and Class," *Social Science & Medicine* 74, no. 11 (2012): 1791–1801, https://doi.org/10.1016/j.socscimed.2011.11.010; Sarah Rosenfield and Dawne M.

Mouzon, "Gender and Mental Health," in *Handbook of the Sociology of Mental Health*, ed. Carol S. Aneshensel, Jo C. Phelan, and Alex Bierman (Dordrecht: Springer Netherlands, 2013), 277–96, https://doi.org/10.1007/978-94-007-4276-5.

13. Janet K. Cater and Jerry Leach, "Veterans, Military Sexual Trauma and PTSD: Rehabilitation Planning Implications," *Journal of Applied Rehabilitation Counseling* 42, no. 2 (2011): 33–41; Paul Higate, "Peacekeepers, Masculinities and Sexual Exploitation," *Men and Masculinities* 10, no. 1 (2007): 99–119.

14. Connell and Messerschmidt, "Hegemonic Masculinity: Rethinking the Concept"; Douglas Schrock and Michael Schwalbe, "Men, Masculinity, and Manhood Acts," *Annual Review of Sociology* 35, no. 2009 (2018): 277–95, https://doi.org/10.1146/annurev-soc-070308-l.

15. Margret E. Bell, Jessica A. Turchik, and Julie A. Karpenko, "Impact of Gender on Reactions to Military Sexual Assault and Harassment," *Health and Social Work* 39, no. 1 (2014): 25–33, https://doi.org/10.1093/hsw/hlu004.

16. Cater and Leach, "Veterans, Military Sexual Trauma and PTSD: Rehabilitation Planning Implications."

Chapter 4

Testing Social Boundaries

We have a general understanding of the issues that comedians face and how much stigma they can encounter. However, before we can examine how comedians confront stigma onstage, we must ask a more fundamental question: how will the audience react when the stigma is revealed? What is acceptable and what is not? In the previous two chapters, we identified the invisible and visible stigmas that comedians navigate onstage. Obviously, why comedians perceived these issues as taboo was somewhat based on audience reactions after discussing them. But much more of it, especially among those issues that had not yet been publicly discussed, were based on their relationships and socialization prior to getting onstage. Before they even took the mic, comedians already had a pretty clear understanding of the scope of stigma through everyday interactions. Those stages that are embedded in specific communities are likely to have similar beliefs; all communities have different perceptions about things like being LGBTQ+, gender, race and ethnicity, marital status, religious association, or any combination of these factors.

However, we still do not know the exact public reaction that would occur when discussing sensitive topics, especially on the comedy stage. Communities do not provide a manual to answer a person's questions about potential discrimination. While some symbols may be scattered throughout a community (such as the rainbow flag versus the Confederate flag), people must test social boundaries to gain a clear understanding. Will they face harassment or violence? Will they be invited to others' homes? Will their children be able to play with others' children? Or will there be no reaction at all? In other words, what are the social boundaries of a stigma?

Selective disclosure is a valuable process because it allows one to block potentially adverse reactions. A person will have to decide (1) whether and to whom to disclose their condition, (2) how much information to communicate, and (3) how to time disclosure.[1] People can selectively disclose information and test others to gauge their reactions. As they gain a deeper understanding of their place in society and potential discrimination, they can then disclose more details and repeat the process as necessary.[2] Let's examine how comedians tested subjects using different strategies, each with its own pros and cons for the prospect of eliminating stigma.

LEADING THE AUDIENCE

Comedians often use leading tactics to introduce a topic to their audience. Their aim is to build empathic support and make the audience comfortable before discussing taboo or stigmatized subjects. By doing so, they hope to make the audience like them personally. If this tactic is successful, the audience will give them the benefit of the doubt and listen without interrupting. This tactic is evident in the case of Bernard, a middle-aged white man who frequently discusses bigotry and advocates for marginalized groups in his comedy. Many of his stories are inspired by his father, who abandoned the family when Bernard was a child:

> Lately, I've been doing this bit about my dad abandoning the family and then me tracking him down as an adult. When I was a kid, my dad was a biker. He was never in a bike gang, but he ran around with a bunch of dudes who were Grim Reapers, which is this meth-dealing bike gang in the Midwest. So, I had a lot of uncles who were Grim Reapers and stuff. He was this crazy, partying, hell-raiser, fighting dude. He had false teeth in the front because all his teeth had been knocked out in a fight in his twenties. So, my mom takes us in the middle of the night because she knows it's a bad situation and my father never bothers to visit us. She tells him where we are, and he never pays child support, never visits. Then as an adult—I don't talk about this part onstage—but I start having dreams about him out of the blue. So, this means something, and I track him down.

Bernard was planning to confront his father, but when he found him, he was surprised to find a man with a spiritual awakening and a serious health issue:

> When I find him, he becomes this super right-wing ultra-conservative, religious nut-bag. Our visits did not go well because he was this right-wing nut-bag. And I made this decision to stop visiting him, which is true, and then he gets sick. And so, I must keep visiting, and I watch him deteriorate over the next few years from ALS. The last time I visit him, he's lost his ability to speak from ALS, he's skin and bones, he can barely do anything. When I'd visit him, we would keep it light. I'd tell him what I was doing, and he would write on a pad and paper.

Bernard had been dealing with his father's bigoted behaviors for some time, but he never confronted him due to intense pity. However, one particular event changed everything. As someone in an interracial marriage, Bernard was particularly distressed by his father's behavior. During his father's battle with ALS, he always seemed to have the strength for something atrocious. One day, he used all his strength to write down a hateful message: "fags caused 9/11." This was the breaking point for Bernard, and he knew he could no longer tolerate his father's bigotry.

It took Bernard almost fifteen years to reach the point where he could publicly tell the story. For more than a decade, he would share what his father did on his deathbed with people, but he couldn't figure out how to make it funny onstage without it being just a sad story. To be successful, Bernard strategically introduces the topic because, as he says, "It does not paint my dad in a particularly good light. But it is an honest light of who he was in my life and what happened." During his set, he spends a long time building tension, eliciting small laughs, and gaining support from the audience before the final shocking revelation:

The joke part, his take on 9/11, it's kind of a sucker punch. The set lays it out. There are a few laugh lines at the beginning where I set up what's going on. There's a couple of jokey laughs about my dad and our relationship. And then it gets into the real heavy part of it, him dying of ALS, and it's silent. When the big reveal comes and the big punch line, it's shocked faces and then laughter.

Bernard has been performing the set for a few years now. While leading the audience effectively, it is one of the most taxing strategies to engage in. Comedians require tremendous skills to lead the audience, which can only be built through years of practice. Consider Hope, a middle-aged woman from the South, whose journey to communal coping began when she experienced emotional and physical abuse at the hands of her ex-boyfriend. She informed me that after the breakup, her ex "started doing scary things, coming around the comedy club, coming around shows. Going through the garbage and looking for receipts." She added that "he would show up at my house. And there was no recourse."

Worse, Hope couldn't escape her ex's abuse, which seeped into her career as a comedian and was amplified by some colleagues:

The hallmark of being trapped in a relationship is being powerless. When he was doing all these things, they [male comics] were making a lot of jokes. Worse, they would invite him into our space when I didn't want them to. They brushed it off a lot as "yeah, they're just a crazy couple." They didn't know all the details, but the horrible things they did see, they made quite a bit of fun of.

Hope felt shame about her relationship and the stigma of being a woman trapped in abuse. She said, "I didn't know how to tell them how terrified I was and how trapped I felt. I didn't tell them a lot of what was going on because I was very embarrassed about being in a relationship that was so bad. I was embarrassed because I didn't want people to think I was an idiot." Her peers' treatment further hindered her ability to communicate with her comedian peers, who lacked empathy. "I didn't know how to communicate with them, and I didn't want to because male comedians don't have a lot of empathy." Overall, Hope was worried about violence from her ex, emotional abuse from her comedian peers, and the potential fallout for her comedy career. "Even though my ex wasn't a comedian, he had really intertwined himself in the theater, and those other comedians didn't understand how getting away from him could affect my comedy career." It took her years before she could confront her issues, needing time and space to carefully understand her experience because, as she described, most victims do not realize that they are victims:

> I sat on it for four years because I was in an abusive relationship and did not fundamentally understand enough to get out of it. I did not understand exactly what abuse was. It changes your mindset in a way that makes it difficult to connect with other people. Because all the things that you think are important about it are not important to the audience, only some distance gives you some ability to present the information. And now I know how to walk them from where they are to where I am. If you are in that moment of abuse, you have no idea what is going on, so you can't bridge that gap between you and the audience. I've seen people try to go up after some trauma, and they are a hot mess up there. It's not that you shouldn't work through it and talk about it, but don't do a show. Get some clarity so you can communicate with people. Trauma makes you like an alien that can't communicate with others.

Throughout her struggles, Hope found the courage to share her story on a comedy stage. She performed hour-long shows where she discussed her trauma, with a particular focus on the comedians who had contributed to her abuse. They were in the audience, and she needed to reach them. Hope carefully crafted her ideas during one show that explored all the emotional and physical abuse she had experienced throughout her life. To tell her Me Too story about her abusive ex, Hope first described her upbringing in a religiously conservative family, feeling like an imposter as a professional healthcare worker, and then the difficulties of being a woman in comedy.

Many comedians attempt to challenge stigmas in public by leading their audience. They take the time to explore the social boundaries of these stigmas and carefully monitor their behavior during this exploration, much like they would when engaging in political conversation. Similar to behavioral and cognitive therapy,[3] the goal of leading the audience is to provide subtle, nonhostile commentary that doesn't provoke the cultural dynamic of the community, but rather guides the audience toward the ideal conclusion.

For this process to succeed, comedians require time between events, clarity from years of self-reflection, and the skill to carefully construct their ideas. Leading the audience takes immense talent, but it may be the most effective way to change hearts and minds. Other tactics are not focused on persuasion or the audience's feelings when approaching a topic.

DISARMING THE AUDIENCE

Comedians often use the tactic of disarming their audience, especially when dealing with visible stigmas related to race, gender, disability, or sexual orientation. They feel compelled to address these topics and make light of them to reduce tension. For example, consider Barb, a white woman in her twenties who is coming to terms with her status as a queer woman and how her romantic relationships affect her identity and relationships with her family. One source of her turmoil is her discomfort with presenting herself as more feminine or masculine. She says, "I talk about society's norms and expectations regarding gender roles or relationships. When it comes to two women in a relationship, people always ask who's the man."

Barb's passion for fashion is derived from her personal experiences. She describes herself as a "flannel shirt, button-down, black jeans, sneakers kind of gal." For many years, she struggled with trying to be feminine. But eventually, she found herself most comfortable in her current boyish, loose-fitting clothes. Today, she can look at her wardrobe and say, "I like this; this is who I am. These are my clothes."

Barb has used the stage to delve into various aspects of her identity, such as her relationships and the process of coming out to her family. However, before she can even begin to share personal anecdotes, she believes it's necessary to address her appearance. According to her, this is important so that "people can identify with it and laugh and sympathize with it." She explains that if someone is preoccupied with something else while she's telling a joke, then they won't find it funny. Therefore, she wants to cover all bases and ensure that her audience is fully engaged.

Barb actively wants to address her identity, which disarms her audience. Other comedians can also disarm their audiences on unrelated subjects. This is especially important when the audience is focused on an irrelevant issue, such as the performer's ethnic background. For example, Emilio is a fifty-three-year-old Latino who grew up in a military family that lived overseas when he was younger:

I'm a military brat, so we moved around a lot. My dad was in the Air Force for twenty years and a Vietnam vet. I lived out in Okinawa for three years during high school. We were there from 1980 to 1983. People always ask me if I speak Japanese and I go "Ie, wakarimasen, No, I don't understand." [laughs]. When I was little, we moved to Washington, D.C. I lived in Fresno.

Due to the military lifestyle, which required frequent relocation, Emilio found that his friendships were only temporary. However, he became very close to his family, whom he described as loving, caring, and the most important part of his life:

In Okinawa in the '80s there was one military channel, and all the other channels were Japanese, but they played American shows. They would play *Dukes of Hazzard* or *CHiPS* or *Three's Company*, but it was all in Japanese. We didn't understand, so we would turn the sound off and read lips and tell our own jokes and tell our own stories. We were making ourselves laugh. We watch TV together. We would point out bloopers and laugh at each other. We've always done things together. My mom and dad were great about going camping and boating and fishing on the weekend. They would get us out of the house and keep us busy. My mantra in life is family, food, and having fun.

Each of Emilio's immediate family members is involved in public service. His brother is a doctor and an officer in the army, his sister is a speech pathologist, his dad is a medical technologist who also works for the armed services, and his mom is a medical assistant. Emilio, however, is the black sheep of the family, the comedian. As he laughs, "I always make fun of it and say, 'My brother is a doctor and colonel, so who do you think is the family favorite during Thanksgiving?' But my mom tells me, 'Son, you cure with your laughter.'"

Even though Emilio and his family are as American as apple pie, with a heritage of serving and sacrificing for our country in multiple wars, and even though he himself has served military personnel by doing a comedy tour in the Middle East for a month, he cannot escape the Latino label that pits him as an outsider. Emilio barely even speaks Spanish. As a standup comedian, Hollywood forces Emilio to play up negative Latino stereotypes, which is direct evidence of the 'modern-day minstrelsy.' Once, a late-night talk show on network television hired Emilio to do a look-alike skit of a prominent Mexican immigrant and sidekick to that host. Emilio is not an immigrant, but as he describes:

In Los Angeles, there is a certain cadence, and I don't do that stereotypical Latino cadence. I don't have that voice. Sometimes I make fun of that voice that they want me to play when I do auditions. They'll ask me, "Can you be more

Latino? Can you be more Hispanic? Can you be more Mexican?" I've talked about those experiences and the stereotypes they want me to play and glamorize.

Emilio's comedy is clean, fun, and family-friendly. He doesn't consider himself solely a Latin comic, as he avoids performing any expected stereotypes or directly addressing the Latino experience. Instead, he often talks about getting older and navigating technology, as well as celebrating his family. Although his experiences are relatable to all, he cannot escape his status as a brown Latino. During a trip to the Midwest, Emilio had to address the racism in the audience in order to talk about his family experiences:

> You don't have to say you're Latino. When you are onstage, I just stand there, and I am Latino. Look at me. I'm brown. So, I'm representing the Latinos, I guess. I did this one show where I was the opener, and then the host bombed. BOMBED! And then the audience started chanting "Bring back the beaner. Bring back the beaner." I was like, is that good or bad? So, I've had to embrace it. When I go up onstage and it's all white conservatives, I'll say, "Hey, I know what you guys are thinking: the lawn guy does comedy?" or "Hey, the cook is doing comedy." And then describe where I'm from in Northern California so they can feel better. Sometimes I'll explain the military brat thing, that I've traveled all over. But even after I say all that, [they think], "You're a Mexican."

Comedians politely and sometimes forcefully disarm their audience. Barb is polite about her status, while Emilio disarms through ludicrous comments to highlight the absurdity of stereotypes and biases in the audience. However, both aim to acknowledge the audience's feelings about a subject, let them know that others share similar thoughts, and then identify the absurdity of those bigoted thoughts. Importantly, disarming is used when the comedian wants to move to a different subject as the audience's inherent bias is blocking a conversation. Barb wants to talk about dating, but must address femininity. Emilio wants to talk about technology and family, but must address his skin tone.

SHOCKING THE AUDIENCE

When disarming an audience, it is important to consider the feeling of the audience. Shocking the audience, on the other hand, is not considerate. This tactic, often described as blue comedy, involves comedians saying something out of place or so vulgar and offensive to ordinary sensibilities that they can simply pass it off as a joke and move on to the next part of their set. For example, Leonel, a Latino from the Texas Valley, experienced an abusive relationship. "I was going out with a Latina. When I grew up, Latinas were really strong, so she would always try to fight me. I was the one getting hit in the face. Her fists were up." Leonel feels that people judge his masculinity when he talks about being abused. To test his experience with the audience, he has created a very offensive and quite shocking joke, which he uses to redirect offense on himself:

> I have a joke about that, how women are abusive toward men. I say women are always complaining men are jerks or they're mean, they treat us like crap. You know what ladies, you are right, we do treat you like crap. But it's not because we want to, it's because we have to. When a guy is too nice to you, you end up jumping him and going with another guy because you are too nice. That's why the next time your husband or your deadbeat boyfriend punches you in the face or kicks you in the stomach; he's a keeper. Then I say, I'm just playing ladies, I'm the one that got hit. I dated a woman who hit me. So, they are like, "Oh my God, he said that!" But no, the truth is I was the one who was getting hit in the face.

Unlike disarming and leading the audience, in which the comedians are generally interested in convincing the audience to agree with their point, comedians who use shock are often not interested in how others feel. Absurdity is their tool to destigmatize, hopefully. It's not always effective. Consider Tiffany, a thirty-year-old white woman. As a child, Tiffany went through a lot of traumas that began with the death of her father:

> My dad committed suicide when I was young. My mom started abusing me when I was eleven or twelve, and I got put into foster care. I was exceptionally ornery. I was very angry all the time. When I was fifteen, my mom sold me to a pedophile. And then I ran away, and I was homeless for about a year. When I was sixteen, I ended up in Arizona and got legally emancipated, and then I started college. During that time, I never fit in with the other homeless people. In my entire life, I've never tasted a sip of alcohol or tried a drug or smoked a cigarette. So, it's weird being in this subculture [standup comedy] of people who have a lot of substance abuse problems. I'm a fly on the wall.

Tiffany has grown into a strong and empowered woman since. She works full-time in adult entertainment as a stripper and takes pride in her profession. In fact, she incorporates her job into her comedy routine, discussing all the details and even stripping during some sets:

> My humor is pretty dark. I joke a lot about the things that people think got me to this point. Like, I'll joke about child molestation. Rape. Those kinds of things. I know people are going to be shocked initially, but quickly people warm up to me. I make a lot of jokes about how people assume that I am a prostitute. Or that I've dealt with being cummed on at work. A lot of my comedy is about

playing the victim, like, "Why did all these crazy things happen to me?" I think shocking people is funny.

Like all other comedians, Tiffany genuinely seeks laughter, but comedians who use shock are more interested in making the audience uncomfortable. Tiffany's goal is to empower other women to be proud of their bodies and sexuality by giving the world the middle finger. She says, "the entire reason that I do standup comedy is to empower women. I want to inspire women to take their life into their own hands. And fuck society's standards. Do what makes them happy. A lot of people give me a hard time about being a stripper and showing my body. And all those people can suck it."

Disregard for the audience's feelings comes as part and parcel of the desire to make others aware of the world's ugliness. Instead of only lifting their own self-esteem, comedians who use shock are partially interested in rattling others' psychological foundations, sometimes as a call to action. Shocking an audience rejects social relationships while leading the audience focuses on gaining acceptance to improve them. Those who shock want to lift themselves emotionally, but they sometimes do so by knocking others down.

Unfortunately, shocking the audience is often the least effective way to start a conversation, promote healing, and truly be understood. Research has shown that individuals who belittle others generally have lower self-esteem than those who do not.[4] While shocking behavior may not necessarily harm the individual, there is plenty of evidence to suggest that it can negatively affect others. Victims of child abuse and school violence, for example, were certainly hurt when they were ridiculed by comedians like Dave Chappelle and Louis C.K. following the Marjory Stoneman Douglas High School shooting.[5] If someone is hurting and chooses to lash out rather than deal with their own personal stressors, then they are not truly addressing the root of the problem. The fact that shock is often used in discussing the most distressing subjects suggests that it is more of a distraction than a means of promoting true healing.

WE ALL TEST THE SOCIAL BOUNDARIES THAT CREATE STIGMA

DesRochers argues that in order to confront and dispel stereotypes, comedians may need to present themselves in certain stereotypical ways that the audience finds most comfortable.[6] To establish an intimate setting with a room full of strangers, comedians use various strategies, such as how they use microphones and their clothing choices, to bridge the spatial and sociocultural distances between themselves and the audience.[7] Culture plays a significant role in how comedians strategically present stigmatized issues. They cannot simply blurt out a topic, even if they are confident about the reaction. Instead, they must gauge all potential reactions, from acceptance to violence. Introductions are crucial, because viewers may not always be ready to engage in a conversation on a subject that may make them feel uncomfortable. If a comedian starts that conversation with an unprepared audience, the public may have an adverse reaction, hindering the comedian's journey to healing.

As I interviewed comedians, I naturally couldn't gather lessons on general stigma reduction without acknowledging the comedy world that provides the data. Comedians exhibit very specific behaviors to understand public reactions and potential discrimination. They exist in a wholly unique world that seeks to feel good. Comedians discuss contentious issues, including religion, death, abuse, and even mental illness, with strangers before selectively disclosing information to family or other associates. This is contrary to early assessments that expected more hostile reactions from strangers.[8] The fact that many comedians disclose information to a "relationally distant" audience and engage in such risky behavior suggests that the practice may not be that risky. For some, a faceless audience may be more forgiving than family.

Although these tactics are unique, they are not dissimilar to what everyone else uses off stage. At some point, you may have used something similar. I certainly have. Sometimes, we slowly convince others of our position to avoid creating social divisions. For example, at the end of my journey to understand my trauma, when I was finally honest with myself, I calmly sat down with my wife and explained everything. It was a long conversation where we both cried and hugged at the end.

Sometimes we express our feelings through shouting, without considering how others may feel. When I was in high school, I had an argument with my parents about something that I cannot even recall. Instead of calmly discussing the issue, I resorted to screaming at them and scraping the bottom of the barrel, "At least I didn't let my child get raped." I'm not sure if they realized the truth behind my words, but they did ask me to leave the house for the night. The next day, when I returned, they avoided discussing the topic of child abuse that wouldn't surface until many years later.

Sometimes we choose to remain silent or only drop hints in the hopes that others will understand. We hope to see a glimmer of empathy so that we can continue those conversations. This was a tactic I used with my parents after interviewing Rafa, a Latino man from Texas, who had experienced abuse at the hands of his father. As an adult, Rafa was finally able to have an open conversation with his father, who deeply apologized. That night, after interviewing Rafa, I attempted to discuss the remarkable growth in Rafa's relationships with my parents. However, in reality, I was testing their reactions and leaving bread crumbs for the abuse that I had endured. Their reaction to the conversation was telling: my mother interrupted me, and my father walked out of the room in the middle of my sentence. In that moment, I knew the boundaries and limits of our conversation.

Once we know that others will react poorly, we hide our issues and try to escape. It took me decades to be open about my abuse. When my parents reacted poorly, we separated, and it would take another two years before I spoke to them again.

Before being seen, individuals need to explore the potential public reactions. They engage in a continuous process of cultural and stigma exploration by using tactics such as leading, disarming, and shocking the audience. The most effective technique appears to be gently leading the audience, as if they are the ones living with trauma, which many of them are. With these conversational tactics, let us now explore the available options for responding to stigma.

NOTES

1. Erving Goffman, *Stigma: Notes on the Management of Spoiled Identity* (New York: Simon & Schuster, Inc, 1963).

2. Peggy A. Thoits, "Resisting the Stigma of Mental Illness," *Social Psychology Quarterly* 74, no. 1 (2011): 6–28, https://doi.org/10.1177/0190272511398019.

3. Ellen Driessen et al., "Does Publication Bias Inflate the Apparent Efficacy of Psychological Treatment for Major Depressive Disorder? A Systematic Review and Meta-Analysis of US National Institutes of Health–Funded Trials," *PLoS ONE* 10, no. 9 (2015): 1–23, https://doi.org/10.1371/journal.pone.0137864; L. Mason et al., "Brain Connectivity Changes Occurring Following Cognitive Behavioural Therapy for Psychosis Predict Long-Term Recovery," *Translational Psychiatry* 7, no. 1 (2017), https://doi.org/10.1038/tp.2016.263.

4. Nathan A. Heflick, "Why Are People Mean?," *Psychology Today*, 2013.

5. Doug Criss, "Comedian Louis C.K. Mocks Parkland Shooting Survivors in Leaked Audio: Parkland Survivors Respond," CNN, 31 2018.

6. DeRochers, *The Comic Offense from Vaudeville to Contemporary Comedy: Larry David, Tina Fey, Stephen Colbert, and Dave Chappelle*.

7. Brodie, *A Vulgar Art: A New Approach to Stand-Up Comedy*.

8. Peggy A. Thoits and Bruce G. Link, "Stigma Resistance and Well-Being among People in Treatment for Psychosis," *Society and Mental Health* 6, no. 1 (2016): 1–20, https://doi.org/10.1177/2156869315591367.

Chapter 5

Tactics to Manage Stigma

Chattoo and Feldman's analysis of social justice in comedy suggests that efforts for social change can range from individual-level changes in attitudes and behaviors to macro-level shifts in social norms, media agendas, and institutional policies.[1] Similarly, stigma resistance can also exist on a spectrum. On one end of the stigma resistance spectrum is Pierson, a young white man who experienced a series of unfortunate events over the past year. Despite getting beat up and receiving a DUI, Pierson found humor in his misfortunes and incorporated them into his comedy routine. The audience's positive response validated Pierson's experiences and made him feel less stigmatized. As he put it, "It's like someone agrees with me, I'm validated, and I'm still here." For Pierson and other comedians, the ability to turn their struggles into comedy can be empowering and help reduce the stigma surrounding their experiences.

Unlike Pierson, who was completely open, others remain silent, including Sef, who hides his child abuse from the comedy world because he is not ready to deal with it publicly. As he describes, he cannot control his emotions or the audience. If he tried and faltered, it may harm his ability to come to closure with his abuse, or even revisit the topic in the future. Avoiding the topic may be creating a better headspace.

It's important to remember that just because someone isn't able to use the optimal tactic, it doesn't mean that other tactics aren't beneficial. Even if Sef refuses to engage in an open conversation, any effort to alleviate stress is still a form of coping.[2] Coping is simply any effort to reduce the effects of stress. When someone is experiencing distress, they can either address the problem or find ways to decrease negative responses like anger, sadness, or anxiety.[3] Tactics for coping could include meditating when a stressor appears, seeking support from friends, or even exercising to feel better. Any sustained effort toward maintaining good health is better than letting health deteriorate. While talking openly like Pierson may be ideal, it's not the only option for everyone.

Therefore, no single coping tactic for dealing with stigma is optimal. Instead, every tactic is best suited for a particular situation. Pierson and Sef demonstrate a wide range of tactics that can be used to achieve the best outcome. While Pierson voices his stigmatized status and seeks validation, people like Sef may choose to conceal their problem entirely because they believe the alternative is worse. On the other hand, others may use more subtle tactics while speaking. Now, let's explore all the ways these comedians managed their stigma in public.

CANDID CONVERSATIONS

Candid conversations are at one end of the spectrum. Comedians openly discuss stressful or taboo topics, and the audience is aware of the comedian's relationship with the issue. In many cases, comedians openly discuss their feelings and allow their emotions to flow. For example, Evelyn, a thirty-two-year-old white woman, describes her father's multiple marriages and alcoholism in her set. Talking about these issues in her standup made her feel better for a time. She says, "That was the closest I've come to doing comedy that felt like therapy. And I hate to say that because it's not therapy."

Next, we meet Jessie, a middle-aged white man who talks about his experience trying to conceive another child with his wife in his comedy routine. "My wife and I are trying to get pregnant right now," he says. "And my comedy is about me dealing with and making sense of doing something like that." Although he still enjoys sex, he finds it strange that it now has the practical purpose of conceiving a child, rather than just being about physical and emotional enjoyment for him and his wife. "Having that much sex with a purpose is weird," he admits. "For so long, the sex was an end to itself, but now it's just a means. I feel okay talking about it, but I want it to be thoughtful and measured when I talk about it." Jessie is careful not to offend his wife when discussing their attempts to conceive, saying, "I don't want it to feel like I am resentful of it, that act or her." Despite the changes in the meaning of sex between him and his wife, they still love each other, and the foundation of their relationship remains strong.

Candid conversations are most effective when the audience feels comfortable. Leading the audience toward candidness is key. For example, Evelyn is able to discuss alcoholism because her father has gotten better, despite the stigma surrounding it. Jessie can talk about sex and marriage because many men experience similar situations. However, calling out racism that pokes fun at white people to their face is unlikely to occur. Similarly, discussions of mental illness or childhood trauma may require a more subtle approach. It's not that these topics can't be discussed, but they may need to be approached with more sensitivity.

VEILED CONVERSATIONS

Others, like Evelyn and Jessi, also want to discuss their issues, but they can't have candid conversations. Instead, they talk about their problems in a way that doesn't fully reveal the validity of their experiences. Some comedians hide the full truth, intentionally leaving out important information to keep the audience in the dark. For example, Torri, a forty-five-year-old white woman, talks about systemic sexism and violence against women in a significant portion of her set:

> When I talk about things that bother me, I have this tendency to paint them out in such weird ways that someone may not realize I'm even saying that, but that's fine with me. One of the bits I've been doing lately is about the 1950s and how I'm on a campaign against the 1950s, which is stupid, who goes on a campaign against a decade. I'm so angry that there are all these 1950s apologists out there. I talk about how men stalking women was totally legal back then and encouraged by the popular music of the day. And I describe the situation where the lady goes to the cop about the stalker, but there is very little difference now for a woman who goes to the police and says she's being stalked.

Torri speaks broadly about sexism and misogyny, drawing from personal experience. However, unlike Jessie, who describes a crisis of masculinity around sex, Torri does not explicitly state that she was a victim of sexual violence. Torri recounts during one set, "I try to make it seem like there are these crazy French-Canadian mall Santas, but the truth is I really did sit on a French-Canadian mall Santa's lap, and he was creepy and copping a feel."

At first glance, the idea of a handsy Santa seems ridiculous and can elicit laughter from audiences. However, what they may not realize is that Torri is not making the joke for shock value—she was actually groped by a mall Santa. Despite the fact that her comedy may not be making any significant changes, Torri feels good being able to talk about her experience and receive laughter from the audience.

Then there's Justus, a young Black man who lives in a liberal college town filled with middle-class white people. Justus believes that the "woke" liberals are the ones causing problems, and he's frustrated by their hypocrisy. He says that they claim to be allies and advocates for Black people, but when it comes down to it, they're just as racist as the people they claim to be fighting against. They talk about diversity and inclusion, but they don't actually practice it:

> I like the bravery of saying "nigga" onstage to a room of only white kids. I'd attack the liberal town's bigotries and shit. Try talking to an audience of liberal white people about virtue signaling. It's a real Uncle Tom thing. Liberal white audiences want to think that after you get offstage, you'll be their Black friend, but their Black friend that they can say the N-word [around] just because they are cool, but don't ever think of them as a racist because they "get it."

Justus understands that calling out his audience for their racism will not be well received, especially by middle-class white people who are particularly sensitive to criticism. He has experienced this firsthand, having been asked to leave the only comedy club in his town after white audience members were uncomfortable with his comments. As a result, he has learned to approach the topic more tactfully and indirectly, using topics that a white audience is more comfortable with:

> I have had to work on my jokes just to see the threshold of what white people can handle. I can't attack or seem as if I am going after you. Where I have found people are okay is fucking movies and music. I can give a Black perspective on that, and the audience doesn't feel embarrassed. Some of the jokes that work 50 percent of the time include, "I like to imagine God is a Black man that judges you for your past racisms." That gets dead silence sometimes because the [liberal white audience] is thinking, "Oh my God, if God was a Black man that judged me for my past racisms, I'm going to hell."

Just because someone is hiding their true feelings or experiences, it doesn't mean they aren't finding some validation. In fact, we discovered that "dishonesty" could be a surprisingly beneficial aspect of certain conversations. Tori, who has experienced sexual abuse, finds that by performing, she can express her emotions about sexism without feeling overwhelmed: "I'm not trying to make a change that I don't think is possible. I'm just trying to exist in my own space." Justus, a Black man who faces racial inequality in a liberal town, feels encouraged by the conversations he has while hiding his true thoughts. He hopes to make white liberals think, even if only for a moment: "I want Black people to feel self-love, and I want white people to think, 'Wow, that's a different perspective. Maybe I like that perspective more.'"

Veiled disclosures are most effective when discussing taboo issues. Child abuse is a clear example of the success of this approach. Jamal, a thirty-nine-year-old Black man, is an excellent example of a positive outcome:

I kind of bury it in a punch line. It wasn't extreme, but I had an uncle that made me feel very uncomfortable. It was one of those things that really messed me up as a kid. It was a one-time thing; it was an inappropriate touch. It really disturbed me. I was old enough to remember it. I had been carrying that around with me for years. Eventually, I figured out how to deal with it, and that was to make it a part of a joke. I told the audience that when I have a kid, I'm going to give him a traditional name. If it's a girl, Marie, and if it's a boy, Uncle Bad Touch. That's how I dealt with that. It was just a punch line that came from a real incident. Nobody knew except my mom and my wife.

Jamal further explained that he felt much better after discussing his experiences through that veiled discussion. The audience was unaware of what he was discussing. However, when he told his truth, he was able to find closure finally:

It was really a cathartic thing for me. I can't think of any other way I could have dealt with that. I guess I could have gone to a therapist and dealt with it there though several sessions, but I don't think I could have dealt with it the way I needed to deal with it. I have been telling that joke for ten years, whenever the audience feels right. Saying it out loud, for whatever reason, it makes it easier to reconcile and let go of that hurt.

Most importantly, when asked if Jamal would provide more information to the public, he firmly stated that he would not. The joke was only for his own amusement. "I was fine with it because no one knew how true that joke was."

Similarly, Connor, a middle-aged white man, uses comedy to discuss abuse. Connor was a victim of child abuse by his father. Every few years, he has attempted to have conversations with his abuser, stating, "I told him that's why we don't hang out. He said I was being too sensitive, that he did whatever he had to." Unfortunately, the apology he seeks has never come: "And all I want is sorry. All I want is a sorry, and it is never there."

While Jamal has received support from his mother, Connor has not received any empathy from his parents. This painful truth has forced him to keep his distance. To express his pain and anger, he discloses all the ugly details of his experiences to the audience, fully revealing his hatred of the abuser:

I've done this numerous times. Sometimes it goes really well. Sometimes it goes really poorly. I would open up with "My dad used to hit me." And people would look around in silence—"And then he would send me to bed, and he would stay up drinking. He would crawl into bed with me and run his fingers through my hair while he cried." People would just sit there, and then I would be like, "Boy, I can't wait for that guy to die."

Both Jamal and Connor's comedy is deeply personal. Jamal designs his jokes with his needs in mind, hoping someone may connect with them, but he doesn't reveal too much detail to maintain control. "Ultimately, I get up onstage to entertain people. If I make it too real, especially a subject that makes people feel uncomfortable, then they are not with me," he explains. In contrast, Connor expresses his anger and is indifferent to the audience's feelings. "I like being the bad guy. Dark humor is kind of funny to me." However, because the subject is taboo, Connor's conversations with the audience usually fall apart due to the pure shock factor.

EXISTING WITHOUT TALKING

Comedians use two tactics to address issues in their conversations: candid and veiled. These tactics actively name the problem that bothers them. However, some people don't feel the need to verbalize issues even if they're disclosing them. For those individuals, merely being visible also discloses the problem. This tactic involves vaguely sprinkling in some information about the taboo topic to ensure the audience is aware of it. For example, Chase, a twenty-seven-year-old trans man, started doing comedy when he identified as a lesbian woman. Like many other comedians, he struggled to find his voice:

> I originally started standup trying to be a lesbian comedian and focusing on that more feminine side of me. And then there were times where I thought I needed to be more feminine onstage, and that was definitely not what I wanted. And later I would try something else. And one day, I decided to crank out every persona that a comedian has, try all of them until something clicks with myself. There were a couple shows that I had serious dad-joke style. And then times when it was a Robin Williams style. I was trying to figure out what I wanted to be onstage. And then I figured out that once I discover who I am offstage first, I can put my own personality onstage. But what is my own personality?

Chase spent several months trying to figure out his identity onstage. He journaled and contemplated life, and eventually came to the conclusion that he is trans. "As soon as I admitted it out loud, everything in my past from when I was a kid started flowing back. 'Oh, that makes sense,'" he happily revealed. After discovering his true identity, Chase needed validation for his newly discovered self-image. He decided to test his trans status onstage before coming out to his family. During a show, he had the host introduce him as a trans man with his new name. The non-reaction from the audience confirmed that the public accepted his status, and Chase finally felt comfortable in his skin. "I found my voice when I did my first set as trans," he concluded. This was the moment when he knew that this was the story he wanted to tell, not what he had been before.

Existing proved to be a very beneficial tactic for LGBTQ+ individuals who were afraid to discuss details and just wanted others to get the hint. This included Alvin, who realized he was gay during his freshman year of college, saying, "I didn't even know I was gay until my freshman year of college. I realized it then." Alvin had sexual feelings toward men as a teenager, but he couldn't explore them due to his family's religious beliefs. He explains, "Because my family was so religious and I didn't want to go to hell, I would purposely watch straight porn and try to be straight. I thought that was the right thing to do. I went a lot of my life trying to be a straight man because I wanted God to be happy with me." When Alvin finally left religion behind and started exploring his sexuality, he was also starting his career in comedy. However, he struggled because he wasn't honest with himself or the audience:

> I was in the closet when I started. My comedy was a lot different when I started three years ago. They [the jokes] weren't as personal. More topical or more absurd. I have a bit about state birds. I seriously talk about state birds for three minutes. The jokes weren't great because they weren't personal. The best comedy is honest and tells your truth.

When Alvin finally understood his sense of self, he tested it in front of the audience by sharing little bits of new information about being gay. He didn't go into much detail like Emilio and Barb did. Instead, he sprinkled in topics and observed their reactions. He added more details as he went along:

> I didn't want anyone to know I was gay, so I was really vague. I was talking about it onstage as the process of me thinking about it. I started by kind of saying I was bisexual onstage. It was an accident. I would say I kind of also like men, and people would think I was bisexual. And then I started saying I just like men. There was this joke where I said I was gay, and then I moved on. That was the first time I said it onstage. Most audiences don't know you until you come up onstage and talk, and I didn't want the audience to know me as the guy who just came out thirty seconds ago. It made more sense to mention it and not elaborate. But it was more of a realization for me and being honest about who I am to myself. It was less of me coming out. Once I accepted it for myself, I wanted to keep doing comedy.

Alvin was able to come out as gay and find acceptance without any discussion. He simply made his status known and existed without going into any details. Most of the time, his comments behind the microphone were ambiguous. However, over time, he became more comfortable talking to others more openly about being gay.

One fascinating aspect of this strategy is that individuals feel better about their issues without discussing the intricacies of any given problem. This passive tactic differs from other active tactics in that comedians do not directly address any prejudice in the audience or try to convince others. Instead, they aim to expel bias by making it a nonissue, just a matter of fact. If they don't address it and the audience moves on, then in their mind, there is no stigma and no problem. They then feel better.

Take Pallavi, a young Indian American woman who discusses surviving cancer onstage, for example. For her, performing standup comedy was a liberating experience. "Making them laugh made me feel empowered," she declared. "That made me feel in control of the situation or control over something. And it reinforced a more positive attitude when enduring the whole health thing."

The key to Pallavi's success was not in the jokes, but in her self-presentation. To resist the stigma, she had to exist and demonstrate tremendous confidence, being very conscious of her every movement. She had to stand strong, dress neatly, not slouch, be clear, and smile from ear to ear. To be seen with cancer onstage, she could not frighten or depress the audience. "It helped me more because they could see that I had a nonchalant attitude," she explained, "and they could see that I was not too worried about it. I could physically show them that I was getting through it. That it was going to be fine. They [her family and audiences] perceive me as strong."

Alvin and Pallavi demonstrate that comedians can gain validation without speaking. They positively affect the stigma without any direct discussion, feeling better about themselves and their position in the world. Another comedian, Chaz, illustrates the power of self-presentation. As a gay man, he knows that his presence onstage can affect his identity and how others perceive him, regardless of the topic. Chaz says, "The fact that I exist in comedy is a political act. The very fact that I'm there talking about my experiences that are different than the norm is political. I think that's super important."

Many comedians engaged in long, thoughtful conversations, while others simply existed in a space that was not traditionally available to them. Through positive interactions, comedians gained validation and felt better about themselves. This is not surprising, as ample evidence has shown that the best way to reduce stigma is through social contact with people who have a stigma. Those who have connections with people who live with mental health problems show fewer negative reactions, fewer discriminatory behaviors, and more tolerant attitudes toward mental illness.[4] Although comedians may be able to talk about their experiences, for those who live in marginalized bodies, their mere presence onstage may be the most impactful way to decrease bigoted beliefs based on false stereotypes. They only need to be seen.

ADVOCACY

Advocacy was another important tactic for self-liberation. Many comedians are aware of discrimination that affects not only themselves but others as well. While they may use personal experiences, advocates are primarily concerned with the well-being of others. When advocates receive a positive response from the audience, they feel as though they have alleviated the suffering of others. For instance, Meghan felt constrained by societal expectations of motherhood. While she was tired of her family's constant pressure to get married and have children, it was more of an annoyance that she pushed to the back of her mind. Advocating for other women onstage partly led her to this mindset:

> That's my favorite thing about comedy. I have had a lot of women come up to me and say, "Thank you for saying that." I've had a ton of women come up to me and say, "I don't want kids either, but I haven't been able to tell anyone." A couple of weeks ago a guy came up to me and said that I got him in trouble with his girlfriend and she just said: "Thank you!" If I can just get one guy in a relationship to treat his girl better from something I said, that's the dream. That's what I want to do.

Meghan is keenly aware that many women struggle with gender-related distress. While she is happy to reduce the stigma associated with being a single woman, she is more concerned with the stress that other women experience. When Meghan makes others laugh, she feels a little better about being a childless and unmarried woman, and she feels even better when she knows that other women are benefiting. Helping others is her path to personal freedom.

However, while Meghan advocates for topics that the audience is aware of, others advocate even when the audience is unaware. Sometimes advocacy is straightforward, while other times it is subtle. Like Meghan, Lora, a white woman in her mid fifties from the East Coast, is an advocate who candidly discloses her stressors. Lora spends much of her comedy advocating for marginalized people. Drawing from her grandmother's traumatic experiences during the Armenian genocide, Lora believes that she needs to spend her time onstage helping those who are less fortunate:

> My grandmother told me that when the Turks came to march them into the desert to die, when the Turks came, they didn't give them a lot of time to empty out their things. There was still bread in the oven. And sixty years later, she was like, "Whatever happened to that bread?" It made her cry because when I was thirteen, I did genealogy for school. And I asked her how many siblings she had. And then I asked, "Where are they?" And she's like "They're dead. Stop talking about it." And I kept pressing her and pressing her. And she was like,

"You got to shut up." And I said, "What was it like? What was the genocide like?" And she said "Well, as we were marched through the desert, there were about two hundred of us. About two hundred Armenians for every one Turkish soldier with a gun." And she was daring me to ask, and I did ask. "There were two hundred of you and one of him? Why didn't you just tackle him and kill him? And she said, "None of us want[ed] to be the first to die, so we all died." My grandmother didn't die. She died in here [pointing at her heart]. She had to watch her siblings die.

Lora expresses to the audience her discomfort in not being able to use her privileges to help others, as she is a respected figure in comedy and an upper-class white woman. She states, "That's why I decided. Nobody gets on those trains, not if I can get in the way. Because it's not okay." Lora is not only upset by the suffering of others, but also by those who refuse to help. Onstage, she copes with her privilege by empowering others.

Simon, a middle-aged white man, differs from Lora in his approach as an advocate. He uses veiled conversations to advocate on behalf of marginalized communities. Like Lora, Simon's comedy aims to convince people that everyone matters. "My goal is to convince this audience that this racist behavior is not only mean and cruel, but also incorrect. It's illogical," he argues. However, Simon veils the shame he feels about coming from a conservative family in the rural South with bigoted views. He draws inspiration from his grandmother, who passed away a few years ago, and advocates for marginalized people in the spirit of her. Simon's grandmother was a devout Christian who grew up in a small town with fundamentalist teachings. Despite this, she had nothing but love in her heart, which was reflected in her actions:

My cousin, her grandson, fell in love with this girl. They didn't want to get married. They were teenagers. And they were going to college, who said they couldn't live together in the same dorm. Well, she [his grandmother] said, "That's dumb. Come live at my house." So, she let them sleep together in the same bed in her own house. And they weren't married, but she loved them. My grandmother, she's not for, you know, homosexuality. But my sister showed up with her girlfriend, and my grandmother stood and said: "You come here and let me hug you." And then my sister told my grandmother that I was going to donate sperm for her baby, and my grandmother said, "When it's born, I want to be right there."

Simon uses comedy to reject the southern bigotry embedded in his own history and confirm for himself that he is a good person. Unlike other advocates who may directly describe their background, Simon hides some of his shameful family history from the audience. He explains, "One of my CDs is about her funeral. From start to finish, I am talking about my grandmother and her funeral. [But] nobody knows it till the end when I'm crying." Simon only discusses and discloses those truths after connecting with others who understand his feelings. Simon describes a recent conversation with a young woman who visited her hometown in the Midwest but now lives in Paris. According to Simon, the girl was ashamed of her home until she realized they were just as racist in Paris. After hearing this, Simon instantly connected and shared with her hidden details of his life. He laughed and said, "Oh my God, when I was a kid growing up in Kentucky, I thought the South was the ignorant part. That's what you hear, that's what the jokes are about. The smart people are in New England. And when I turned eighteen, I got in my car and drove to Boston and realized they are just as racist as we are."

CONCEALING AND WITHDRAWING

Although there are various conversation tactics, not everyone can engage in them successfully. Despite their skills, some individuals may face negative reactions from the public. As a result, many comedians silently suffer onstage, unable to discuss their issues. Unfortunately, concealing their problems is also linked to other negative coping strategies, as demonstrated by two comedians. The first, Amelia, is a white woman in her twenties who explains, "I prefer not to talk about personal stuff onstage. I want to talk about things that are sillier and more lighthearted because I think so much of comedy is saturated with sadness." For Amelia, comedy serves a purpose, and she firmly believes in the unspoken agreement between herself and her audience. "I want that for my audience too, rather than having them accompany me through the pain."

Amelia's sadness is partly due to dropping out of college, which has worsened her eating disorders. The stress she's been under has caused her to adopt negative coping mechanisms. She explains, "I have a myriad of coping mechanisms. They range from taking a bath to substance abuse. I have been hospitalized before, been in treatment programs for drugs and eating disorders." Moreover, the comedy world has contributed to Amelia's dangerous behavior. She says, "It became a problem when I turned eighteen and left for school. A lot of my fellow comics are people that I have done drugs with. Comedy is a huge catalyst for my usage."

Then, there is Mark, who has been reflecting on his childhood upbringing. He comes from a middle-class, white background, and while his family is loving and not abusive, there are some underlying issues. For instance, his dad suffered from depression, which was an open secret in the family. As a result, their relationships were very disconnected:

My dad suffered a lot from depression. He was out of work for a couple of years, as far as I remember, he stayed in bed for a couple of years. I think in a way, my dad's depression had all the effects of an absent dad. Like I remember—and this is a really weird and specific example—I didn't know until I was twelve that women didn't have penises. Which is a super weird thing, but it was this sheltered life. Like, I cannot imagine being a kid, being so detached from the important part of their upbringing that that kind of information would slide. Or that there would never be that kind of conversation about it.

Later, when Mark entered high school, his family was shaken daily as they tried to cope with their older brother's mental illness and health:

By the time I was a sophomore in high school, things weren't great. My brother had a pretty bad heroin addiction, and he has always been my closest friend. So high school was pretty dark days. That had an effect on the family structure. I remember seeing my mom cry every day for years, literally the last half of my high school. They were so beside themselves, not knowing how to handle the addictions. For me, it was personally destructive because of the stigma surrounding that. There was such a focus of keeping this thing silent, that it was a pretty destructive secret. It's hard to have healthy coping mechanisms for something of that magnitude when you are that young. When I finished high school, only three people knew about it, so it was a very well-kept secret.

The family's pains still remain undisclosed to this day. Although there have been some discussions, they have not been as thorough as Mark needs or wants. Additionally, Mark do not bring up these issues in public, as they fear it could harm their family. At present, he depends on unhealthy coping mechanisms. On his good days, Mark exercises at the gym, but on most days, he resorts to drinking, which is made worse by his job as a bartender.

It's important to note that not all concealers resort to extreme measures, and concealing can be beneficial in situations where being open could lead to violence or discrimination. However, the stories of Amelia and Mark highlight a correlation between concealing and deep emotional pain caused by the reactions of the world around them. Neither of them actively copes with their problems in a positive way, such as seeking communal support or finding alternative solutions. Instead, they turn to negative behaviors in order to feel better. Amelia continues to use illegal drugs, some of which are facilitated through the comedy community, while Mark abuses alcohol. The stressors they face are so taboo within the comedy community that they feel unable to find liberation. At best, they can only try to make it through each day by any means necessary.

The one benefit that both Amelia and Mark enjoy is their ability to hide their issues. While hiding will never allow them to find closure, it at least maintains the status quo—albeit a very sick status. Others cannot hide, including Treyvaughn, who was pushed out of comedy by homophobia. While stigma toward homosexuality has decreased, the Black community has been one of the slowest to accept those who are LGBTQ+, which he still feels. Treyvaughn has recently returned to comedy, but is only able to perform in drag, veiling his status as a gay man behind a caricature. Treyvaughn is as funny as they come, but his skill was not enough.

USING THESE TACTICS IN THE REAL WORLD

Stigma resistance tactics exist on a spectrum, and it's important to note that everyone engages in these tactics, not just comedians. For example, concealing and withdrawing are so common that we even have a term for it: "hiding in the closet."[5] While some discussions are very open and honest, others are more subtle. Veiled disclosure in comedy is similar to when someone says, "my friend has a problem," but they are actually referring to themselves. Some people speak up for marginalized individuals and defend them, while others resist stigma without saying a word. They simply walk into a space and exist, their mere presence serving as an act of defiance and social connection that breaks down stigma.

Before telling Hiromi the truth, I spent months actively facing my trauma through journaling, reading, and sharing stories with strangers. When conducting intimate interviews in my research, it can be helpful to share parts of oneself as a two-way conversation to build trust. However, I also used this tactic to test social boundaries with comedians for personal growth. For example, when Heather shared losing family relationships after coming out as a lesbian, I shared that my relationship with my parents was contentious. When Bernard shared his struggles with depression, I disclosed my own experiences with suicidal ideation after my divorce. While these empathetic comedians provided some relief from my pain, none of their stories quite matched my own.

One conversation stands out as the most important for my growth, as it helped me address stigma. I had the opportunity for a veiled discussion when I ran into a dear friend in our graduate office at Indiana University. Like most conversations, we started by catching up. In the middle of our conversation, I mentioned that I enjoyed seeing her wedding photos on Facebook, but I hadn't seen any updates in a while. She then explained that she had disabled her social media accounts because of conflicts that had arisen with her family. Like so many people living during the Trump years, his election exposed many volatile divides in families. These conflicts had made her feel very lonely within her own family, especially when they refused to consider the real-world trauma that she faced as a woman. After nights of crying following angry exchanges, she decided to leave social media to try and salvage some of those family relationships.

Sitting in the graduate room, with her crying and my eyes watering, I was reminded of the pain I felt among the comedian participants. The comedians were discussing all kinds of traumatic issues. Every time I spoke with another comedian who told me something deeply personal, I felt the urge to share my own experience. But each time that urge built up, I couldn't speak my truth. However, because she was a friend, I felt free to be a little more honest and try to alleviate some of the pain I was holding. During a lull in her painful story, I calmly told her that she wasn't alone. "I know it doesn't seem like it, but there are many people who know what you are going through. A lot of people have lived through tremendous trauma, even men." I paused and thought carefully about my next words. I swallowed the lump in my throat (the same lump I feel now as I write these words) and then pushed out the next words, "We just aren't ready to tell the world." She wiped her eyes as I continued, "I'm always here to listen if you need anything." She sniffled and smiled, and for the first time, I felt like someone was hearing me. Even though I didn't say much, I'm sure to this day that she has no idea what I was really talking about. I'm sure she had no idea that I was carrying a little less weight on my shoulders.

Opportunities to stand out and be noticed may be rare for some, but they can still be found. Many people spend their whole lives searching for someone with compassionate ears to reveal their painful truth. Often, the only people we can confide in are those who have experienced the same trauma and can perfectly empathize with us. Unfortunately, because of stigma, many of these empathetic individuals will never be known, and the silence around trauma persists. Context may be a predictor of this silence, as a person's socioeconomic background can play a role.

NOTES

1. Chattoo and Feldman, *A Comedian and an Activist Walk into a Bar: The Serious Role of Comedy in Social Justice*, 23.

2. There are four recognized coping categories: meaning-focused, emotion-focused, problem-focused, and compensatory coping.

3. Charles S. Carver, Michael F. Scheier, and Jagdish K Weintraub, "Assessing Coping Strategies: A Theoretically Based Approach," *Journal of Personality and Social Psychology* 56, no. 2 (1989): 267–83, https://doi.org/10.1037/0022-3514.56.2 .267; Leonard I. Pearlin and Carmi Schooler, "The Structure of Coping," *Journal of Health and Social Behavior* 19, no. 1 (1978): 2–21; Jo Lynne W. Robins et al., "Mindfulness: An Effective Coaching Tool for Improving Physical and Mental Health,"

Journal of the American Association of Nurse Practitioners 26, no. 9 (2014): 511–18, https://doi.org/10.1002/2327-6924.12086.

4. Pescosolido et al., "'A Disease Like Any Other'? A Decade of Change in Public Reactions to Schizophrenia, Depression, and Alcohol Dependence."

5. Patrick W. Corrigan and Amy C. Watson, "The Paradox of Self-Stigma and Mental Illness," *Clinical Psychology: Science and Practice* 9, no. 1 (2002): 35–53, https://doi.org/10.1093/clipsy/9.1.35.

Chapter 6

Context Matters

Black and Latino Lives

The book has presented a complex perspective on the stigma coping process so far. In the "ideal" coping process in comedy, individuals are honest, receive positive feedback, feel empathy, and gain a new and improved outlook on themselves and the world around them. There are varying degrees of stigma attached to different experiences, and different people experience them in different ways. People test social boundaries in different ways and use various tactics to engage in conversations about stigmatized topics. Some individuals may try to fully confront those who stigmatize, while others may withdraw to avoid potential violence. However, not everyone has equal access to a platform to speak out. Some individuals may live in a body that is harshly critiqued, forcing them to withdraw from an unsympathetic community. Others may live in a community where simply mentioning a stigma could result in violence, leaving them with no choice but to suffer in silence.

When addressing stigma, it's important to recognize that people are all unique. Viewing differences in trauma, stress, inequality, and discrimination in binary terms fails to acknowledge the diversity within groups and locations.[1] While individuals may face visible and invisible stigma, there are countless potential differences in how people experience it. For example, a Latino man's experience with depression stigma will differ greatly from that of a woman. Similarly, a woman's experience will vary depending on her race, with a Black woman's experience differing greatly from that of a white woman. Even within a particular race, differences in background and composition can affect how someone experiences gender and race. For instance, someone like Jamal may experience his "Blackness" differently in New York compared to a southern state he recently moved to. As he describes it, these variables not only affect how we communicate, but also how we experience something as integral as our identity:

In New York, you are just a comic. You might be a Black comic, but New York produces a certain kind of comedian because it's this melting pot and mixed in together. You talk about race from "this is what my family is like, and these are what my friends are like." But not from tension from people of another race. Down South, everything is race. When I go to a club, it's either a white club or a Black club, and they are always that. It's the location and the crowd that tends to show up. There are certain jokes I can't do in front of Black crowds. They aren't receptive to it. So, I don't perform in a lot of Black rooms.

Jamal highlights a significant fact: universal discrimination is different for everyone, as seen in chapter 3's discussion of parenthood. Jamal experiences "Blackness" regardless of where he lives, but his experiences as a Black person are less prominent in New York than in the South. Black people, Latinx people, women, men, and LGBTQ+ individuals are not homogenous groups. They may share similar cultural experiences of discrimination, but their experiences are unique to them. They are united in the distinctiveness of their experiences.

The best way to understand complexity is by using an intersectional lens. The intersectional approach emphasizes that even though there may be broad patterns of inequality, it's not fair to generalize about everyone. Different systems of stratification—such as race, caste, religion, ability/disability, and location—all "intersect" to create unique and varied outcomes.[2] Sometimes these systems lead to discrimination, like the higher unemployment rates among Black people. Other times they don't, like the lower rates of mental illness among Black people or higher rates of education among Black women. Sometimes a person can be advantaged, like white men who are less likely than Black men to be imprisoned for the same crime. Other times they are harmed, like white men who have the highest suicide rate. People are different, their experiences are different, and how they fit into the world is different. Because of all these intersecting variables, how they experience discrimination and the potential for liberation will vary. To illustrate these complexities, let's examine the vastly different experiences of Black and Latino comedians in front of different audiences, considering their race, ethnicity, and gender.

BLACK COMEDIANS PERFORMING
FOR WHITE AUDIENCES

For individuals of color who took part in the study, discussing or dealing with any subject matter is more complex due to their race and ethnicity. They are also more likely to face outright discrimination. Every Black comedian in the study talked about instances of discrimination and personal management onstage, but when these issues arose varied greatly depending on various factors. The first factor that appeared to moderate experiences onstage was the audience's race. It's not surprising that some comedians felt most comfortable in front of audiences that looked like them when discussing social justice issues. For example, Tracy took to the stage to share her experiences working:

> I have a very tender heart for social justice issues, especially in medicine and for those who are wrongfully convicted. I work in healthcare, and for a very short time, I was a nurse in jail. Unfortunately, I have seen a lot of hurt people, their experiences with the healthcare system, and I talk [onstage] about my own frustrations with working in it. Seeing some of that opened my eyes to the prison industrial complex.

Tracy, a middle-class queer white woman, feels most comfortable connecting with either a middle-class white crowd or an LGBTQ+ crowd. She has nothing against any other audience, but as she explains, "I tend to gravitate toward LGBTQ+ audiences." On the other hand, many Black comedians feel more comfortable performing in front of Black crowds, such as Tiana, who also talks about racial justice. Empathy is the driving factor. Tiana dislikes talking to certain types of white people because she feels like they cannot truly connect with her lived experiences:

> An older Black crowd takes it differently than a bunch of hipsters, white people. If I am in an all-Black crowd and I talk about police brutality, they are like, yes, they understand what I'm talking about. They are clapping. I feel so good in front of the Black crowd. They understand that it's this young woman and they come up to me like, "great job young lady." But if it's twenty-one-year-old college students, they are just like, "what! Oh no" [mockingly]. They don't even want to talk about it because they don't get the struggle. They don't give a fuck because it doesn't apply to them. They want me to talk about "issues" that aren't issues. People are dying, that's an issue.

While some Black comedians hated talking to certain white crowds, others didn't mind, but they understood the need to carefully frame their conversations in front of white audiences. They were aware of public biases, especially the stigma attached to race. As a result, Black comedians spent considerable energy working through their sets to avoid audience misinterpretation. Comedians of color knew that if they didn't frame the conversation correctly, their discussion might reinforce racial stereotypes rather than diminish them.

Consider Ciara, who is in a deeply loving and supportive marriage with her Black husband. Every Saturday morning, they have a special date where they get coffee, choosing a different place each weekend. Additionally, they make it a point to have a date night three or four times a month, whether it's just dinner or going dancing. "I love to dance," she explained, "and he loves to take me." Ciara's husband is also a deeply caring person, sometimes to a fault. "The one frustrating thing is that he's a fixer," she continued. "Instead of listening and just hearing me, he's trying to fix it or find the words to make it all better when I just want to vent and express my feelings. Sometimes I just want him to hold me, which he does." She paused before adding, "All you men are the same," jokingly accusing me of the same problem (which, truthfully, is accurate; I try too often to fix things when my wife just wants me to listen). As a significant focal point in her life, some of Ciara's comedy involves her husband. Like all marriages, they've had typical conflicts that have helped them build a closer partnership:

> My husband and I have been married for almost seventeen years this year. And every marriage goes through a dry spell where you just can't stand that person. I talk about that in my comedy, how even the little things that he did would annoy me. Even when I told him to do something, and he did it, it still would annoy me. It's funny now, but it would annoy me more when he would do what I asked him to do. When he's in the audience, he laughs the hardest because he knows it's true. He's glad that we can talk about it now.

Although her relationship is no different than any other, when she talks about her husband and typical marital conflicts on the comedy stage, she is acutely aware of the stereotypes attached to Black men. It's important to her to frame those conversations in a way that keeps her husband's reputation intact. Ciara explains, "I make jokes about him, and I think about how he looks as a man, as a Black man, with the words that come out of my mouth. So, I am very particular." She's afraid that not framing her husband correctly could harm him, their marriage, and other Black people.

Certainly, the racial makeup of the audience not only impacted whether or not a Black person could be visible, but it also influenced how they spoke. Ciara did not alter her subject matter for either a white or Black audience, but instead adapted her language accordingly:

> One way I restrict myself is I don't use certain words. I know my audience. If I am in front of an audience that is majority white people, I won't use the n-word. But if I have an all-Black audience, I can. I feel okay. But when I get onstage, and I feel a whole bunch of white people looking at me, I cannot use that word. I cannot. It's like not being able to curse in front of my parents. If I see a white person laughing when I use the n-word, it's going to make me mad.

Performing in front of a Black audience allowed Ciara and Tiana to be themselves fully, but for other Black comedians, the region and subject matter also played a role in addition to the audience's race. Candice, who uses comedy to discuss having an interracial child, finds liberal communities more welcoming as a Black woman. In New York, she can speak her mind freely, saying, "New York allows me much more license to be who I want to be." However, when Candice performs outside New York, she must present herself in specific ways to ensure her voice is heard:

> The mentality about race is different in the Midwest, where I grew up. In a state like Alabama that is sensitive about race, or a state that voted for Trump and doesn't want to hear any anti-Trump rhetoric or doesn't care about New York liberals, I downplay the New York side and play up my Midwestern side. I've learned how to tailor my act a little different, but you don't change the jokes, you change how you relate to the audience in between the jokes. They need to see that you are not threatening. You are on their side. You are here to make them laugh. You are not here to judge them. And maybe that's a self-preservation thing that I shouldn't need to make a priority. But I have to do it to be heard. In New York, if they don't laugh, you can be like, "fuck you, that's funny." But I mind my Ps and Qs when I am on the road.

But her perception of the South was not universal. While some Black comedians, like Candace, find it difficult to navigate southern white audiences, others actually describe those conversations as the most fruitful. Nyah spends most of her time touring the South. I interviewed her over Zoom when she was traveling between venues in the South. While passing through some of the most red, Trump country, Nyah pulled over to the side of the road to join our meeting. Here, she explains her view of these communities as a little misguided: "When I do rural shows, a lot of the people in the audience are not around minorities in their life. I'm it. I'm the spokesperson. They find out that I'm a veteran and a mother. They find out that I'm divorced, but I'm trying to move forward with my life. And they love me." She goes on to say that being a Black woman is not the inherent problem. Rather, the problem is that there is a stereotype in their head that creates a division: "The stereotype that I have to fight all the time is the Def Jam comedy style. People expect minorities and people of color to behave in this cartoonish, buffoonery way. When they find out that I'm not that grille-wearing, bandana-wearing gangster from the hip-hop videos, they understand that's not all Black people, and we're good." Nyah's success with white southern crowds is a product of her background and self-presentation. As a military veteran, she is instantly legitimized as a less-threatening Black woman. To be sure, that trope is confining, but Nyah is more than willing to perform, as she described:

> I joke that I have a Claire Huxtable vibe. It makes the discussion a little less threatening for some that I am articulate, a veteran, and I am a "main street" Black woman. But that's not what we were theoretically taught as kids, what

Afro-people should be. I've literally met people who have never been around minorities or have even talked to us as human beings. I've literally seen the lightbulb switch on for a few people. It's kind of weird that in 2019, people don't understand that everyone is an individual.

Like Nyah, Marcus has found that presenting himself in a certain way allows him to better connect with white audiences when advocating for race issues. As a Black man, Marcus has experienced racism firsthand. "I have been called a nigger. I have been called a nigger lover because of my father." However, as a multiracial man—his mother is white and his father is Black—Marcus can present himself as white by shaving his head and keeping his facial hair trimmed. This, combined with his status as a veteran, gives him more leeway to connect with audiences and avoid discrimination:

> As much as that has impacted and hurt me, it's my responsibility to make things a little better for those who can't escape that. If I want to, I can go anywhere, and no one will have any idea. Because it is so easy for me to exist in the world without dealing with it, I think it's my responsibility to deal with it. It sucks, but as white-presenting, I think it's very important for me to add my voice to the race conversation because, unfortunately, others listen to me more. So, when I talk, other white straight men are more likely to listen.

Marcus has the potential to be an influential advocate for racial equity due to his skin tone, which allows him to connect with white people. However, his whiteness also creates a different barrier. Many marginalized individuals are hesitant about his perspective and are unaware of his lived experiences. As he puts it, "I have found other demographics will approach me with more caution." As a result, he spends more time trying to amplify the voices of other marginalized individuals rather than discussing his own valid personal grievances:

> As a white-presenting, straight man, I try to approach every interaction like I have ideas, but I don't want to behave like what I say matters more. When someone is also mixed but not white-presenting, or someone is a person of color, when they talk, it's not that I give deference, but I absolutely do not argue with their experiences. I might say that I've had a different experience, but I will never try to silence, quiet, or deflect from someone else's experience because they are the ones who've suffered. I was a guest on a podcast that was done by a poly-bisexual woman and an asexual woman. It was a podcast about male-centric movies. We talked about *A Few Good Men* because being military does color all my interactions with the military. But they knew that I was a safe person to talk and that I would add insight from a different perspective without discounting theirs.

Self-presentation plays a role in how Marcus and Nyah interact with their audiences, but the audience's lived experience also matters. While liberal audiences may seem more open to discussing difficult racial conversations, this is only true to a certain extent, particularly when they feel implicated. Justus believes that white audiences are not ready to hear conversations about racism from Black comedians. He explains that if a Black comedian talks about race, the audience responds, "'Why do you have to talk about that?' As if you are going out of your way to conjure up these experiences. If I just tell you about my day, I'm going to tell you about some racist stuff." Justus argues that even though these experiences are his own, white people are more likely to be celebrated for taking on racial injustice that impacts Black lives. He points out that when "when White comics tackle race, typically, the audience is impressed. "it's like, 'Wow, what a great joke. What a brave person you.'" However, he adds, "When you are Black, and you do it, it's like you are bitter and hacky."

BLACK COMEDIANS PERFORMING
FOR BLACK AUDIENCES

Some Black comedians felt seen in front of a white audience, while others found it to be a maze. Interacting with southern audiences brought success to some, but not all. Speaking with liberal audiences provided complete liberation for some, but others were banned for making them uncomfortable. There was no universal discrimination in front of white audiences. However, Black audiences posed different challenges for different comedians. One issue that arose was the style. Many felt they didn't have the right style for "urban" rooms. As Jamal explains:

> The kind of jokes that work in Black rooms are different than the jokes that work in white rooms. I tell the jokes that work in white rooms. I've had a couple of bad experiences in the Black rooms, and I figured out that nobody in those rooms cares about my jokes. There is a pace and a cadence that works in Black rooms in the South. You can venture on the edge of that cadence and style, but if you get outside their range, they are not going to be on board. Even though the joke is a good joke, the host is upset because the audience wasn't into it, and they dismiss it.

The problem Jamal faces originates from a stereotype that Black comedy has perpetuated. He believes that while platforms like Def Comedy Jam were crucial in bringing Black comedians to the forefront, they also limited their performances:

Being in standup this long, I feel like Def Comedy Jam shaped that in a very specific way. I don't know what came first, the chicken or the egg, but people were watching DCJ before they ever went to a live show, and they saw a style of Black comics and the audience. Now, when they go to the show, they expect that live. It's perpetuating.

Jamal doesn't face much hostility from Black audiences, but he feels a lack of support from the Black comedy community, particularly from other comedians. According to Jamal, even if he performs exceptionally well for a predominantly white audience, there's no guarantee that Black comedians will book him for shows with predominantly Black audiences. "If I ask them, they'll say sure, but they won't approach me, and I won't hear back from them."

To clarify, many people, including white people, struggle to perform on stages with a predominantly Black audience. Tiffany, a comedian who also works as a stripper, has had some terrible experiences and now actively avoids such situations due to anxiety. "I'm a blonde, white girl, and I'm not willing to deal with that," she says. "I've been in situations where I'm in a predominantly Black audience, and they won't even let me open my mouth to tell one joke. That has been a very stressful part of comedy; how Black audiences will perceive me before I even speak."

But despite those hardships, Tiffany persevered and has finally established a connection with Black audiences. She attributes the positive change to both her improved skills and her decision to incorporate her full, authentic self— which includes her past as a stripper. She described:

> The first couple of times that I did comedy in a predominantly Black audience, I was still new to comedy, and I used to dress professionally. I was in a dress with my hair done, and I would talk into a microphone the way that comedy is traditionally performed. But then I really developed into the headlining act where I have my stripper pole on the stage with me. During the show, I start off dressed normally, and then relatively quickly, I start taking off my clothes. I do most of the act in a bra and underwear.

The question of why some white comedians succeed in Black comedy rooms while some Black comedians do not may be due to perceptions that can be dispelled. When a white person enters the Black community, the community may be hesitant and distrustful of the intruder. However, with persistence and even a little hardship, white people can change those perceptions and be viewed as allies, especially among those who humble themselves. This seems to be happening for Tiffany. Instead of being a white lady talking to an audience of Black people, she has evolved into a white lady who is performing with an audience of Black people. Whether or not she is aware of it, she certainly demonstrates that shift when she explains, "I think that changes the way the audience perceives me. They perceive me to be less pretentious and more vulnerable, and they can laugh with that vulnerability."

On the other hand, specific stereotypes in "Black" comedy cause Jamal and Nyah to be seen as rejecting their Black identity. This phenomenon, known as self-oppression, is when racial hostility is directed horizontally within the same group.[3] Instead of recognizing their similarities and uniting, some groups argue amongst themselves.[4] This conflict can arise when individuals within a group do not conform to stereotypes, and other members interpret this as criticism.[5] This perception may even explain why some in the Black community criticized Barack and Michelle Obama for not being "Black enough."[6] Nyah explains that her identity as a Black woman from an interracial relationship was not accepted in some Black communities, ultimately silencing her voice:

> Urban rooms hate me. They HATE me. That grates me to no end. It really does because these are the same people who, when they get called the stereotype, they call it out: "Don't you dare call me Kesha." But the minute I talk about my ex-husband being white, "I don't want to hear shit that this bitch has got to say." I'm still a Black person. Why do I not get to tell my story? It is because I'm not peppering it with "I got dicked down by this big ass Black dude?" No disrespect to that comedy, but that's not me and it would not be genuine.

LOCATION AND SKIN TONE DEFINE
THE LATINO EXPERIENCE

Like Black comedians, Latino comedians also grapple with their ethnic identity and how it affects their interactions with the world. They often find themselves navigating stereotypes in the comedy world, particularly that of being an outsider. Despite having deep roots in America, Latinos are still commonly perceived as foreigners. Rafa, a middle-aged Latino man living in Texas, sheds light on this misconception of Latino heritage. He explains, "People don't understand our culture. It's like, 'Yo, dummies, we've been here longer than you in some cases. And in other cases, we had to come back. Some of us were already here, and then you changed the border, and we had to come back.' And they are treating us like we are always outsiders. We've been here longer than you have, and we are still here, and we're still just as American, if not more, than a lot of you."

Other Latinos were scrutinized in ways that their nonethnic counterparts were not. Isabella, a thirty-five-year-old Afro-Latina from New York, explained how she cannot simply exist without her physical features being scrutinized. She explains that even something as simple as her speech patterns affects how the audience perceives her as a Latina woman:

> I'm in this weird racial gray area. It's hard to tell what I am when you first look at me. Latinos know that I'm Latino, immediately. But when it comes to other ethnic groups, they don't know what the fuck this is [herself]. They don't understand this. Americans don't know what "Latino" is. They don't get it. They still think we're a race.

Many Latinos have faced hurdles due to pervasive stereotypes, causing some to avoid the label altogether. In fact, some Latino performers felt they needed to conform to certain stereotypes just to get stage time. Mateo is one such performer who treats his heritage like a stigma he has to hide away. "I don't want to be known as a Latino comic," he admits. "So I don't talk about race at all. I try to be as nonethnic as possible. I don't reveal my ethnicity onstage. I don't want to be pigeonholed as a Latino comic because that puts me in a box."

Mateo avoids discussing his ethnicity, while Isabella takes it a step further by modifying her speech. "I've noticed that as I've become more confident in my speech," she explains, "the audience is less likely to assume I'm Hispanic. When I was still very shy, Latinos in particular were more likely to think, 'Of course, you're Latino.' But the more assertive I've become in presenting myself, the more people assume that I'm white."

Latinos acknowledge the existence of stereotypes and how they impact their lives universally. Being Latino is a significant part of their social identity that transcends other experiences. However, the extent to which they feel the effects of these stereotypes depends on specific variables such as their location and skin tone. For instance, the Latinos in this sample from the Southwest rarely faced explicit discrimination for being Latino. While they are proud of their heritage and often celebrate it as unique, they did not often experience tension for presenting their culture. Ignacio, a Latino man in his mid-twenties from Texas, explains that in his community, Latinos can choose to embrace their heritage. "You are only a Latino comic if you do Latino material." He adds, "I didn't grow up very Latino at all. I grew up in a white farming community where the only other brown people were cattle. I've never lost an opportunity for not being 'Latino' enough."

However, some people feel that their ethnicity has created obstacles for them. In regions outside of the Southwest, Latinos frequently have to address their heritage for their audience and peers. Alejandra, who resides in the Midwest, not only has to perform the stereotype for her audience, but some of her peers have also attempted to educate her on her own identity:

Most people who hear me think I'm from Northside, California. Nope, I'm from the Midwest. I'm super honky and I don't speak Spanish. But because my race barely comes up in my standup, a lot of comics, mostly white dudes, tell me that I should talk more about race. They try to give me tips on how to tell jokes about being Hispanic. Don't tell me how to do my shit. Sometimes, they like to use me as a token brown person. They'll introduce me like, "we're not racist, we have someone . . . " I feel like that's a big thing. A lot of my experiences have been people telling me how to tell jokes, and then if I do something, they'll say something like, "That's just you. You are so spicy." I don't like how that sits.

The potential reactions of the audience force Latinos to adjust their approach to certain topics. However, the negative social pressure is even stronger among Latinos who live outside the Southwest, like Lola who resides in Chicago. Like members of other minority groups, Lola explains that she talks about race by comparing her experiences to those of white people. However, she admits that she is sometimes hesitant to discuss white people because the majority of her audience or other comedians may be white. She worries that they may become upset, which prevents her from being as honest as she would like to be.

It's important to note that the ability to shed the Latino label wasn't a point of contention between liberal and conservative communities. Rather, it was a defining characteristic of the Southwest that set it apart from other regions. Valentino grew up in rural southern Texas before moving to San Antonio, and he never felt like an outsider. Although he was aware of racism and inequality, and even studied them in graduate school, he didn't experience direct or explicit discrimination until he visited New York City as an adult. The memory of that experience is still fresh in his mind:

The first time I flew on a plane, I was not ready for a post-911 interaction with a TSA agent. That was the first time I had to wrestle with ethnic identity. My whole life, I grew up and thought, I'm Latino, whatever. But then I get to this airport—JFK—and they are like, "You have to step aside." And the dude, who luckily was Latino, was looking at my ID and realizes I am Latino, I have a Latino last name, and he says, "Oh shit dude, I thought you were Muslim." He straight up said that to me. At the time, I was very confused; that has never happened to me before. I'm from Texas. I moved from the Valley [Rio Grande Valley, both southern Texas and northern Mexico] to San Antonio, and our city is just a bigger Valley. Growing up where I'm from, I didn't even know that I was "other" in most of the rest of the country. Initially, I thought I had a pretty good political awareness, based on my educational background. And then experiencing that from a Latino dude—I knew he was, I could tell—for him to realize, "Oh fuck." To be asked to pull to the side is nerve-racking enough, but then to add this new variable that I was not anticipating at all. "Hey, I thought you were Muslim. Sorry." Other people see me differently than I've ever seen myself. From that point forward, I could identify every time that happened, which was an eye-opener. It's something that I have repeatedly experienced since traveling outside of Texas.

Many Latino standup comedians, like Valentino, have faced challenges with their ethnic identity when performing outside of the Southwest. They often feel limited and forced into a box, instead of being celebrated for the diversity of their backgrounds. Isabella, for example, comes from a rich heritage that includes Puerto Rican, Ecuadorian, Haitian, Mexican, and Brazilian roots. However, even when performing in front of Latino audiences, she feels pressured to conform to stereotypes:

> The Latin night, that one's worse for me because at least in rooms where it may not be ethnically diverse, but they are trying, at least they don't have any expectations about me ethnically. So, I can be more myself, I can deviate from the "Latino" standard of comedy. I struggle at Latin nights because it's one type of Latino. And a lot of Latinos, especially more Americanized Latinos, well, anything that comes from that more standard Latino archetype is not appreciated. It's like they expect everybody to be a fucking beaner, everybody is supposed to be a fucking cholo. Even the Puerto Ricans are doing some variation of cholo. It's weird. I struggle because I am not that. I have enough Latino jokes where I can hold my own in a room like that, but it definitely feels like I have to subvert parts of myself to fit in.

Isabella struggles to fit in among specific Latino comedy communities due to discrimination, so she avoids those stages. Instead, she prefers to perform for suburban and multiracial audiences that are diverse, or at least try to be. She admits that performing for multiracial audiences may still result in her being tokenized, but she tries to brush off this internal stigma. As she says, "you are being tokenized by the very fact that you are on that stage. But the way you can feel tokenized depends on the room."

Furthermore, Isabella's straightforwardness in acknowledging the trope of the "fucking beaner[s]" is significant as it is a stereotype that many Latinos face. This caricature is a direct result of Latino stereotypes perpetuated by some famous comedians from Southern California, which have come to define all Latinos despite our diversity. Other comedians also share her perspective. Rafa, for instance, not only acknowledges these stereotypes but also recognizes the liberty that Texas has afforded him as a performer and Latino after moving from California:

> When I was in San Francisco, I went to a show to find out how I could get on. The white guy who ran the show literally just looks at me in the eye and says, "I'm sorry, but this isn't one of those Mexican shows. We do comedy." I was

shocked. The fact that he said that was so ugly. This shit keeps popping up all the time. Hollywood and clubs don't know how to work with us.

Rafa explained that he enjoyed his time in California and appreciated the liberal clubs in San Francisco. However, he faced difficulties as a standup comedian because bookers only wanted to book him with other Latino comics. Fortunately, he had friends who could vouch for him, which helped him get gigs. But the real turning point came when he made the decision to move out of California. Since relocating to Texas, Rafa has faced fewer of those pressures. He finds that diverse Latino experiences are more common and celebrated in Texas:

> If you go to a karaoke bar in Texas with a bunch of Latinos, you'll see Latinos sing death metal. And then three songs later, they'll sing Vicente Fernandes. And then later they'll sing Frank Sinatra. What they don't realize is that, yes, we are Latino, it is part of our culture. But we are also American as fuck. We grew up alongside you. We grew up experiencing the same culture you all did. We like everything you like. Throw us in it.

Another defining factor for Latino standup comedians was their skin tone. Specifically, those with darker skin tones faced more challenges. This is not to say that Latinos with lighter skin completely avoided discrimination outside of the Southwest, but it was more evident when they had darker skin. When traveling outside of the Southwest, comedians with darker skin tones were more likely to be met with skepticism or even outright hatred. For instance, Emilio from the first chapter had to disarm a Midwestern audience who was chanting "bring back the beaner" when the host bombed. Emilio was very explicit about why they identified him as Latino. As he describes, "I'm brown."

The ability of Latinos with a light skin tone to deflect animosity is an important advantage. However, once their Latino identity is revealed, having a lighter skin tone can present unique challenges, especially when discussing issues of race. Without obvious physical markers of their Latino heritage, it can be much harder for Latinos to engage in conversations about their background. In fact, they may even be accused of racism, as Fernanda explains:

> I am very comfortable with the parts of my family and me that are Latinx. But as far as being Latina, I'm pretty much just white. I've talked about race, but I'm still finding my way. Latin people that read as Latin can say jokes about people of color that may actually be quite racist. I have some jokes about being Latinx that I think are funny, and some people think they are funny, but I can feel that some in the audience don't know if they are allowed to laugh at it, and it's because of how I look.

Many other Latinos have had similar experiences with skin tone. It has affected some of them in their decision to become "Latin" comics, while others have endured outright discrimination in standup. One comedian's insight is particularly illuminating. Like other Latinos from the Southwest, Leonel expressed that he had never experienced explicit discrimination until he left the safety of his community and decided to go on tour across the country. When he did experience discrimination, it was not directed at him, but at his best friend, a fellow Southwestern Latino:

> I don't think I'm dark enough to get it. I think if I was a little darker and my accent was a little thicker, sure. I'm a little light skinned and I can get away with it. My best friend, he's dark as fuck. One time, we went to visit a friend in Pittsburgh, and he literally got discriminated against. They wouldn't let him in the club and go onstage. I had never seen it before. I was shocked. I was like, "Bro, you are legitimately getting discriminated against." It was weird. We grew up together. We have the same family, but he got it, not me. And I knew it was because he was dark.

BLACK AND LATINA WOMEN

Black and Latino individuals expressed universal experiences of discrimination, but their ability to speak was often limited by various factors, including the political leanings of their community, the racial makeup of their audience, their perceived level of "Blackness," skin tone, and even region. One inescapable and powerful variable highlights the complexity of inequality experienced by these groups. For example, Jamal and Nyah share many similarities. They share similar ages. They perform best on similar stages, in front of similar audiences. They both have a similar educational levels. They both engage in healthy behaviors such as exercise, eating right, and little to no alcohol use. In fact, they both abhor alcohol and substance abuse in the standup world. And they had about the same support from families to practice the art that they love. The one glaring difference between the two is gender. Regardless of their alikeness, Nyah is a woman, which dramatically affected her relationships with the audience making it, by far, more vitriolic. In fact, gender was the single most important variable that seemed to define and amplify both race and ethnicity for all the participants. Racial biases were much more definable for Black women in this study, making it more difficult to be authentic because of specific stereotypes. Best described by Jada, she reports that compared to other groups, "Black women don't always get to represent themselves as they want to because there is so much stigma attached to being a Black woman. You can't come off as even slightly that *angry Black woman.*"

Trina confirms Jada's assessment on the stigma attached to Black women. She explains that there is always someone negative toward women and that they think Black women have an attitude. Unfortunately, Black women have to "tone it down." Trina argues that Black men get a pass for the same behavior that she may display onstage. She notes that male Trina can go onstage and say the exact same thing that female Trina says, and it will be better received. Most importantly, Black women are not only limited by how they present themselves, but they are also limited by what they can present. Sexual issues seem to be the biggest taboo. Trina further explains this point:

> I've noticed that it is okay for Black male comedians to be sexually explicit, but when we do it, it's kind of frowned upon. You shouldn't talk about sex to be funny, but some shit about sex is funny, so why should it make a difference when a woman is talking about it? If a woman gets too raunchy, they see it as taking away from her funny.

The well-documented stigma faced by Black women has a historical precedent for mistreatment. Jada explains, "Back in the day, they thought of Black women as sex fiends. They put hypersexuality on Black women since the time of slavery. We have healthy sexual appetites; we are not super freaks. Just because a Black woman has a little ratchet moment doesn't mean she's all ghetto all the time."

Latinas, like Black women, also faced stereotypes that made it more difficult to speak onstage. However, like their Latino men counterparts, they were also shielded from overall prejudice in the Southwest. Carmen, for instance, not only experiences immense liberation in her Southwestern Texas community, but she also notes that her previous home in California was far less freeing:

> How do you marginalize me here? We are the majority. Maybe the only thing that doesn't help is that I'm a Latina comic who doesn't do comedy in Spanish. But I've never felt it. I can't even imagine it. I've never felt the stigma of being a Latina. I've never felt it was held against me. I've never felt marginalized. I've never felt discriminated against—knock on wood. Someone may have called me a beaner once in road rage traffic, but I've never been to Michigan. I've never been to Oklahoma. White places: I've never been there, so I don't know.

Latinas in the Southwest report experiencing less stigma attached to their ethnicity, but gendered ethnic stereotypes still play a significant role in their lives, as seen in Carmen's experience. Despite this, Latina women like

Carmen work hard to overcome the stigma associated with their ethnicity, particularly the stereotype that portrays them as obedient:

> The stereotype of me as Latina women, I was supposed to stay at home, I was supposed to stay married, I was supposed to be happy being a wife and being a housekeeper. And fuck all that shit. I'm none of those things. I've been married multiple times. I have tattoos. I'm a single woman. I hate to clean my house. And I wish my kids would raise themselves. I've tried to be that subservient "sí, señor" kind of woman. But there is this bitch in me, and it's not going to happen.

For other Latins, skin tone is often the defining factor that amplifies gender-based discrimination, even in the Southwest. While men with dark skin tones can avoid Latino stereotypes in this region, darker skin tones can amplify stereotypes for women. Once these stereotypes become salient in the audience's mind, Latina women are stuck in a Catch-22: either play up stereotypes that are not authentic to themselves or avoid them and lose some opportunities to communicate and cope. Luna describes this problem:

> People putting me in a category that they are not quite sure about. I'm brown. I'm tattooed. I look really young. Sometimes, people book me because I have a white name, and then they are surprised: "Damn, you're brown as fuck!" And I'm like "I'm Peruvian. I took my husband's name." It is ever-present, especially when they were only booking me on Latina shows at the beginning. Oh my God. Can't I just do the comedy night? I try to stay steer clear of it, but I'll get onstage, apologize for not being white. I could smack my lips like a Latina and get an easy laugh, but that's not me.

Having a dark skin tone made Latina stereotypes more noticeable, but for some Latinas, having a light skin tone was equally problematic when discussing their heritage. Some light-skinned men felt more accepted in certain communities, as they were seen as just another white guy. However, if a woman was seen as white, she would be grouped into a different category that faces challenges in comedy: white women. Fernanda, from Chicago, shared her experience at a recent open mic:

> I was at the end of the list, and I was like, "Oh my God, it's going to be one in the morning before I can go on." And the host says, "Nah, it won't take that long." And he gets up onstage and says, "A white lady came up to me and complained that she's going to be going to bed at one in the morning." Because I come off initially as a white lady, everything I say comes off as, for lack of a better phrase, as a white bitch. You are a run-of-the-mill white bitch. What's so funny is that I hate white bitches. I don't like those women that have this sense of entitlement. But I look like that girl.

The animosity directed at white-passing Latino women is not limited to a specific region or white audience. It is also experienced in front of Latino audiences. Even Bianca, a child of Peruvian immigrants, has faced rejection from her community because of her skin tone. "I love performing in front of Latino audiences," she explains. "I'll throw in a few words like 'chancla,' and they just get it. And I go to Mexico often, and I love performing there, so I love bridging that gap. But at the same time, some audiences don't consider me Latino enough. They say, 'oh, she's a white girl.' And I'm like, 'no, I'm more Latino than you are. My parents were born in Peru. Your parents were born here.'"

While gender was much more consequential for Black and Latina women, it is not to suggest that gender did not affect Black men or Latino men. It absolutely changed the context of the situations that they were experiencing in the comedy world. Rafa accurately explains how men of color are typically perceived:

> One of my mentors, when I got off the stage, told me, "Bro, you got to smile." I was confused, and he said, "You got to smile. Look at you. You're a big Latino male. If you don't smile, you're scary. Think about the audience; they have prejudices. When you don't smile, all they see is a big scary Latino." And then he adds, "that's why you see a lot of Black comics smiling because they have to disarm the general white public. It's unfortunate, but you have to do that."

Race was a significant factor for Latinos and Black men, but it was women who often felt the negative consequences. The most important context that affected the ability to achieve equality in comedy was gender. Ultimately, minority women in this study reported spending more time performing comedy routines that they did not want to perform. They spent more time disarming the audience so that they could have a moment to discuss something of real importance. They also spent more time considering the ramifications of their speech on others, as demonstrated by Ciara from earlier chapters who felt that it was her responsibility to frame her Black husband in a better light. Unfortunately, for most, including Jada, that moment of honest and sincere conversation is still far away. "You have to start out performing things you don't want to do forever," Jada explains. "Eddie Griffith jokes about Michael Jackson on crack early on. Now he talks about all these intellectual things. Michael Jackson on crack was just a way to get to what matters. So, me talking about this ignorant shit about Black women is just a way in so that I can educate later. It has to be that way," she sighed, "but it can be stressful. Sometimes I'm tired."

MARGINALIZED PEOPLE ARE UNIVERSALLY
DIFFERENT AND SIMILAR

It may be true that Black and Latino individuals have universal experiences of discrimination that limit their voice, even among those who are economically successful. For example, Eddie Murphy, a comedian with cross-cultural appeal, was able to comment on liberal racism and the voyeuristic portrayal of minorities.[7] However, his skits had to be subversive. While he could be as 'Black' as he wanted to be in front of an urban standup audience, he had to present as a 'non-threatening' Black man in front of the mostly white SNL audience."

On the other hand, Eddie Murphy's subtle differences in self-presentation also emphasize that minorities are unique in their own way. They all may have experienced racism or discrimination, but the extent and frequency of these experiences can vary greatly depending on different factors. Candace acknowledges that no group is universally oppressed:

> It's not as simple as "because I'm a Black woman I sit at the back of the bus. I have to sit in the front to get my voice heard." It's a little less obvious than that. The discrimination is more nuanced. I'm privileged. I'm college educated. I've had jobs. I've been able to eat. I have my health. I didn't have a kid until I was in my thirties. Single moms that have baby's fathers, or drug-addicted family members in their life, financial struggles. There are women in comedy that have a much more uphill battle than me.

Haggins argues that performers are forced to navigate "ambiguous and fragmented notions of blackness" and a new cultural landscape in which white audiences consume Black cultural products, but not necessarily out of an affinity for Black culture.[8] While the participants in this study would agree with her assessment, our findings also demonstrate that Black audiences sometimes do not have an affinity for the Black body standing in front of them. The comedians featured in this book reveal that marginalized people are not universally empowered by their community. Every Black comedian in this book has experienced some form of oppression, whether it be for being "too Black" or "not Black enough," or for overcoming the stereotypes of being a Black woman or man. Similarly, Latinos are often confined by their ethnicity, but unlike Black people who are always viewed as such, Latinos sometimes have the ability to choose whether to present themselves as Latino onstage, especially if they are white-passing or live in the Southwest. For Latinos, skin tone is a marker of being "desirable" or "undesirable," an experience shared by many Latinos in the United States.[9]

People are not just their race or gender. Sometimes, Black and Latino voices are allowed to thrive, while other times they are unable to share their voices, even within their own communities. Liberation is neither always denied nor always achievable, as it depends on multiple variables and background characteristics that are present simultaneously. The experiences of people of color, women, men, and those who are LGBTQ+ are vast and complex. A perspective that conceptualizes differences in trauma or stress, inequality, and discrimination in binary terms of "us versus them" fails to acknowledge differences within a group or by location. While individuals with mental illness may universally experience stigma, each person experiences it differently. For instance, how I as a Latino man experience the stigma of depression will be different from how a woman experiences it. Similarly, a woman's experience of stigma will vary depending on whether she is white or Black. Moreover, a Black woman living in an affluent, middle-class American suburb will experience that stigma differently from a Black woman in an urban metropolis. Different variables, including background and composition, can affect not only whether we can communicate, but also how we experience something as integral as gender and race.

The perspective presented in this chapter is one of acknowledging complexity rather than simply victimhood. Although I faced difficulties when I began actively coping, I recognize that my struggles were minimal compared to those of others. While I have experienced racism, I am white-passing and fortunate enough to not constantly feel targeted. Although I have lived from paycheck to paycheck, I have never had to worry about where my next meal would come from. While I have been afraid of being judged, my career has never been at risk like those of the women featured in this book. While my time may be limited, I have always lived in safe neighborhoods where I can exercise outside without fear of violence. Although I have a responsibility to support my wife, we do not have children who can consume our lives emotionally and socially. Communal coping can be a valuable tool in eliminating stigma, but we must also recognize and respect cultural differences that create unequal opportunities to manage stigma. The next chapter explores how comedy, like all communities, can provide opportunities for liberation and the expulsion of stigma.

NOTES

1. Phillip Atiba Goff and Kimberly Barsamian Kahn, "How Psychological Science Impedes Intersectional Thinking," *Du Bois Review* 10, no. 2 (2013): 365–84, https://doi.org/10.1017/S1742058X13000313; Patricia Hill Collins, "Intersectionality's Definitional Dilemmas," *Annual Review of Public Health* 41 (2015): 1–20, https://

doi.org/10.1146/annurev-soc-073014-112142; Kimberlé Crenshaw, "Mapping the Margins: Intersectionality, Identity Politics, and Violence against Women of Color," *Stanford Law Review* 43, no. 6 (1991): 1241–99.

2. Crenshaw, "Mapping the Margins: Intersectionality, Identity Politics, and Violence against Women of Color"; Elizabeth R. Cole and Alyssa N. Zucker, "Black and White Women's Perspectives on Femininity," *Cultural Diversity and Ethnic Minority Psychology* 13, no. 1 (2007): 1–9, https://doi.org/10.1037/1099-9809.13.1.1; Pamela Y. Collins, Hella von Unger, and Adria Armbrister, "Church Ladies, Good Girls, and Locas: Stigma and the Intersection of Gender, Ethnicity, Mental Illness, and Sexuality in Relation to HIV Risk," *Social Science & Medicine* 67, no. 3 (2008): 389–97, https://doi.org/10.1016/j.socscimed.2008.03.013; Patricia Hill Collins and Sirma Bilge, *Intersectionality* (Cambridge, MA: Polity Press, 2016); Flavia Agnes, "From Shahbano to Kausar Bano-Contextualizing the 'Muslim Woman' within a Communalised Polity," n.d; Bridget K. Gorman et al., "A New Piece of the Puzzle: Sexual Orientation, Gender, and Physical Health Status.," *Demography* 52, no. 4 (2015): 1357–82, https://doi.org/10.1007/s13524-015-0406-1; Stevi Jackson, "Gender, Sexuality and Heterosexuality: The Complexity (and Limits) of Heteronormativity," *Feminist Theory* 7, no. 1 (2006): 105–21, https://doi.org/10.1177/1464700106061462; Combahee River Collective, "The Combahee River Collective Statement," in *Home Girls, A Black Feminist Anthology*, ed. Barbara Smith (New York: Kitchen Table: Women of Color Press, 1983), 29–37, https://doi.org/10.4324/9780429494277-3.

3. Karen D. Pyke, "What Is Internalized Racial Oppression and Why Don't We Study It? Acknowledging Racism's Hidden Injuries," *Sociological Perspectives* 53, no. 4 (2010): 551–72, https://doi.org/10.1525/sop.2010.53.4.551.SOP5304; Teeomm K Williams, "Understanding Internalized Oppression: A Theoretical Conceptualization of Internalized Subordination," *Open Access Dissertations* (2012); Judith B. White and Ellen J. Langer, "Horizontal Hostility: Relations between Similar Minority Groups," *Journal of Social Issues* 55, no. 3 (1999): 537–59, https://doi.org/10.1111/0022-4537.00132:

4. Kristine M. Molina and Drexler James, "Discrimination, Internalized Racism, and Depression: A Comparative Study of African American and Afro-Caribbean Adults in the US Kristine," *Group Process and Intergroup Relations* 19, no. 4 (2017): 439–61, https://doi.org/10.1016/j.physbeh.2017.03.040.

5. Wesley W. Bryant, "Internalized Racism's Association with African American Male Youth's Propensity for Violence," *Journal of Black Studies* 42, no. 4 (2011): 690–707.

6. Tina R. Opie and Katherine W. Phillips, "Hair Penalties: The Negative Influence of Afrocentric Hair on Ratings of Black Women's Dominance and Professionalism," *Frontiers in Psychology* 6, no. August (2015): 1–14, https://doi.org/10.3389/fpsyg.2015.01311; Karis Campion, "'You Think You're Black?' Exploring Black Mixed-Race Experiences of Black Rejection," *Ethnic and Racial Studies* 42, no. 16 (2019): 196–213, https://doi.org/10.1080/01419870.2019.1642503: Martha Augoustinos and Stephanie De Garis, "'Too Black or Not Black Enough': Social Identity Complexity in the Political Rhetoric of Barack Obama," *European Journal of Social Psychology* 42, no. 5 (2012): 564–77, https://doi.org/10.1002/ejsp.1868.

7. Raquel Gates, "Bringing the Black: Eddie Murphy and African American Humor on Saturday Night Live," in *Saturday Night Live and TV*, ed. Nick Marx, Matt Sienkiewicz, and Ron Becker (Bloomington, IN: Indiana University Press, 2013).

8. Haggins, *Laughing Mad The Black Comic Persona in Post-Soul America*. Pg 233

9. Andrés Villarreal, "Stratification by Skin Color in Contemporary Mexico," *American Sociological Review* 75, no. 5 (2010): 652–78, https://doi.org/10.1177/0003122410378232; Frederick J. Hollister, "Skin Color and Life Chances of Puerto Ricans," *Caribbean Studies* 9, no. 3 (1969): 87–94, https://doi.org/10.1177/0306312708091929.

Chapter 7

Cultivating Positive Outcomes

Chapter 5 presented the range of tactics that standup comedians use to manage stigma, which was then complicated by adding social context at the intersection of race, ethnicity, gender, and location in Chapter 6. During optimal process of this "charged" comedy, standup comedians both educate people about a stigma and challenge stereotypes attached to a stigma. Comedians verbalize the taboo out loud for the audience, purposefully to help a comedian feel better about a stigma that they have. When a comedian elicits a positive response, they are explicitly seeking validation for their idea, enhancing their self-efficacy. The optimal process is not dissimilar to a meaning focused coping, whereby comedians are reinterpreting the meaning of a stressor so that it is less impactful (e.g., devaluing the value of personal belongings or money).[1] Meaning focused coping is a strategy that is embraced in therapy including mindfulness meditation where people builds self-reflection skills related to the world that they inhabit.[2] Similarly, religious people engage in benevolent religious reappraisal in which stressful circumstances are less adverse because they have been interpreted as "part of God's plan."[3] For comedians, it is necessary to perform; they have to find humor in incidents even if those experiences are painful or traumatic.

Most important, Rebecca, who opened the book, and others are trying to create a sense that they matter to others through this coping process. Mattering, which is the feeling that one's welfare is important to another person, is crucial for health and well-being.[4] Everyone wants to feel like they matter to someone else, to feel loved, cared for, and supported by their community. Stigma, on the other hand, is the opposite of mattering. If a person experiences discrimination, they are living in a world that tells them that they don't matter.

Improving a sense of mattering can be achieved through communal conversations, but it's not the only strategy. While laughter can heal and relieve stress,[5] not everyone can engage in the optimal coping process due to stigma. The next few chapters will explore the darker aspects of the comedy world, including discrimination and violence, which create barriers to coping. Despite these challenges, many people still participate in comedy. One might argue that comedians, like other artists, seek fame and fortune, but fundamentally, their goals indicate a desire to matter.

There are two broad categories of resources that affect a sense of mattering: social and psychological. Psychological resources include self-esteem and a sense of mastery, which is a person's perceived ability to positively influence life circumstances.[6] Social resources include social integration, which is the size of a network and frequency of interactions, enacted social support, which is the receipt of assistance, and anticipated support, which is the expectation that members of one's support network can be relied upon if needed.[7]

Moreover, each type of resource can have independent, direct positive effects on health. Furthermore, these resources are intertwined and can build upon or amplify one another. For example, individuals with more mastery have greater confidence in their ability to address a wide range of stressors, including financial strain.[8] As a result, events are less stressful. Additionally, those with a higher sense of mastery are more likely to anticipate problems and call upon friends, for instance, to help manage them.[9] Stronger social ties mean having someone to reach out to for tangible support, such as loans, jobs, or a place to sleep, when they, for example, lose a job.[10] More interactions may lead to less isolation, and thus a greater sense of mattering.[11]

There are many ways that a vast social network, like comedy, provides these resources to improve a person's sense of mattering beyond coping alone. Let's look at some of the ways that comedians have countered stigma and built a stronger sense of self.

CULTIVATING SELF-ESTEEM THROUGH PERFORMING

It's not surprising to find that that standup comedy can help build self-esteem, especially when dealing with specific traumatic or troubling circumstances. Many participants have described using comedy to boost their self-esteem by directly addressing the stigma associated with their experiences onstage. Performing in front of an audience allows for validation through their approval, and the laughter helps to make the stigma less threatening. For example, Zahra, a young Black woman, found acceptance as a lesbian woman from the audience in her college town, something she never received at home:

> I was in the closet throughout high school. When I got to college, I didn't want to be in the closet anymore. I also never felt comfortable talking about my sexuality with my parents. The first time I performed, I made a quick quip about enjoying a Tegan and Sara album and lying to my mom, "I'm straight, I just

really like this music." It felt good. I don't think I got any negative reactions to being gay. I don't think I got any reactions about my set. It was a college set, so people had low expectations. But it did feel good. It felt nice to know that that my friends had accepted me at that point. It's always nice to have people laugh at your jokes.

Our participants revealed that standup comedy improved a comedian's self-esteem by providing a safe space for them to perform. For example, Joji, a trans man of color, described how the stage protects him. "I walk down the street as a gender-nonconforming person of color who gets read as a Black person or Latinx man," Joji said, describing the fear of violence he faces in the real world. "Walking down the street was always an anxiety-provoking thing. Just walking down the fucking street." However, "The stage is the safest place on this planet because I'm not anxious about being shot or killed or bashed. I may get an occasional heckler, but the stage is very sacred for me to express myself and not feel in danger. I don't think I would be walking through this world with a sprinkle of the amount of confidence that I have if it weren't for the fact that I know my power is the greatest in performance."

For some people, being onstage boosts their self-esteem because of the way they are perceived. Research shows that self-esteem can improve when a person achieves tasks that are highly regarded, especially if recognized by people whose opinions matter to them. For comedians, their performance is the task, and the audience's approval is the authoritative opinion. As Hazel describes it, this relationship is exhilarating. She says, "You feel the rush beforehand, the adrenaline of accomplishing something, and the release of that feeling after you're done. No matter what happens, you did something. It's like a hack. It tricks your brain into thinking you accomplished something every day, even when you didn't do anything."

The participants commonly used the drug/comedy analogy, with some specifically stating that the feeling of performing comedy was like a direct relief from pain. Mateo acknowledged this, saying, "I always think back and remember the horrible time in my life . . . and now you take that funny thing and you are showing it to strangers, and they laugh at it. I've never done heroin, but I would assume heroin is like. Oh, my God, this is great!" The analogy highlights the powerful and addictive nature of comedy, as well as the cathartic release it can provide for both performers and audiences.

Having a good performance was also transportive; it allows comedians the opportunity to relive good times. Consider Bianca, who was introduced in an earlier chapter. She says, "My household was just so sad and abusive." Bianca grew up in a household full of violence, and comedy was often the only reprieve. "My dad got this VHS tape of Bill Cosby, so it just came out, and I was watching my family," she continues. "For an hour to an hour and a half, my whole family was laughing. No one was crying. No one was yelling. No one was being hit. Nothing was being thrown." For Bianca, performing standup today allows her to numb painful memories and relive those precious moments of joy when her family was at peace.

For other comedians, comedy is not just a job; it encompasses their entire existence. Comedy gives their life meaning and purpose. Hope is one of those people. Before comedy, she devoted her life to caring for others at the expense of her own health. Hope revealed that her white parents were "adopted" children in the South in the 1960s. According to her, many farmers in her parents' community adopted children who were then forced into child labor, or in other words, slavery. Her parents were never educated and were made to work as farmhands until they fled as children. As uneducated, runaway children, they eventually had children of their own, and Hope was the firstborn. As the oldest of their kids, Hope spent her childhood raising her siblings and caring for her parents. And that life of service to her family did not end with her parents and siblings. It continued into college, where she cared for her partner, who suffered from an incurable illness. Hope describes:

> My partner and I moved together so that I could get my graduate degree. After about a year, he got sick. He was sick for a year, and it turned out to be some extremely rare incurable cancer. I was caring for him, and he died about two months after I finished graduate school. It was a horrendous year, because I was trying to finish grad school and care for him. He was doing his best, but he was so sick. When he died, I was so busy taking care of him that I did not realize what life was going to be like when he was not there anymore. I had no idea how much my identity was wrapped up in nursing him."

After Hope's partner died, she fell into a deep state of mourning and became completely disconnected from everyone around her. She described:

> When he died, and I was trying to enter the workforce as a therapist, which was an insane thing to do considering my mental status. But I was poor, and I needed a job. And I was alone in a city hundreds of miles from everyone I knew. I kind of paced around the city, totally numb like a zombie. All the mourners came, and all the mourners left. When they left, it was just me with my own thoughts in my empty apartment—no one to look after and no support. I was aimless and lost my faith in the work I was trying to do. I had no interest, and I couldn't help people. I couldn't sleep. My hygiene was a mess. There were plenty of people who were concerned for me, but I wasn't allowing it. I was in my apartment with my door locked:

Hope gave up on life completely, left with nothing and no purpose, living in a new reality of alienated loneliness:

Everything lost its meaning, everything I used to care about that I used to worry about if they were gone. I didn't care about going to work. I didn't care about where the money was going to come from to pay my rent. Nothing in the world mattered. It was like the *Matrix* when you see that it's all just a ruse. All the things that people were doing, all day long, going to work trying to pay bills, taking care of their houses, going to movies, going out together, looking for relationships, doing all these things didn't mean anything. I could care less. I could have laid on that floor and rotted. Apathy crept into the point that I got very calm. I thought, "Well, I think I'm done here." And it wasn't some dramatic decision, "I want to die. I can't take this." Nothing like that. It was total and complete calm—settled.

Hope was ready to give up on life, but she decided to give herself one last chance to live. She thought about what she still needed to do before she could allow herself to die:

I thought to myself, is there anything that I want to do before I die? I thought about everything that used to be on my bucket list like I want to go to India, or I want to see the Maldives. Nothing. All of that meant nothing. I was so tired. I was so exhausted from just picking my body up every morning and moving it around. So, I sat around and said, "Think, is there anything that you need to do?" And the only thing that came to mind was I never went onstage. I never did standup. It was something that was always on the back of my mind. So, I made a deal with myself on my floor; "You will go and sign up for an open mic. If it's not what you thought, or it's terrible, you are allowed to die."

Hope made it to a club and prepared herself. She finally got up onstage and explained, "Like most people's first time, it went fine. It wasn't great. It wasn't bad. It was fine." After she finished, she felt a little bit of motivation to try again. She said to herself, "Okay, I'm going to go up one more time and see if I can fix those jokes, but if it doesn't go well, I can die." She spent the next few years performing at open mics and shows, living microphone to microphone, until she was able to perform for herself without being burdened by her despair. "I'd step off the stage and know what to do to make it better," Hope explains. "I'd think it was good, but not great, but I think I can make it great. I would stay alive until the next open mic or the next show." It took about two years before she started having fun and it became easier to get up in the morning. "Cut to thirteen years later, and that's where I am. It is the actual reason why I am alive."

Hope is still alive and thriving in comedy, touring across the country. However, it is important to note that while her comedy has been valuable in her life and remains a life line in many respects, it was not the only resource integral to her health. We will learn more about her later.

CULTIVATING MASTERY THROUGH SKILL BUILDING

Comedians experience a growth in mastery, specifically in their ability to control others' negative reactions toward their stigma, much like the apparent improvement in self-esteem. Standup provides a place where they can manage negative behaviors that many find difficult to navigate in the regular world. For instance, Heather, a lesbian woman, uses comedy to talk about the total rejection from some of her conservative family. "Some of the reactions I have had to coming out, those are prevalent in my standup. I lost people I cared about and who I thought cared about me, but then I realized that they felt a part of me was wrong and they rejected me." Heather explains how she uses comedy to come to terms with her loss of family and control the narrative about who they are. She says, "I joke in one bit about my extended family's reaction to me coming out. I can't just accept that those were never good people and then let them go."

Most importantly, by controlling the narrative around her family onstage, she can control the audience members and manage their homophobia. "It's a place for me to be me. I can control every word I say. I know that when I say certain things, people will have certain reactions, and I can choose how to convey each idea. It gives me confidence that if the same issue comes up in the future, I have thought about every aspect of it. What can be funny about this? How can I twist this?"

Other comedians have shown how they achieved mastery by developing skills, specifically by being able to anticipate negative reactions and problem-solve for those negative public reactions. It was crucial to view their problems from multiple audience perspectives. For instance, Lola, a Latina woman who has lived with mental illness for most of her life and was recently hospitalized, can attest to this. Despite having a loving family, mental health remains a taboo topic for many Latinos. "I always thought my family was more open to mental health because they knew I had been going to a therapist for years," she explains. However, when the hospitalization occurred, her family was not supportive and became very upset, making it a shameful thing. As a result, she lost some of the essential family support after her hospitalization. "Things were really tense, and I didn't speak to a lot of family for a while."

Despite losing family members, Lola has been able to bounce back by using multiple aspects of the comedy process. First, she learned how to conceptualize her problems by seeing them through the eyes of different audiences. "One audience will be on board and like it, but a different audience will be more hesitant," she explains, "so I have to try and put each audience in a space where they are okay to laugh." Second, reflecting on her experiences during the creative process helped her to "better understand what had occurred." Now, she feels empowered and in control. "I do feel empowered and in control; I can prevent that in the future," she assured me, "because, in that situation, I felt very out of control. I do feel like I can handle a future situation better. That was the key. If I didn't have this outlet where I could creatively respond to it."

The process of comedy that Lola described involves cultivating interpersonal skills. This includes developing an idea, performing it onstage, evaluating the audience response, reconfiguring the set, and then reperforming the set. Through this process, comedians enhance their active listening skills so they can respond to stigmatizing audiences in real-time, as described by Mateo. "Audiences are different and the comedy is different," he explains. "If it's an older, white crowd versus a young urban crowd, versus a group that is LGBT, I'm going to say the same jokes, but I will deliver them a little differently because I need them to understand where I am coming from. I can get others to listen because comedy delivers my ideas to different people correctly."

Moreover, various comedians have explained how comedy helped them understand how the public perceives them. For many comedians, mastering the art of public speaking was crucial to their performances. For example, let's consider Marcus, a veteran who struggles with PTSD:

> I was an interrogator in the Army. Nothing I did while I was in Iraq was illegal at the time even though a lot of it shook my morality. Some of it is illegal now. I remember telling my dad that I spent years making people afraid, scream and cry. I have a joke written about waterboarding. The thesis of it is true. I was dating a girl who wanted to know what it was like, which is weird, and unhealthy relationships is a separate thing. But I had written a joke where the punch line is waterboarding is ridiculous and unnecessary, and it doesn't work.

After separating from the Army, Marcus had a successful career as a civilian contractor teaching interrogation tactics to active-duty service members. However, the constant reminder of his trauma from practicing the tactics took a toll on him. It took about seven months before he hit rock bottom and attempted suicide. "Rock bottom was a suicide attempt," he shared. Despite taking a tremendous amount of pills, including sixty Xanax and an unknown number of Trazadone, while drunk on a bottle of Crown Royal, he miraculously survived. "I don't know how I survived," he said.

Marcus struggles to display emotions due to his PTSD, which makes him appear cold and distant. "I'm not the most facially expressive person," he admits. This lack of emotion worsens the stigma surrounding his mental illness. "People have walked on eggshells around me because they're worried about making noise," he explains. "They're concerned about who I am because of the military." However, after years of doing standup comedy, he has learned to recognize his problem and improve his communication skills to put others at ease. "I work hard to be extra silly and do a preemptive strike against the stigma by being goofy onstage. I have strong opinions about Disney movies and play Hannah Montana on the jukebox." Today, Marcus feels more confident in his ability to approach and engage with people positively, and he applies these skills to his everyday life:

> Years ago, I made a joke about being hungover at work and my commander sent me to the Army alcohol control program. Five years later, I joked about being drunk at work, and everyone clapped. Comedy has given me the tools to ease people into the areas that people aren't comfortable with. If I wasn't a comedian and I was just walking around, people would be at best confused, more likely to be concerned. Comedy has given me the tools to engage in interpersonal communication in a way that lets people get to know the real me at a slower pace.

Importantly, Marcus has experienced incredible recovery in the decade since his psychological collapse, not just because of comedy, but also thanks to a myriad of resources, including therapy, counseling, and tremendous family support, especially from his father. When Marcus attempted suicide, his father rushed to his aid and brought him to California, where he nursed him back to health. Since then, Marcus's father has been his biggest champion, supporting his son's career as a comedian and providing necessary skills for managing his PTSD. Social and family support are not just important; they are often the defining reason why some people can positively cope through standup.

FINDINGS FRIENDS IN COMEDY AND
IMPROVING SELF-ESTEEM AND MASTERY

Comedians developed their social support by cultivating self-esteem and mastery. Initially, many comedians made friends when they joined the comedy world. For some, comedy felt like home right from the start. Liam, a middle-aged white man, enjoys spending time with his friends, meeting new people, and using the social aspect of comedy to relieve stress. When I met him, he was planning to hang out with another comedian, deciding whether to watch a new movie in the theater or stream it at home. Liam's social life revolves around comedy, and he enjoys thrifting, flea markets, and used bookstores with his comedy friends. They often grab lunch and watch the Pittsburgh Pirates, or just talk. While Liam tries to attend open mics every week, it's not because he wants to perform comedy. He goes to meet his friends and catch up with them, since their schedules are different.

Social support played a vital role in the comedy scene for the participants. Later, we will see that some people, particularly women and minorities in smaller communities, took longer to develop these social connections. However, even those who were marginalized gradually made friends, like Fernanda. "I just moved here and have only been in this scene for a few months. It's fine, I'm making connections so far," she said. "I've hung out with a few friends, and one time we got together at this girl's house to practice our standup sets for a show we were doing together."

Similarly, Lola describes finding several diverse and supportive stages. "I connected with a group of comedian women who would send emails about all-women mics. Then there was one supposed to be all-inclusive but had one all-women night. I started going to that one a lot because it was a very supportive environment." Lola also explains, "Without them, I would have been more hesitant, and it would have taken longer. I'm not sure I would have continued doing standup fully. Most women seek more supportive environments because standup can get uncomfortable."

The issue that women face when finding social support is bigotry. Fernanda shares, "I've made that mistake before where we hang out as a group, and then find out, oh shit, this guy is a racist or a sexist." She expresses her reluctance to build connections, stating, "I have to be a little bit of a spectator to feel people out before I find my people." This hesitation is further discussed in chapter 9 on lost resources.

Despite the prevalence of sexism in standup comedy, many women found solidarity with other women. This solidarity extended beyond demographics such as race, ethnicity, age, or class differences. Women felt that all women were their allies in comedy, as Trina summarized: "I find that I get a lot of support from the women comics in general. I feel that's a big sisterly thing. I feel positive about it. I still have to weed out the ones who are not there for me and are looking to get something from me, but women comedians stick together more. And it's not just the male comedians; the men in my life don't support my comedy. I think it's just a general sexist thing. They still think women aren't funny and should not be onstage telling jokes. Women support each other. Men don't. Men are the biggest haters. That's just the fact. They are the biggest haters. And they shouldn't be, because we are all in this together."

Most comedians experienced an increase in their social support networks after joining comedy, whether their networks were robust and incredibly supportive like Liam's or slim but slowly building like Fernanda and Lola's. Cara, a middle-aged transwoman who initially moved to Memphis for a music career, found comedy to be more welcoming and switched to it instead:

In 2012, I visited Memphis for the first time in fifteen years. I liked it, so I stayed here for a month, and I fell in love with the place all over again. I'm also a musician so I wanted to see how far I could go. While I was here, I found out there was open mic for comedy. I went just as a fan. I befriended some of the comics, and they let me play some music during the shows. So, I decided to move in 2013. And then, when I was at an open mic, the founder of the festival was looking for volunteers. I told her I was a musician, not a comic, but I would love to volunteer. She took my information, and a week went by, but I didn't hear anything. I see her again and she apologies. Then again, I don't hear from her for a couple of weeks, and I thought, "fuck it, they don't want me." Then I get this email saying, "oh, I'm so sorry, please get ahold of me." I don't know what possessed me, but I wrote this really smart-ass response "I don't know if I can work for someone who doesn't meet my emotional needs, but since I have no sense of dignity, I can do the comedy fest." She writes back to me and says she loves me.

Cara explains that her friends are what keep her around and have significantly boosted her self-esteem and overall well-being. She was gradually drawn into performing comedy and producing shows. "Memphis has a different comedy scene than other places," she says. "We're not so dog-eat-dog. We're like a family. I'm the oldest person in the scene; I turn sixty in July. But I am well-loved in this city. When I am around the other comics, it's a good time."

While it's not surprising to discover that relationships build comedians' self-esteem, what's interesting is that many describe how those relationships also improve their sense of mastery. Comedians openly discuss their feelings with each other to hone their craft. Mateo explains, "We'll talk a little about our family and what we're going through." Those candid discussions, although not intentionally designed to reduce the stress, absolutely had that effect, by first, understanding the issues, focusing their ideas, and eventually, bringing those stigmas to the public stage:

> It's not like I'll call up and ask what the doctor told them or ask about their marriage. It's never that. It's always, "Hey, I got his new bit. I got this new sketch." But it's deeper. We unravel why the joke is funny, why the setup is funny, why it's not funny. In a way, I can tell them the worst things I have ever been through or done or have ever experienced, and they won't judge me. They won't say, "Oh, you're a bad person." They'll see it as "Ah, that would be a great bit." It's a deeper understanding of each other.

Valentino explained how journaling ideas, which played a crucial role in his comedy process, also improved his psychological well-being. "I started journaling before I got into standup," he said. He then explained how this process helped him cope with a disturbing sexual experience he had with his ex-girlfriend:

> At some point, we [he and his girlfriend] ended up at this fetish sex thing. That's what she wanted to do. Looking back, I know it was insane. What happened in the actual basement of that place, it was weird. Basically, I couldn't perform [sexually] because of a bunch of guys who were watching me. Because I am part of this comedy group, they get together and talk about the material. After I journaled it, I ran it by other people to get an idea of the bit, where to take it.

Valentino has moved on and he stated, "I am at a place now I don't have to carry with me for the rest of my life. It's an experience that I had, and it's now really funny to me."

IMPROVING RELATIONSHIPS OUTSIDE COMEDY

Many comedians have reported that the standup comedy process not only provides friendships within the industry but also helps improve relationships in the real world. With improved self-esteem and a sense of mastery, comedians are able to positively engage with family, friends, and strangers. Some comedians can even address stigmas with stigmatizing people, such as family, friends, or coworkers, directly onstage. This process is multiphase, beginning with testing their material in front of strangers. After gaining confidence, they invite family and friends to their shows. Seeing these performances can then lead to more discussions at home.

A great example of building a relationship outside comedy can be seen with Marcus. Marcus used comedy to address issues about his military career with his brother, whom he had not seen in over twenty years since their parents separated. "I reconnected with my brother about two years ago," he said. Describing the uncomfortable first encounter, he said, "When I met him, it was me and a friend, and him and his wife. We had dinner before the show. It was a very surface-level conversation." But, "During the show, I chose to do military material to try and give him some background. He knew some of it. He knew I was a vet. He knew I had some PTSD, but he didn't know all of it. This was a way to give him some background in a palatable way without making him have to ask." After the set, Marcus described how they were then able to continue that conversation in a substantive way.

Another way that comedians improved relationships was resisting the stigma onstage without directly addressing a taboo with a particular person. They used the stage as a space to tell their truth and talk about taboo topics without interruption. This was a space where they could convey information without any necessary follow-up. For example, Alvin came out as gay onstage. Initially, he tried to reveal his sexuality to his parents by creating a show and only booking gay comics. Although his parents enjoyed the show and were supportive, they didn't get the hint. Later, Alvin's mom told him that she had a fun evening, even though "it was a really gay show." Similarly, Mateo used the stage to talk about his late uncle who died from HIV:

> I had an uncle who died in '91 of AIDS. He was gay. I remember hating him because he would push me away. He would lock me out of my grandma's house—that type of stuff. And I thought he just hated me. But he didn't know how HIV was spread, and he didn't want to give me the disease. He loved me so much, and I wanted him to die because he was mean. And at five years old, I thought that I killed my uncle; that I had wished it upon him. I remember being at his funeral, everyone was crying, and I was the only one who was happy. Finally, this fucker is dead. And then years later, when I was twelve, my cousin told me what he died of. That really fucked me up for years.

Mateo's uncle's death was a traumatic experience for him. Besides his wife, he hasn't shared his feelings with his family, which he believes is due to the Latino culture. "They don't want to hear it," he explains. "In a Latino family, you don't talk about that kind of stuff. You keep it buried. I want to have those conversations, but I know I can't."

During one of his comedy sets, Mateo talked about his uncle, but unfortunately, some of his family members heard about the set and became angry after hearing secondhand descriptions of the jokes posted online. Mateo's aunt was especially upset, saying, "How dare you say those things about my brother." After some initial drama, he was finally able to convince his mother to listen to the set. "She listened to it and said, 'I don't like it, but you are right. You didn't say anything bad about him,'" Mateo recalls. His mother has since come around to his standup routine.

Many standup comedians have used comedy to improve their self-esteem and mastery, and later to address relationships involving stigmatizing individuals. In many cases, these relationships grew stronger as a result. For Ethan, the coping process helped him overcome barriers that were preventing him and his father from having an emotionally vulnerable relationship:

> I used comedy to work through the feelings I had about my father. Neglect issues. He didn't abandon me; we just didn't talk. I thought he hated me. Until I started doing comedy and he started talking to me more, partly because I was making fun of him a lot, we didn't have a relationship. We understand each other much more now than we ever did. He likes to fish. I hate fishing. I like to make fun of him, and he hates that. I don't think comedy was everything, but after he heard my set, he understood how I felt.

Like Ethan, Rafa also had a similar relationship with his father that was sometimes physically violent. "We threw down," he nervously laughed. "It was a very physical, emotional moment. I was young and he was tossing me around. That was our culture; that's how you become a man. You get your ass beat now and again." Part of his healing and confronting the trauma was talking about the issue in public with his father present. "I remember saying that joke onstage, and people loved it," he explained. "Afterward, my family was talking to me about it. A couple of them looked at my dad and asked, 'Did you do that to him?' And he says, 'I don't remember shit, but I'm sure it happened if he's talking about it.'" Most importantly, he used comedy to demonstrate understanding, rather than only chastising, his father. Rafa explains how he used comedy to explicitly show his father that he understood his feelings as well:

> My father is not a very emotional person. I told them about a time when he walked in on me, crying [after a breakup] in the garage, and he doesn't know how to deal with that. I'm feeling awkward because he's seeing me in this vulnerable moment. We're two machismo Mexicanos. He's like, "I'm going to get a beer, are you good?" I let it all out and he doesn't know how to deal with it, and he goes, "Hey man, fuck it, there are more chicks. Go find another one." At some point, we come together, but we don't know how to hug. So we come around a tool chest, with the one arm around each other. We had to do something manly, so we touched the tool chest. He says, "Grab a beer and come inside.

After publicly acknowledging the positive moments and condemning the violent ones, Rafa's father has witnessed the possibility of a better relationship, which has brought them closer together. Rafa says, "He doesn't talk to me the same way he used to. He talks to me as an adult now, whereas before he talked to me as his son, someone who was beneath him." Rafa's openness about his emotional experiences with his family onstage has made his father confront his own behavior and wonder if he had hurt his son.

Some people use comedy to mend family relationships, while others use it to confront toxic relationships within the comedy industry. For example, Hope suffered emotional abuse from her ex-partner. Although their relationship had ended, she continued to relive the trauma because of her colleagues in the comedy world. They not only allowed her abuser into their community (he was not a comedian and had no connection to comedy except through Hope), but they also teased her about the abuse for years. After enduring years of harassment, she finally had the opportunity to tell her story onstage and confront one particular person:

> It turns out my fellow male comedians were standing in the back, waiting to see how the show would go. I knew they were listening so I made sure to hit it very

hard about the way that people perceived that relationship, the way that they would talk about it, and the way they would invite him into our space when I didn't want him to. I was very resentful of them. I wanted to make sure they all understood why I made the choices I made and why I couldn't leave comedy to get away from him. It took about thirty minutes to tell the story, and it was the only time I could say it without getting interrupted. One of the male comedians was there. He may have been the worst one. I know a million white men, but he thinks like a white man more than any other white man I know. After the show, we came backstage to tell me that I did great and "good job." And he hugs me, and he starts crying. Crying! "If I ever did anything, if I ever was not supportive of you during that time. If I ever made you feel like you couldn't talk to us or that you weren't safe. I'm so sorry. I had no idea. I had no idea it was that bad." But it was so funny that he was crying about my pain, and I didn't feel anything anymore. I felt great after that show, and I used to cry every day for four years. What if I transferred all the pain out of me onto the people who really need to receive it? He felt like a real asshole, and boy did I love that.

Stories like those of Hope, Rafa, Ethan, Mateo, and Alvin give us hope for the restorative power of communal conversations. Unfortunately, many others have not been as fortunate. They are still unable to mend those gaps because the people who stigmatize them, such as family, friends, and peers, are unwilling to meet them even halfway. For example, Joji wants to empathize with his parents, even though he is the one facing homophobia as a queer person of color. "I come from a culture where people don't talk about their feelings," he explains. "In 2004, my parents and I were not okay. My mother kept trying to change me—basically, conversion therapy." Notice how he takes great care to shoulder his mother's burden, even though he is a queer person of color who faces violence daily:

> I was in my parents' home county, and I was asked to perform, and my mother came. I did a monologue based on her, how she was not able to accept my queerness fully, and how she struggles. I think it was the first time she heard somebody speaking her story and people not judging her for it. So, my sister died when I was very young, and in the monologue, she [my mother] says, "Maybe I wouldn't be so hard on Joji if my first daughter hadn't died." I described my mother's pain, and she was essentially being witnessed in this world, expressing thoughts she never outwardly expressed. The limelight was on her, but in this weird way, she saw herself outside of her own body. She saw it, and she saw how people gravitated to me and were laughing at my stories. She saw how I wasn't hated for talking about my queerness in front of a bunch of conservatives.

Despite achieving professional success and connecting with his conservative community, Joji's relationship with his family has not improved significantly. He is especially hurt that his mother still does not give him the love he needs.

"Were there moments where there might have been an understanding, particularly with my mother?" he asked. "I don't know." While comedy provided some relief for Joji and others, they relied on other strategies as well.

COMPARTMENTALIZING PROBLEMS AND COMPLIMENTING COMEDY

There are many ways to actively cope with one's problems through comedy. Having conversations, even subtle ones, can produce positive outcomes. However, it's important to remember that comedy is not made to heal; it's made to entertain. Some comedians have internalized this fact and are vehemently opposed to the idea of coping through comedy, like Franklin. "Some people say that comedy is their therapy, which doesn't make sense," he argues. "You get to talk about your stuff, but you aren't getting any feedback other than laughter. Getting trauma off your chest is one thing, but getting it off your chest with someone who is there to help is something else. How is standup providing that?" Although he discusses subjects like depression and suicide attempts with the audience, he doesn't use them to gain any mental validation.

Compartmentalizers, like Franklin, take charge of their lives by seeking alternative coping strategies for emotional or personal problems. They actively seek help outside of comedy through counseling, psychiatric services, mediation, religious coping, and even family and friends. They have taken charge of their health and will not leave it to chance with an audience who wants to be entertained, not to heal others. For instance, Stephanie, a middle-aged white woman, described all the preventive health measures she takes:

> I work a twelve-step program, so I go to meetings. I have a sponsor. I meditate. I have a very particular meditation practice that focuses on body sensation. My self-care included a lot of rest and trying not to push too hard in any direction. Trying to do basic things like take a walk and eat and sleep. And for me, those three things are sometimes the hardest to do. I am very aware of what was going on in me, and I was actively do what I could to help myself. To try and self-soothe.

Health management practices become even more important when, as Stephanie describes, comedy is the biggest stressor in her life. "I was terrified that I wouldn't be good enough and that my show wouldn't be good," she laments. "Every day, all I could think about was whether I was okay and whether I could actually do this. It was like carrying a heavy weight inside my body. I didn't sleep well, and I generated a lot of emotional stress in my body because I was obsessive."

Many of the participants find that compartmentalizing their problems and seeking healthy alternatives are the best options, especially if they plan to bring their issues to the stage. For example, Hazel, a middle-aged white woman, jokes about the traumatic experiences she had at the hands of her mother:

> I have a lot of stuff about my mom. She has bipolar personality and narcissistic personality disorders. Sometimes she is the most loving person in the world, and then sometimes she would be horrible. Plus, she was always putting us in dangerous situations. I make it funny now, like when she got arrested in her clown uniform on the lawn of our house because she was fighting with her boyfriend. But I used to be terribly sad. I had to leave when I was thirteen; I had to divorce her. So much of that stuff I could not talk about. I had to just pretend it didn't happen.

Therapy helped Hazel cope as an adult, and she often discusses her issues onstage, complementing the benefits of therapy. Comedy plays an active role in her coping process. She explains, "I did it because I was in therapy, and I was thinking, what was the scariest thing I could do? And the scariest thing—besides self-harm—was to get up in front of people and just talk." Moreover, comedy acted as a catalyst to put those events behind her. "But getting through that and making it funny was really therapeutic for me. We [her and her mom] just started talking now. I couldn't talk to her the whole time I was doing trauma therapy. Then, when I started doing comedy, I started telling everyone about it. It felt great." Hazel continues by directly comparing the two: "That was the therapy for me. I was just able to be honest about my past. I feel like I present myself as a put-together person most of the time. And when people found out about my history, I would feel judged. But in comedy, this way, I can control the narrative."

Many participants use alternative coping strategies, but these are not always effective. Some people compartmentalize their issues, while others use complementary coping mechanisms, such as speaking onstage. However, it is crucial to have complementary coping strategies when the space is not designed to provide equality and is explicitly structured to harm certain individuals. Comedy alone does not provide enough opportunity to fully understand the intricacies of any issue. Without these alternatives, sharing problems with an unknown audience is like target shooting in the dark while blindfolded. You may hit the bull's-eye, but you are more likely to miss.

COPING IS VALUABLE, BUT NOT THE ONLY OPTION, AND NOT EFFECTIVE ALONE

In every community, people can accumulate social and psychological resources to feel valued by others. Comedians demonstrate that this process doesn't happen in isolation. Some comedians gain self-esteem from their performances, while others use comedy to strengthen relationships with people who have hurt them. For non-comedians, the most significant impact of comedy may be the development of interpersonal skills. Interpersonal skills include communication, assertiveness, conflict resolution, and anger management.[12] People with higher interpersonal skills have higher self-esteem, fewer psychopathologies, less stress, and fewer negative behaviors like binge eating or alcohol abuse. They also have better emotional responses to challenging situations, such as PTSD.[13] Better communication skills lead to less stress in romantic relationships and better interactions between doctors and patients.[14]

Many participants in this study have expert interpersonal skills, which they developed and enhanced through consistent practice. With these newly developed skills, some felt more comfortable discussing taboos with family and friends and challenging their stigma. I will revisit the topic of interpersonal skills in the conclusion of this book because I believe they are incredibly important. As individuals, how can we hope to find liberation from stigma if we don't have the necessary skills to do so?

But most importantly, the participants demonstrate the necessity of a supportive community that provides many resources and opportunities to heal. Coping never occurs by itself, and the best coping outcomes occur in tandem with a supportive group that allows them to suffer, understand, and grow. Social support is the key to coping, a fact that I can attest to. While I was processing my trauma, I first started through my conversations with comedians. I also had unconditional love and immense knowledge from my spouse. As a former abuse advocate, she knew where to get free professional counseling at the Rape Crisis Center. Her knowledge was vital after I came out to her because we didn't have any health insurance at the time. Unfortunately, most people do not know that free counseling resources do exist. And even if they did know, they probably face a multitude of other barriers, including cultural stigma that will deter or prohibit the use of those resources.

I also had very supportive family members who were there to shoulder some of the weight when my parents could not. When we told my grandparents and aunt that my relationship with my parents had soured, they dropped everything to come to our aid and shower us with hugs and affection. They gave us love and support every day with no strings attached. They even gave us board for a couple of months until our jobs started, which would allow us to afford rent for our own place. Without family support and my wife's knowledge and determination to use proven health resources, I would still be hiding my pain. It wouldn't have mattered that I was able to communally cope with some of the comedians in this study. There is never only one answer, and one answer is usually not enough.

NOTES

1. Susan Folkman and Judith Tedlie Moskowitz, "Coping: Pitfalls and Promise," *Annual Review of Psychology* 55 (2004): 745–74.

2. Jo Lynne W. Robins et al., "Mindfulness: An Effective Coaching Tool for Improving Physical and Mental Health," *Journal of the American Association of Nurse Practitioners* 26, no. 9 (2014): 511–18, https://doi.org/10.1002/2327-6924 .12086; Jill E. Bormann et al., "Spiritual Wellbeing Mediates PTSD Change in Veterans with Military-Related PTSD," *International Journal of Behavioral Medicine* 19, no. 4 (2012): 496–502, https://doi.org/10.1007/s12529-011-9186-1.

3. Christopher G. Ellison and Andrea K. Henderson, "Religious and Mental Health: Through the Lens of the Stress Process," in *Toward a Sociological Theory of Religion and Health*, ed. Anthony J. Blasi (Boston: Brill, 2011), 11–43.

4. Elena M. Fazio, "Sense of Mattering in Late Life," in *Advances in the Conceptualization of the Stress Process: Essays in Honor of Leonard I. Pearlin*, ed. William R. Avison et al. (New York: Springer, 2010), 149–76; Morris Rosenberg and B. Claire McCullough, "Mattering: Inferred Significance and Mental Health among Adolescents," *Research in Community and Mental Health* 2 (1981): 163–82; John Taylor and R. Jay Turner, "A Longitudinal Study of the Role and Significance of Mattering to Others for Depressive Symptoms," *Journal of Health and Social Behavior* 42, no. 3 (2001): 310–25; Peggy A. Thoits, "Stress, Coping, and Social Support Processes: Where Are We? What Next?," *Journal of Health and Social Behavior* Extra Issue, no. 1995 (1995): 53–79.

5. McGraw and Warner, *The Humor Code: A Global Search for What Makes Things Funny.*

6. Leonard I. Pearlin and Alex Bierman, "Current Issues and Future Directions in Research into the Stress Process," in *Handbook of the Sociology of Mental Health*, ed. Carol S. Aneshensel, Jo C. Phelan, and Alex Bierman (Dordrecht: Springer Netherlands, 2013), 325–40, https://doi.org/10.1007/978-94-007-4276-5; Abraham Rudnick et al., "Humour-Related Interventions for People with Mental Illness: A Randomized Controlled Pilot Study," *Community Mental Health Journal* 50 (2014): 737–42, https: //doi.org/10.1007/s10597-013-9685-4.

7. Blair Wheaton, "Models for the Stress-Buffering Functions of Coping Resources," *Journal of Health and Social Behavior* 26, no. 4 (1985): 352–64; Nan Lin and Walter M. Ensel, "Life Stress and Health: Stressors and Resources," *American Sociological Review* 54, no. 3 (1989): 382–99.

8. Tetyana Pudrovska et al., "The Sense of Mastery as a Mediator and Moderator in the Association Between Economic Hardship and Health in Late Life," *Journal of Aging and Health* 17, no. 5 (2005): 634–60, https://doi.org/10.1177/0898264305279874; Scott Schieman, Tetyana Pudrovska, and Melissa A. Milkie, "The Sense of Divine Control and the Self-Concept: A Study of Race Differences in Late Life," *Research on Aging* 27, no. 2 (2005): 165–96, https://doi.org/10.1177/0164027504270489.

9. John Mirowsky and Catherine E. Ross, "Measurement for a Human Science," *Journal of Health and Social Behavior* 43 (2002): 152–70, https://doi.org/10.2753/JEI0021-3624430226.

10. Matt Bradshaw and Christopher G. Ellison, "Financial Hardship and Psychological Distress: Exploring the Buffering Effects of Religion," *Social Science & Medicine* 71, no. 1 (2010): 196–204, https://doi.org/10.1016/j.socscimed.2010.03.015.

11. Teresa E. Seeman, "Social Ties and Health: The Benefits of Social Integration," *Annals of Epidemiology* 6, no. 5 (1996): 442–51, https://doi.org/10.1016/S1047-2797(96)00095-6: Lisa F. Berkman, "The Relationship of Social Networks and Social Support to Morbidity and Mortality," in *Social Support and Health*, ed. Sheldon Cohen and S. Leonard Syme (New York: Academic Press, 1985); Lisa F. Berkman, "Social Networks and Health," *Annual Review of Sociology* 34, no. 2008 (2008): 405–18; Lonnie R. Snowden, "Social Embeddedness and Psychological Well-Being among African Americans and Whites," *American Journal of Community Psychology* 29, no. 4 (2001): 519–36.

12. NC State University Counseling Center, "Interpersonal Skills," accessed January 9, 2020, https://counseling.dasa.ncsu.edu/interpersonal-skills/.

13. David A. Kenny et al., "Interpersonal Perception in the Context of Doctor-Patient Relationships: A Dyadic Analysis of Doctor-Patient Communication," *Social Science & Medicine* 70, no. 5 (2010): 763–68, https://doi.org/10.1016/j.socscimed.2009.10.065; Marylene Cloitre et al., "Skills Training in Affective and Interpersonal Regulation Followed by Exposure: A Phase-Based Treatment for PTSD Related to Childhood Abuse," *Journal of Consulting and Clinical Psychology* 70, no. 5 (2002): 1067–74, https://doi.org/10.1037/0022-006X.70.5.1067.

14. Thomas Ledermann et al., "Stress, Communication, and Marital Quality in Couples," *Family Relations* 59, no. 2 (2010): 195–206; Vahid Kohpeima Jahromi et al., "Active Listening: The Key of Successful Communication in Hospital Managers," *Electronic Physician* 8, no. 3 (2016): 2123–28, https://doi.org/10.19082/2123.

Chapter 8

The Structure and
Culture of Inequality

In the previous chapter, I emphasized that open conversations are not the only way some people combat the effects of stigma. The comedy community offers a variety of "flexible resources" such as money, knowledge, power, prestige, and beneficial social connections that can be used to directly eliminate stigma or counter its negative effects.[1] Some performers use the stage to build self-esteem, while others develop skills that are necessary to build confidence and self-worth. Some find a sense of camaraderie with like-minded individuals, while others improve their relationships with family and friends. Still others find a sense of purpose. All of these tactics and resources are valid ways to become healthier and happier individuals.

However, the stage is not a level playing field. While there may be an optimal way for comedians to cope communally, their experiences, background, and the audience can all hinder their freedom behind the microphone. Throughout this book, we've examined how stigma affects comedians' ability to speak, how they manage cultural conceptions, and how some people are dealing with more issues. Even if someone is funny and skilled, the audience may not laugh, and people cannot heal. Fernanda's story perfectly illustrates these constrained voices. As a former professional ballerina, Fernanda is physically fit and appears to be a very emotionally and psychologically healthy individual. But she lives with anxiety that was fostered in her dance culture. Body-image issues and subsequent eating disorders are common for young women, and they are amplified for ballerinas, as Fernanda describes the pressures she faced from a young age:

> When I was in ballerina school, they brought me into the office again. The principal said, "You need to lose weight, and you need to do it however you can do it. When I was your age, I used to have a cigarette for lunch." So, I started taking diet pills as a child. I lost all this weight. I weighed 110 pounds and got down to 104 pounds, which for me at 5 [foot] 3 [inches] that was not great. I

lost all this weight, but my parents found the pills under the bed. My mom called the school and was like, "Oh my God, my daughter is taking diet pills. What do we do?" Then this same woman tells my mom, "Oh my God, your daughter is taking pills? That's so terrible."

Fernanda intends to bring her disturbing experiences to the comedy stage, but she's struggling to find the best way to convey her message. "I haven't found ways to make it funny," she admits. In a world that's obsessed with gender and fitness, even someone like Fernanda, who is probably in the top 1 percent of fittest people on earth, is judged based on her appearance. "I still weigh 110 or 115 pounds. I still have a great figure," she says. And because of this, she's judged just like other women, but differently. "If I were to get onstage and tell people I was called fat and that I have body issues, the audience will absolutely turn against me. If I tell a room full of people with normal bodies of various sizes, nine times out of ten, they'll think I'm a monster." By not exploring her true self onstage, Fernanda feels like she's lost some of her voice, her ability to cope, and ultimately her ability to address stigma. Ultimately, managing one's voice is a form of self-stigmatization. Fernanda and others lose opportunities because of immense pressures to create a perfectly cultivated self-presentation that doesn't offend. To eliminate stigma, people require positive social contact. For comedians, talking on a stage may be optimal, but at minimum, they need to actually set foot in a comedy space and make social contact. In the same way that a community can provide alternative means to counter the effects of stigma beyond speech alone, it also creates other ways that hinder our ability to address stigma. The comedy world is producing many different resources and avenues to counter stigma, but we also need to consider the many other ways the community may hinder growth.

The stigma process indicates that there is discrimination, and unequal access to resources tied to health outcomes is fundamental to discrimination.[2] Fundamental causality shows that health inequality persists because individuals with less social status are less likely to access flexible resources such as knowledge, money, power, prestige, and beneficial social connections that can improve health. For example, healthcare is crucial, but healthcare options are limited in the poorest communities. Even if healthcare is available, those who are poorest often have the fewest options to get to hospitals. Additionally, if transportation is readily available, those who are poorest are less likely to be able to afford a day off work. Regarding comedians, while they may be able to access the stage freely, the community prevents participation in other structural ways.

Furthermore, individuals with lower statuses are more prone to experiencing stressors. Any group that faces discrimination, stigma, and lack of resources experiences worse health outcomes than those who do not.[3] For instance, mothers often face occupational denial or are hired at lower income levels.[4] Additionally, Black Americans have higher morbidity rates and are more likely to suffer from all-cause mortality compared to whites.[5] Gays and lesbians face higher rates of mental illness, such as depression, and suicide.[6] Transgender adults have a significantly higher risk of poor physical health, disability, depressive symptomatology, and perceived stress compared to non-transgender adults.[7] Women may enjoy longer lives than men, but they suffer from higher morbidity and illness.[8] While an individual may be able to address stigma, they may also experience so much harm that the consequences offset any gains from stigma management.

Although there is still debate about what constitutes the "fundamental cause" of inequality, strong evidence suggests that economic status, racism, sexism, and segregation are all consistent predictors of health inequality.[9] This book and other research in comedy have documented many examples of these types of inequality and discrimination. Negative social pressures and structures counter any stigma reduction and deter open conversations. However, what is more important is not whether it exists, but the extent to which it does. Inequality exists everywhere, but it manifests at different magnitudes. Therefore, before we can understand how structural inequality has harmed the comedians in this book (explored in chapter 9), we need to have a clear understanding of how the participants in this study experience inequality and how the community may explicitly exacerbate poor health.

FINANCIAL EXPLOITATION

First and foremost, comedy is a profession that comes with low pay and high stakes, as all the comedians in this study described workplace exploitation. For example, Zoey has a contract to perform on Friday nights at a prestigious LA comedy club, but she only expects to be paid $15 for the night. If she performs on the main stage, she could earn $30. This club is nationally recognized and makes upwards of $100 million in revenue annually. Headliners at the club get specials on Netflix, HBO, and Comedy Central, and some even sell out arenas. Despite the club's value and owner's wealth, Zoey's annual income is less than $10,000, leaving her impoverished and relying on food stamps and welfare to survive in one of the most expensive cities in the world.

On the opposite end of the spectrum, Lora is a highly successful comedian who tours the country and has multiple television specials and late-night appearances. However, like Zoey, she also frequently performs for next to nothing, often losing money to perform on stages she feels pressured to perform on. "Standup comedy should not cost you money," Lora explains.

"I'll pick up sets in Los Angeles and then have to drive forty-five minutes, so I'll take a Lyft. That means it costs me sixty dollars just to do a set in Los Angeles. It's not sustainable."

Although all participants indicated that they experienced financial hardships from comedy, full-time comics seemed to suffer the most and be the most impoverished. Part-time comedians may be balancing other jobs, which makes it more difficult to be a full-time comedian. However, for those who make comedy a full-time profession, transitioning out of their previous job is a tenuous proposition with food and shelter at stake. Felipe describes the transition to a full-time comic when he gave up a very lucrative job. "When I started standup ten years ago, I was in real estate," he explains. "I was making double or triple what I am now. To make it in comedy, I needed to let go of that lifestyle, that career. So I let my license go." His hope was that after time and success, comedy would allow him to support his family. But it's difficult because he's constantly caught between missing opportunities or making money to feed his family. "I've had to cancel a couple of shows because they didn't pay." Adding that he hasn't become much more stable in the decades since he started: "It's the career that I am working on, and hopefully it will allow us to live better."

The lack of pay is not a choice; many performers feel obligated to work for free in order to get onstage. Even the most prestigious and wealthy clubs participate in this exploitative behavior, and some even use personal connections to take advantage of their workers. As Lance explains:

> My biggest stress in life comes from comedy, mostly from working with the club owner. He tends to take advantage of people's labor and time. Last summer, he'd call once a week and ask me to come in and run the club since he was gone or doing something. It was always at the last minute and never paid. My boyfriend would get in free, which is the "compensation." I get paid well at my main job, and I don't mind helping out a friend, but it's a constant. I'd work ten hours of work during the day then I'd have to go to the club till one in the morning, no pay, all because the club owner wanted to watch football.

It's important to note that while Lance was only annoyed by the lack of compensation because he has a full-time job, other comedians who rely exclusively on comedy income are indeed harmed. Evelyn, who makes about $10,000 annually and has performed on late-night, primetime talk shows including *Late Night with Stephen Colbert*, lives off food stamps and Medicaid. "I'm very lucky that New York provides these resources," she explains. "I don't know where I would be without them, because comedy sure doesn't provide." Evelyn is single and lives with roommates. She is certainly struggling, reporting that she has gone a couple of days without food.

But her responsibility is to herself. For those with familial responsibilities, their situation is far worse. For instance, Jeremy had to make some very difficult decisions about his family's well-being when he and his wife both lost their healthcare coverage. "A few weeks before my daughter was born, my wife and I lost SAG, actors' insurance," he explained. "Luckily, my daughter was covered, because California does an excellent job of ensuring children under the age of five." He then added, "We would take her to the pediatrician and try to weave in questions about ourselves. They would tell us she gained three pounds and grew a couple of inches, and I would say, 'Yeah, she got acid reflux after four beers.' I am insured now, but at the time, that lack of coverage was terrifying."

Healthcare remains one of the top problems in America. Unfortunately, comedy is not a viable way for many Americans to obtain health coverage. As a result, many aspiring comedians, like Valentino, give up on their dreams. Despite recently receiving full health benefits in a new job, Valentino remains determined to pursue his passion for comedy. He acknowledges that the industry is tough to break into, stating, "There are a few people at the top, and then there are the rest of us." Monetizing standup comedy is already difficult, as many people do not view it as a legitimate art form. Valentino explains, "It's just this crazy person who goes onstage and starts rambling some bullshit." However, he remains optimistic about the possibility of making a career out of comedy and living comfortably. He admits that it is not a secure path unless one reaches the top. Without a regular paying job, most comedians are unable to afford health insurance.

The comedians in this study expressed a continuing problem of lacking legal protection. Only a tiny minority of them have reached the level of notoriety where they can rest comfortably, with some easily purchasing their own healthcare coverage. A few others belong to elite comedy troupes that provide some benefits. However, the vast majority are independent contractors with no workplace protection, including Simon. Simon is one of the few comedians who headlines across the country, even performing multiple times on late night. He reported that even at his status, club owners take advantage of him. "A club in Idaho still owes me $1,200 from ten years ago. I'll never see that money," he said. While $1,200 may not seem like a lot, for someone who makes as little as $20,000 annually as a full-time comedian, it's a few months of mortgage payments for Simon. Unfortunately, Simon's hardships are the norm. "If they don't pay us, we don't have any recourse. We don't have a contract. We can't sue. We're all poor; we don't have the money to sue."

Moreover, comedians face outright abuse from gatekeepers who are happy to harm their workers, with little protection. Chacha reported such workplace abuse, stating that about a year prior, a manager at one of the biggest clubs in Texas had beef with her. "He came after me, and I felt alone. I was blacklisted. He was publicly speaking for the club on Facebook, mentioning my name and saying I was a horrible comedian." She elaborated that it started because she tried to defend women who were abused at his hand. "There were other women that he was aggressive toward, very touchy." She then revealed that she was also a victim but tried to put a stop to it. "One time, he made a comment about my ass to my face, and I told him to stop being an asshole." Chacha continued, "I was told that I would never work in a comedy club again. This guy is the manager of the biggest clubs in Texas. People feared him. People would call me and say, 'Chacha, what are you doing? You can't go against this manager.' But he's wrong. What he's doing is so horribly unprofessional and illegal, but all the other comedians were like, 'What's wrong with you?'"

Because of the power imbalance, club owners not only financially exploit their employees but also instill fear in other employees. Some have even attempted to use these tactics on people outside of the club industry. During my project, I personally experienced attempted exploitation from club owners and agents. While most clubs and agents ignored me, some responded with perplexing behavior. One agent asked me how much the research paid, and when I informed him that it was voluntary and I would provide a $10 Starbucks gift card as a token of gratitude, he mocked my profession and said that he wouldn't waste his time with this "bullshit." In another instance, a club owner promised to help spread the word about the study but then demanded payment to talk to comedians who frequented his club. If I refused, he threatened to make it difficult for me to continue my scientific inquiry. Although I never returned to that club, I continued to interview people who had been employed by him. It's important to address these issues and bring attention to the exploitation that occurs in the club industry, because as will be revealed, they are driving the inequality and unequal representation.

DRINKING, DRUG USE, AND TERRIBLE DIETS

Comedians often struggle financially and lack access to healthcare, which is particularly concerning given the unhealthy lifestyle that comes with the job. Standup comedy is typically performed in dark bars and clubs late at night, which can attract unsavory crowds. This lifestyle is not conducive to good health, as comedian Jamal points out: "With that, you got a bar tab. You could order whatever you want with this tab. They had burgers and sodas and alcohol, back-to-back. Think about that, weeks and weeks and weeks of eating nothing but over-the-top food." It's clear that the comedy industry needs to do more to support the health and well-being of its performers.

Not only does the club provide unhealthy food and drinks, but they also make it free for him and other comedians. According to Jamal, standup clubs directly facilitate those negative behaviors by offering free drinks and bar food, which are neither healthy nor beneficial for the performers. As a middle-aged, married man, Jamal recognizes these poor habits and makes a point to make healthy choices. "Now when I go out," he explains, "I'll order soda water or a salad because I know better." Unfortunately, standup seems to reward bad health. "It's almost an advantage if you don't take care of yourself. Having the 'oh, I'm out of shape, I'm so fat' jokes. That's funny, and that works."

To be sure, poor diets are a problem that is facilitated in standup, but it pales in comparison to the exorbitant amount of alcohol consumption that the comedians report. According to Nyah. "So many comics think they can't perform unless they've been drinking or high." She adds, "Only after getting to the brink of killing themselves or ruining their lives do they try to be sober in standup. I wish it didn't take that because there are so many brilliant people who are dying." Bianca goes further, saying that alcohol is mild compared to some of the other drug use. "There would be the comics that are really strung out on drugs," she says. She explained that that club owners didn't seem to mind. "There is a decent number of comics that really abuse hard drugs when they perform."

Another comedian, Dylan, describes the pervasive substance use in the community. He went so far as to place a number and say, "Over half of them are heavy drug users who rely on substances for comedy." According to him, many comedians are so drugged up while performing that they are completely detached from reality. As someone who comes from a very clean community, Sikh, the problem is so pervasive that he has difficulty making positive professional connections. Often, he simply avoids stages, even those that are most prestigious.

People are getting high, getting wasted, doing drugs, or going onstage drunk. I have nothing against them. Do what you wish; to each their own. But when they are getting high, and I have a coffee, it doesn't go well. They can't even engage with me. Where is my mind, where is their mind? It may be part of my upbringing, but if you are not in 100 percent here, I don't want to have a conversation with you. A drink or two is fine, but anything that messes with their capability of being present, that's what scares me. Comedians are unpredictable when they are that drugged. And that's half of the community, which is why I don't hang out with them as friends.

The amount of alcohol use in comedy has been confirmed time and time again by participants who have struggled with these problems. Recall Pierson, who was arrested for a DUI, shared his experience: "I didn't realize how bad my drinking problem was. I've since been arrested again, went to rehab, quit drinking, and just celebrated a year of sobriety." He then pointed out that his drinking problem started when he got into comedy. "I started drinking before I went onstage to deal with the nerves, as I think most do. The culture kind of elevated my drinking habits."

Others have confirmed their drug use, including Amelia. Amelia, whose home comedy club is one of the most prestigious clubs in America, stated, "Standup is a huge catalyst for my usage." She went on to say, "Drugs are always around. And it's not just weed, it's cocaine, it's Adderall." She finally added, "A lot of my fellow comics are people that I have done drugs with." Even worse, Amelia describes how her comedy peers simply didn't care. Even after her hospitalization for depression and substance abuse, her fellow comedians actively encouraged more drug use. "They have a hard time taking it seriously. Some of my best friends in the scene, and they are my best friends outside of comedy, continue to offer me drugs after I was in rehab," adding, "or, while I was in rehab."

Drinking and substance use are serious problems in standup comedy. Among the participants in this study, both men and women had a 50 percent rate of hazardous drinking (see appendix B). In comparison, only 12 percent of men and 9 percent of women in the regular population met the criteria for hazardous drinking. It's notable that none of the participants in this study who discussed substance abuse knew each other or lived in the same region. They came from all corners of the country, including New York and the Northeast, Chicago and the Midwest, Texas and the Southwest, and Atlanta in the Deep South. While it's impossible to determine the exact extent of substance use in standup, this study, along with other evidence, suggests that it is a significant issue in the industry.

AN UNHEALTHY CULTURE THAT
ATTRACTS UNHEALTHY PEOPLE

Comedy enables many unhealthy behaviors, such as drinking, drug use, and poor diets. It's not surprising that a culture of self-deprecation is more likely to celebrate dangerous behavior rather than assist those in distress. However, while there is certainly a culture that contributes to poor health outcomes, can we solely blame the culture itself? I discovered several cases of people resisting these unhealthy temptations. Jamal explains:

Health? Standup comedy is kind of brutal. There is no physical requirement to get into standup. You don't have to take care of yourself to be good at standup comedy. There are comics that are overweight, have high blood pressure. I know a couple of comics who've had a stroke. All this stuff because they don't take care of themselves. But, you have to be the kind of person who is already thinking about eating right and exercising before you do standup comedy. If not, standup will make it worse.

Jamal believes that comedy is inherently unhealthy, so to maintain good health, comedians must take charge. This raises the question: is comedy itself unhealthy, or does it attract unhealthy behavior? It's clear that there is some degree of the latter. For instance, club owners could take responsibility and prohibit alcohol use among performers, rather than feeding many vulnerable comedians drink after drink all night.

But at the same time, it is also true that the unhealthy comedy community may attract troubled people. Stephanie believes as much:

> I don't think anything is naturally toxic about the environment, but we all bring baggage to the relationships. Whatever is going on, that is not occurring organically out of comedy. That's about people. Many of us have parts of ourselves that are very wounded. They prevent us from making healthy connections. Working in comedy has some conditions that can be very persuasive, but it is worse if you don't have your voice or own sense of self.

Stephanie and Jamal are both very health-conscious individuals who take an active role in managing their well-being. While Jamal focuses on maintaining a healthy diet and exercising regularly, Stephanie goes a step further by actively seeking therapy and joining support groups when necessary. Their careers in the health field have developed over the years, and they believe that this maturity is something that many comedians lack.

Jamal, who is almost forty, explains that many young comedians do not fully recognize the long-term consequences of neglecting their health. "Comics that are young, they don't care. They are just out there living," he says. Stephanie agrees and adds that most comedians who suffer from health issues are younger than her. She believes that part of growing up involves distancing oneself from certain relationships, a process that many people in their twenties are still figuring out. Stephanie herself is in recovery and has been for a long time, but she acknowledges that some people may not realize they are unwell until later in life.

Stephanie showed sympathy toward the challenges that young comedians face, but some of her fellow comedians were more straightforward in their evaluation of their peers. As Valentino put it, "In comedy, you deal with a lot of mentally ill people who need help, and they are not receiving it in the right way." He went on to say, "Even if they appear to be well-adjusted, they are all mentally ill. That's my overall impression."

Justus agrees with the overall assessment that comedy attracts unhealthy people. However, he takes it one step further by adding a dimension of masculinity to explain the mental state of many of his comedy peers. According to him:

> Most of the comedians are incel [involuntarily celibate][10] dudes. The people who actually have sex with women, there aren't that many of us. There are a couple types of bits these guys do. There are the guys that snagged a relationship but are like, "I don't know how I got her. We don't have sex because my dick don't work." Or it's the "Women are weird, I don't understand them. I have a small penis."

The fact that Justus and other participants identified their comedy peers as incels is disturbing, considering that this group of young men has a high rate of depression and suicide and openly promotes violence against women.[11] Their existence further demonstrates that comedy not only attracts unhealthy people and exposes them to unhealthy behaviors, but it also may not socially protect those who are mentally ill.

During the conversations, many comedians discussed the passing of Brody Stevens to suicide. He had been beloved comedian in the comedy scene. According to several of the comics, including Sophia, it was all the more sad because he was an advocate for those living with mental illness. "Brody was very open about mental illness and struggling with depression. He did a show about it and would talk about it often." According to her and others, "He decided to stop taking his medication to be more 'creative,' and a few days later, he took his life." She then added, "He told a few other comics, but no one stopped him."

We need to be clear that the comedians who talked about Brody are only speculating. Even if their accounts are true, no one is to blame, including those who could have intervened. Some things are uncontrollable. As Stephanie stated, "Brody lost the battle." However, the evidence shows that those with larger and more supportive networks have better mental health because they have a safety net to fall into when there's a problem. Unfortunately, the comedy community doesn't provide adequate support and pits artists against each other. Ciara explains, "Mental health is a real issue for all types of performers. Comedians are hardest hit because we don't have a community. It's not a team sport, and everybody is fighting for a slot, and there are not that many slots." She links competition to health issues and continues by saying, "You go through ups and downs when you are booked for a couple of months, you are hot, and then you are not, and then you are hot again. I've seen it. I've had friends who disappeared for a long time, then I see them performing, and

I ask, 'Where have you been?' 'Well, I was depressed, and I needed to go get back on my meds.'"

The participants report that the overall standup culture does not take health as seriously as it should, considering the global conditions that people experience in comedy. Those with deep social supports outside of comedy seem to thrive the most. "I'm one of the lucky ones," Ciara describes. "I have such a good family, my husband, my pastors, and therapy. I'm a little better off than others—but just a little." Even after times of tragedy, standup does not seem to get its act together. Immediately after Brody's death, when the comedy world was hyperaware of mental illness among its ranks, many tried to take action, as reported by Sophia. "After Brody passed, several of us were trying to start a mental health support group for comics. We raised a little bit of money and would have a monthly meetup where we could just give each other resources." While valiant, it fell through. "It didn't work because with comedians, it's always a punch line, especially with the guys. It's always a pissing contest where they are trying to be funnier than each other even at their detriment." According to those participants, standup seems to stymie real help for those in need because it simply doesn't care about the mental health of its artists.

DISCRIMINATION

Comedy, as a profession, often exploits its workers and leads them toward unhealthy behaviors, such as drinking, drug use, and poor diets. While it's not impossible to find reasonable and well-adjusted people in this toxic community, it does tend to attract those who engage in such practices. This, in turn, may deter healthy individuals from pursuing a career in comedy. Dylan is a top comedian who avoids substance use, partly due to his Sikh heritage. However, he struggles to make connections within the comedy community because he avoids those who engage in unhealthy behaviors. Furthermore, he finds it difficult to convince his family and friends to participate in the comedy community due to the practices that they find culturally and morally objectionable.

Beyond the unhealthy lifestyle, the community has created a very strong deterrent: discrimination. Women and minority comedians reported examples of racism, sexism, and bigotry without prompting. Everyone in the study experienced discrimination because of their gender, race, ethnic identity, or LGBTQ+ identity. Even legally protected groups faced discriminatory practices, including those who live with disabilities. Nathaniel, who lives with cerebral palsy and uses a wheelchair, explained that many venues are not handicap accessible. "I can't go on tour because half the clubs are up and downstairs. It's hard to get booked places because no matter how good my comedy is, it's like, 'Oh shit. Do we have to rent handicap-accessible equipment? Do we have to get a ramp for the stage?'"

Furthermore, Nathaniel faces accessibility issues even at some of the country's most influential comedy clubs. "For example, I can't perform at the Comedy Attic in Bloomington. I have a real problem with that place because I can't perform there," he stated. He then goes on to note that this club, like many others, is located in a very liberal area. "I find it strange," he continues, "because if there was a place where women and people of color couldn't perform, people would boycott." Nathaniel is in a unique position because federal law requires protection for individuals with disabilities. Under the ADA, businesses are required to accommodate those with disabilities so that they can participate equally. As a result, all of the locations mentioned by Nathaniel are simply violating the law.

However, some individuals are not given opportunities due to discriminatory behaviors that may not necessarily be illegal. Jada, for example, lives with a chronic condition that requires weekly dialysis treatment. "I have to do dialysis three times a week, which limits spur-of-the-moment travel. I have to work around my health problems, which is limiting," she explains. "Before, I could take a show and drive to Louisiana for a thirty-minute show. But now, I can't just do that. If I have to go out of state, I have to know at least two weeks ahead of time so I can set up a treatment schedule." While her illness makes performing comedy difficult, the solution is simple: club owners need to give her enough notice so she can participate. "I have seen comics with dialysis, and bookers and owners work with them," she says. "I know of one comic woman in Austin, and everybody knows her issues. People come to the clinic with her during treatment."

However, Jada's comedy community has been of little help to her. "When I got sick, people stopped booking me," she says. To make matters worse, some individuals have actively worked to sabotage her ability to participate. "There is a club owner who knows about my issue. He purposely calls me on the day of a show so I can't make it. I tell him that 'You know I have this issue. I have told you that if you want to work with me, there are certain accommodations I need.'"

Jada and others deserve help, not only because it's required by the American with Disabilities Act, but also because it's the morally right thing to do. Similarly, other marginalized groups face discriminatory behavior that prevents them from accessing mainstream opportunities, including LGBTQ+ comedians who are often segregated to less- prestigious venues.

Homophobia

We previously observed how LGBTQ+ comedians had to navigate the audience's biases due to their explicit discrimination, as described by Cara, a trans comedian from Tennessee. "There is still so much misogyny, transphobia. It's still there. It's not every comic, but I'll hear stuff come out all the time. I had a show the other night, and an older dude from New York asked to get on my show." Despite being a kind person, she regretted welcoming him to the stage because "That motherfucker called me a transvestite from the stage." Apart from outright homophobia, LGBTQ+ comedians frequently encountered segregation, one of the most common cultural behaviors affecting them. Instead of welcoming seasoned comics to the main stage, they were often confined to queer comedy shows. For example, Cam was initially approached to perform on the main stage on a Friday show at a renowned comedy club in Los Angeles. He recalls, "The Laugh Factory in LA found my videos and messaged me on Twitter. 'Hey, we want to talk about booking you to do some shows on our stage.' I was like, 'Great! I'm glad you liked my shows.' 'Yeah, you are super funny, let's get you out here.'"

But when the booker discovered that he was gay, they conveniently claimed that they couldn't accommodate him. "When we talked, he asked me if all my jokes were gay jokes. And I said, no, not by a long shot, but we could talk about it more when I got out to LA later that month. He responded by saying that Rainbow Pop wasn't happening at that time. Rainbow Pop is their monthly LGBT standup show." The bookers then told Cam they could book him, but they just stopped responding.

Many people, including Barb, have had similar experiences. Living in New York, she is frequently forced to perform on queer comedy shows. "I've auditioned for clubs where I only get booked on their gay shows instead of a regular house show," she explains. "They never say it, but you can tell they only book one gay person per main; if there are two of us, then it's a gay show." Flustered by the missed opportunities, Barb Laments, "I'm glad there are shows featuring LGBTQ comics, but I don't necessarily want to be a gay comic performing on a gay show. I want to be a comic performing for people."

Instead of openly expressing homophobia, comedy was often communicated through covert language that denied opportunities. LGBTQ+ comedians, such as Lawshawn, recognized this covert language. Lawshawn shared, "I was told very early in my career that a booker couldn't sell me because his audiences wouldn't connect with me. He was doing everything short of saying the magic lawsuit words 'it's because you are Black. It's because you are gay.'" LGBTQ+ comedians face a culture of homogeneity among gatekeepers. Holly described how power brokers all operate similarly due to their similar backgrounds:

> The industry has gatekeepers like any industry. And in the comedy world, those gatekeepers are programmers and producers of festivals, television, Netflix, other streaming services. Unfortunately, within the comedy industry, across the board, cisgendered heterosexual white people hold those positions. Mostly men, some women, but those women tend to operate like those men. So, there is not much difference.

In the end, access to the stage for queer comedians is precarious. They are not granted access to the same stages, and as we will see, this poses a significant problem for both advancing their careers and resisting stigma. Ironically, despite the fact that comedy gatekeepers believe that LGBTQ+ individuals cannot connect with audiences, in most places, there are no queer stages, and they only have the opportunity to hone their craft in front of "cis-gendered, heterosexual audiences. And they love it." Thus, the denial of these voices is clearly a product of homophobia. As Holly states, "I've always killed it. And I've killed it in front of these gatekeepers. I don't know what more to do to prove to them that I am worthy of the next level?"

Performing the Latino Stereotype

Comedian Latinos, much like those who identify as LGBTQ+, have spoken about being typecast in front of specific audiences and facing limited opportunities. Felipe, for instance, shared his experience of being labeled as a Latin comedian and only being booked for Latin shows. He noted that there is still a stigma attached to it and that women also face gender inequality in the industry. He said, "Women are only booked on all-woman shows. You can't help but look at lineups and see mostly white people in Hollywood. There are some Latinos sprinkled in there." It's clear that there is a need for greater diversity and inclusivity in the entertainment industry.

But unlike LGBTQ+ participants who are sometimes forced onto stages due to their identity, Latinos often express that they were unable to be themselves and were instead forced into playing negative stereotypes. This pattern has been confirmed in other research that has examined Latino representation in media.[12] Mateo explains, "What sucks is that they are looking for a specific type that screams this guy is 'ethnic.' It's changing a little, and I try not to think about it, but I feel it. They are trying to fill their quota of a specific type of comedian."

Many Latinos in this study view comedy as a form of "modern-day minstrelsy" that forces them to play "brown face" characters. Felipe, in particular, hates this type of comedy and exclaims, "I'll shoot the next guy who does the joke with the chancla." The situation is a catch-22 because many Latinos miss out on opportunities if they don't play these roles. Mateo explains, "Because I don't talk about those issues, I lose things here and there. I could do those bits and jokes, but that's not who I am. I wouldn't want to get booked, play that card, and think yuck, I don't like this."

On the other hand, if comedians play into stereotypes, they risk being pigeonholed in front of one particular audience. As Felipe advises many young Latino comedians, "Don't get stuck in that Latino Bermuda triangle. If you keep doing Latino jokes and working for Latino crowds, that's where you are going to stay." He suggests that they go to Hollywood and perform in front of diverse audiences, telling jokes that everyone can relate to, rather than relying solely on their cultural background. "Get out of the box," he urges. While he understands that newcomers may have to use their cultural identity as a starting point, he is proud to say that he himself was not booked on a Latin comedy show during the last Cinco de Mayo celebration.

Black Men versus Black Women.

It's not surprising that Black comedians also report experiencing discrimination. Demarcus, for example, feels like he's constantly working overtime both in his life and in his comedy to achieve any kind of success. He described:

> I've always been raised to work twice as hard and get half as far. The highest we can get is the floor for a lot of people. Chris Rock has this great bit about how he lived in the neighborhood, and the Black people who live in the neighborhood were Mary J Blige, and Eddie Murphy, people at the top of their field who rose from rags to riches. But the white people in his neighborhood are dentists. In general, it feels like that as a Black person, you have to work really, really, hard for some stability. You have to dodge early death or prison, or just poverty. If you don't do something very special, your life is going to end in that way.

Every Black comedian in this book has experienced discrimination in this industry, but the types of discrimination they face depend on the region they're in. Those who travel outside of major cities face even worse consequences for simply being Black. For many Black comedians, like Candace, the possibility of violence is emotionally and psychologically draining:

> I was the only Black person on an all-female tour, and we were performing in Maryland, and the host came to our table and said, "don't make any ignorant jokes." And I said, "what does that mean." He says, "Ignorant about race." I respond, "oh, like the Asians are bad drivers. That kind of crap." And he goes, "oh, no, no, no. That's funny. I mean dot do ignorant stuff about white

people. White people are this. White people are that." I was so confused; they were totally cool with discriminating against any other ethnicity, but you can't challenge whites. And he says, "There are a couple of KKK chapters here in Maryland, and we don't want to offend anyone in the audience." It's like, the fuck I don't! I felt very unsafe. What the heck am I going to say that is going to set them off and then suddenly it's a hate crime happening here.

While every participant in comedy may have experienced discrimination, Black men seem to have a slight advantage in their ability to navigate the industry. As Demarcus explains, Black comedian men are often viewed as entertainers first, with their race being a secondary consideration. According to him, many people don't differentiate between the best white comedian men and their Black counterparts:

> Hetero, cisgendered Black men, were second in the comedy world. It's likes first are hetero cisgendered white dudes; they still have the most privilege. But close right after that is us. If I were to ask most people to name five successful comedians, they could easily name five Black dudes even if you don't ask them to name five Black men specifically. It's going to be Kevin Hart, Eddie Murphy, Steve Harvey. Kanye has this line, "I thought I chose a field where they couldn't sack me." I've always kind of felt that way about comedy. I have an excellent chance in comedy to be all the things I want to be.

Demarcus further elaborates on the status of Black men in comedy, explaining that despite his race, the audience can still relate to his experiences. However, he notes that other comedians are not given the same benefit of the doubt:

> I can be doing poorly in a room of racist people who do not want to connect with me because I'm a Black dude. But then I mention I have a wife, and they are just a little less tense about me because they also have a wife. I have comic friends who are members of the queer community. When my lesbian friends want to tell jokes about their wives, it has the complete opposite effect. It's like, "Oh, my God, you have a wife? I don't like this. I don't want to hear that you and your wife engage in normal activities like my wife and me because I don't want to think of you as normal."

Demarcus's assessment of gender and race dynamics was confirmed by several other comedians. Although Demarcus expressed his opinion politely, Black comedian women were more straightforward in their views, as Ciara stated:

> Me as a Black woman in the comedy world, we don't get much respect. It's so hard. I swear I have to put in so much more work and be ten times better than other comics just because I'm a Black woman. Approaching comedy clubs, I'm

sure I get looked over no matter how many tapes I send in, no matter how many standing ovations I get at other clubs, no matter how often I get booked for private shows. They always want just a little bit more. "Oh, just a little bit more before you can get on this stage." They don't that we can capture an audience and story tell. They don't think we can shine, and that people want to hear us. Generally, white men don't believe that Black women should be heard in any aspect of life. Comedy is just another thing. "Oh, you're not funny. You're just mean. You're a Black woman. You're just mean." We can make anything funny; they just don't want us there.

While many Black women report being denied opportunities onstage, Lola finds a certain type of comedy even more insulting. She is particularly upset by Black men who use satire to mock women, especially because it means she loses opportunities to them:

One thing I hate in the Black comedy, is the Black guys who wear dresses and talk about Black women. That kills me. It's not helping us at all. They think it's funny; it's not. It's derogatory. A gay Black dude in a dress? I can kind of deal with that. To a certain point, gay Black men appreciate women. I can understand if they are using it to talk about themselves. But a straight Black dude in a dress, making fun of women. The very same comedy clubs that barely have any Black women headliners will book them? It's easier for a Black man in a dress to get booked than actual woman. Everything that I am, they don't want; they just want to make fun of us.

Sexism: Universally Damaging to Women

While Black women experience a unique form of discrimination, much of it may be related to gender. This is not to downplay their unique lived experiences as Black women. Evidence shows that they are more likely to be sexualized and stereotyped as aggressive compared to their other feminine counterparts. Other research has even found that it took much longer for Black women to be seen in comedy. However, gender in general seems to be the defining factor in prejudice that harms all women comedians regardless of race or ethnicity, amplifying other inequalities. For instance, financial exploitation is the norm in comedy and it seems to cross gender lines. But women are more likely to report being stiffed when it comes to compensation, which is easily recognized when men get paid at the same shows. As Sharice reported:

People are sinful. Because I'm a woman, they don't want to pay me as much, or at all. They think we're suckers. People always want to holla, "That's the game. That's just the way it goes." A man gets paid for the show, and I have to sell tickets? They are not more seasoned than me! We're at the same level in our careers! And then you want me to buy two drinks to stand on your shit stage? I will dine and dash so fast.

Women faced various forms of sexism, beyond being financially exploited. One of the ways participants experienced sexism was through the expectation placed on their appearance. This aligns with existing research in comedy that argues women cannot be funny-looking, or they won't get selected for certain roles.[13] While men could appear unkempt, standup comedian women had to dress nicely and present themselves as attractive and sexually available, a pattern that is prevalent in most societies.[14] When they didn't conform to these expected norms or even discussed them in public, comedian women were penalized harshly. For instance, Sharice recalls being explicitly told to avoid mentioning her body. "I've been big my whole life, and I was told that I shouldn't focus on my weight. I wanted to talk about myself and anything about me." She added, "They wouldn't tell a man that. A lot of Kevin Hart's material revolves around being small."

All the women in the study were judged for their appearance, not just those who were people of size. Even if they were considered conventionally "fit" or "pretty," they still experienced body shaming. No woman could escape the pressures of appearance, which profoundly shape their lives, self-esteem, and careers. This was a fact that the women in the study were acutely aware of. As Fernanda explained, "If we didn't put on makeup and wear high heels, we'd fall many levels in this business."

The public shaming was a minefield, no matter what choices these women make. Lydia, for instance, uses fitness to maintain control over the sexist body standards that could harm her career in comedy. However, even losing weight and becoming healthier has its downsides for women's comedy careers. As Lydia describes it:

> I exercise not just for my mental health, but because if I want to keep telling the jokes that I want to tell, there is a range where my body must be at for me to keep telling those jokes. I'm smaller and fitter, and I have to make different jokes because people don't like to hear pretty women talk about how ugly they feel. Audiences don't want to hear how they don't think they are hot or how they can't get a man. That means well, "she looks good. If she can't get someone, then I can't either." A friend of mine went through that too. She lost a bunch of weight, and everyone hated her. But men? I've seen so many men get up, and they'll say something like, "My wife's vagina is all stretched out from having my two kids." And I'm looking at him thinking, what stretched you out, you fucking pig.

Moreover, the stigma associated with gender continues throughout one's life, and it may even worsen with age. Hope describes how, despite being in the best phase of her life and being a better comic than ever before, her age is a significant obstacle to professional growth. Her age was the determining factor in securing a job on a nationally recognized, syndicated sketch comedy show:

> When people are casting me for things, they are wondering how many years of fuckability I have left. Looks have nothing to do with being funny, but not to bookers. I just got another question about my age today for [Sketch show]. Someone was looking at my mission video and they said "We love all her characters, she has such a range, she is such a good writer, did she right all this. We really want to consider her for next season. We need to find out how old she is." And I was like, "you just watched me do 13 different characters, that's got to answer all your questions. And I was not this cute at 27; I'm much hotter now. I've not experienced a loss of looks. This [pointing at herself] just keeps getting better. I'm at the top of my game in every single way. Physically, emotionally, mentally, financially, and professionally. I'm great. If it weren't for my arthritic bones, this would be the highest functioning I've ever been. So that fact that someone would want to judge my capability off the date of my birth is just shocking to me. That's why I don't dye my hair. I understand my gray hair makes people question my age, but I'm really proud to be 40. To me, 40 is shorthand for I am so much smarter than I used to be.

Sexual Harassment and Violence

The final area where women's experiences stood out from men was the level of sexual harassment and violence they endured in standup. Women face dangerous situations at worst and unfriendly stages at best. Cara described one instance.

> I did a show with my friend, and when we rolled up to this place, it was at a pizzeria right next to a trailer park. It's full of all these aging bikers who look like they have had rough lives. And we are thinking, oh shit. When we walk in the door, a guy opens the door for us and says, "Welcome ladies." And I look at my friend like, is he being an asshole. And all these bikers are yelling at the stage. One of the owners was a guy named Pineapple who had three teeth to his name, drunk off his ass. While my friend was onstage, he goes up to her and says, "Can I smell your pussy?"

While faceless strangers can be terrible, the biggest threat comes from peers within the community. Sexual harassment is prevalent in standup comedy. Many comedian women, including Dahlia, have described being propositioned by comedian men peers to engage in sexual favors. "I had a very

famous male comedian, years ago, who told me he would take me on tour
if I fucked him." Moreover, race, ethnicity, location, and age do not seem to
moderate the likelihood that comedian women peers will be sexually propositioned by comedian men. Virtually every woman in this study reported
such vile incidents, including Candace from New York. "I've been sexually
harassed," she sighs. "I've had a headliner only take me on the road so he can
try to sleep with me. That's a specific woman problem that rarely happens
with men. They are invited to do the road so they can be taken advantage of."

The problem of sexual harassment and violence is a well-known secret.
It is so pervasive that many believe the world is actively protecting vile
people. According to Dahlia, nothing is off-limits, including rape. "Women
can't complain to male comics about how they're treated," she explains. "I
learned to only talk to other female comedians. And when they do, they get
ostracized. A lot of these clubs protect sexual harassers. Known rapists still
work at clubs. Nobody stops booking them."

Comedian women not only face the threat of violence and sexual harassment but also the risk of professional backlash, as Zoey experienced. Zoey
runs a prestigious, invitation-only club in Los Angeles that is home to
world-famous comedians. However, at this club, Zoey was assaulted by
another comedian who was highly regarded and professionally successful.
To make matters worse, the incident was not hidden as the man groped her
backstage in full view of many other comedians and even used a homophobic
slur. Zoey describes the ordeal:

> There are no resources for women. I was sexually assaulted by this comic. And
> everyone knew, and they had his back. I was scared; what am I going to do?
> Tell the owner and then they just say, well, you can just not come back. I can't
> do that. Not only do I need to pay the bills, but I can't lose other gigs. So, I was
> assaulted and then attacked again and again.

The assailant was a prolific predator who had received numerous complaints
for sexually assaulting other comedian women. Other venues had already
banned him due to this issue. On the night of the incident, Zoey reported it
to the club managers. However, they took no action against the assailant and
even booked Zoey, without her knowledge, for later shows with her attacker.
The predator used these shows to continue harassing her, making Zoey want
to drop out of comedy. The perpetrator even recruited others to take part in
the harassment. Zoey stated, "He tried to hurt me. He wanted to have me
kicked out of that and other places. Others tried to speak out, but many were
scared." Despite Zoey's attempts to report the incident, she received no help
from other comedians, the club management, or the club owner. After enduring weeks of harassment without any assistance from the industry, Zoey took

matters into her own hands and publicly shamed her assailant onstage. She went into detail about the incident, his mistreatment of other women, and how the club was protecting him. Only after the story began to spread on social media did the club finally take action and do the right thing. However, Zoey reports that she has received fewer bookings at the club since the ordeal.

The violence against women in comedy is disgusting, but it should come as no surprise to anyone who spends a little bit of time in that world. The topics discussed onstage are so abhorrent that many women are simply scared to visit those clubs. Furthermore, there seems to be a sexist atmosphere that permeates both the amateur and professional levels, as described by Tori:

> Comedians tell a lot of extremely offensive jokes. They tell a lot of rape jokes. They tell a lot of jokes about beating women. They tell jokes about dead hookers. And at the professional level, it's still not all the way better. You got so many people like Bill Burr. I mean, I don't hate the guy, I've laughed at him. I think he's pretty funny and he's an amazing performer to watch. He's so energetic and really mesmerizing, but he denigrates women really bad. His whole comedy is "women are stupid." It's just so frustrating because a lot of the people who are expressing these kinds of sentiments are extremely beloved and so it keeps perpetuating it.

Sexual harassment and violence permeate many corners of our society, so some may dismiss the problem in standup as no worse than anywhere else. However, the levels of drinking, drug use, mental illness, and gender segregation should make us take notice. Additionally, the fact that violent, sexist humor is celebrated lends credence to the idea that the problem may be worse in comedy than in other places. Remember Rebecca from the introduction; she was assaulted downstairs from her hometown comedy club, where she had performed just a few hours prior. Still, while the voices of women should be enough, their experiences were backed by most other comedian men in this study. According to some, the entire hegemonic culture is rotten. Demarcus explains:

> Sexism, to me, is way more prevalent than racism. Racism is bad, don't get me wrong. I was at improv, and the audience wanted me to do a scene about lynching. But for women, women of color? There is a whole nasty culture against them in comedy for sure. It's very blatant. It's very aggressive. People really are malicious and hateful toward women comics. It's so much harder for them to find allies. And the whole predator thing is extremely real. People want to sleep with them or take advantage of them, or sexually assault them, or sexually humiliate them, and embarrass them. Women deal with that all time. And it's so normal; the baseline for what is decent behavior in this industry is despicably low. It's really disgusting.

BAD BEHAVIORS, BAD PEOPLE, BAD CULTURE

Inequality persists in many places, with some being worse than others. The goal of this chapter is to illustrate some of the countless negative behaviors and provide a broad sense of the community. According to the participants in this book, the comedy community is rated as one of the worst for health and well-being, a fact supported by ample research.[15] The comedy community facilitates deadly behaviors such as excessive drinking, smoking, drug use, long hours, and low pay, all of which are hallmarks of poor health. Additionally, the community exacerbates these issues by financially exploiting its workers. Comedians describe how they are little more than free labor, there to pad the bank accounts of bookers, agents, and club owners. The harm of financial insecurity cannot be overstated. It directly harms people by exposing them to poor and unsafe living conditions and increases the risk of homelessness and food insecurity.

Sadly, the structure of the comedy community often forces comedians to perform a "modern-day minstrelsy," which is detrimental to equality. Comedians of Latino descent face a difficult choice: either play into harmful stereotypes and reinforce stigma, or avoid those stereotypes and risk losing opportunities and resources, which can create further segregation and stigma. Both options perpetuate a cycle of stigma reinforcement. Additionally, violence against women is a real problem in the standup comedy community. Some comedians have been identified as rapists, while others use the stage to air their grievances toward women. Justus's description of these men as "incels" (involuntary celibates) is accurate, as they are often lonely men who feel entitled to women's bodies. These men have coalesced on online forums to post hate speech and call for violence, including acid attacks and mass rape. Unfortunately, some incels have acted on these threats, committing heinous acts such as mass shootings.[16] If the comedy community is indeed full of incels, then it is facing a very real and frightening problem.

None of these accounts are surprising, although they are shocking. At one end of the spectrum, comedy is at best an unwelcoming place, as demonstrated by *SNL*.[17] When it was first created in the 1970s, prominent comedy figures like John Belushi claimed that women aren't funny, while writers would decorate their office walls with the panties of female fans. Years later, things had not changed, as described by cast member Janeane Garofalo, who endured "fag-bashing and [colleagues] using the words 'bitch' and 'whore'" in as many sketches as possible. According to Murphy,[18]

A scathing *New York* magazine piece on that season reported that Farley was making prank phone calls from the writers' room during which he released flatulence into the receiver, Norm Macdonald punched a writer "in the head, knocking him to the floor," male colleagues taunted Laura Kightlinger (an SNL feature player) with obscenities until she cried, and a group of male writers debated the merits of a sketch joke about *60 Minutes* commentator Andy Rooney raping his colleague Lesley Stahl.

On the opposite end of the spectrum from abhorrent toxic masculinity are the open secrets of sexual predators at the top of the comedy industry. Comedians such as Roseanne Barr and Tig Notaro had called out Louis C.K. years prior, with Marc Maron directly confronting C.K. who lied through his teeth to Maron.[19] Fellow comedians have responded to allegations against Chris D'Elia with statements like, "I guess it's always the first person you suspect" and "Who could've known Chris D'Elia was a creep other than anyone who's ever looked at him or heard him say things."[20] Bill Cosby had been accused of rape years prior, but the breaking point in public acceptance of Cosby as a rapist came after Hannibal Buress called him out. Additionally, there are clips of Cosby joking about drugging women in his comedy and on *Larry King Live*.[21] This is the racist and patriarchal history of comedy that women and minorities have endured.

In this space of the chapter, I usually share my own experiences to try and relate comedy back to you, the reader. As a Latino man, I have certainly experienced my fair share of racism and bigotry. However, after reading all these accounts, my voice is entirely unnecessary. Instead, I will leave you with the assessment of Valentino, who summarizes a common collective perspective on the state of comedy:

At the main stage in this town, there are comics that I don't want to be affiliated with. The stage has an open mic, and I don't go to it because I know that club enables bad comedians and bad people in general: people who should be in jail. The comedy world is scum full of scum bags.

NOTES

1. Bruce G Link and Jo C. Phelan, "Social Conditions as Fundamental Causes of Disease," *Journal of Health and Social Behavior* 35, no. 1995 (2009): 80–94; Jo C. Phelan and Bruce G. Link, "Is Racism a Fundamental Cause of Inequalities in Health?," *Annual Review of Sociology* 41 (2015): 311–30, https://doi.org/10.1146/annurev-soc-073014-112305; Jen'nan Ghazal Read and Bridget K. Gorman, "Gender and Health Inequality," *Annual Review of Sociology* 36, no. 1 (2010): 371–86, https://doi.org/10.1146/annurev.soc.012809.102535.
2. Link and Phelan, "Social Conditions as Fundamental Causes of Disease."
3. Jane D. McLeod, "The Meanings of Stress: Expanding the Stress Process Model," *Society and Mental Health* 2, no. 3 (2012): 172–86, https://doi.org/10

.1177/2156869312452877; Leonard I. Pearlin et al., "The Stress Process," *Journal of Health and Social Behavior* 22, no. 4 (1981): 337–56; Leonard I. Pearlin, "The Sociological Study of Stress," *Journal of Health and Social Behavior* 30, no. 3 (1989): 241–56.

4. Correll, Benard, and Paik, "Getting a Job: Is There a Motherhood Penalty?": Wei-Hsin Yu and Janet Chen-Lan Kuo, "The Motherhood Wage Penalty by Work Conditions: How Do Occupational Characteristics Hinder or Empower Mothers?," *American Sociological Review* 82, no. 4 (2017): 744–69, https://doi.org/10.1177 /0003122417712729.

5. David T. Takeuchi, Emily Walton, and ManChui Leung, "Race, Social Contexts, and Health: Examining Geographic Spaces and Places," in *Handbook of Medical Sociology*, ed. Chloe E. Bird et al. (Nashville, TN: Vanderbilt University Press, 2010), 92–105.

6. U.S. Department of Health and Human Services, "Why Is LGBT Health Important?," HealthyPeople.gov, 2019, https://www.healthypeople.gov/2020/topics -objectives/topic/lesbian-gay-bisexual-and-transgender-health.

7. Karen I. Fredriksen-Goldsen et al., "Physical and Mental Health of Transgender Older Adults: An At-Risk and Underserved Population," *The Gerontologist* 54, no. 3 (2014): 488–500, https://doi.org/10.1093/geront/gnt021.

8. Jen'nan Ghazal Read and Bridget K. Gorman, "Gender and Health Revisited," in *Handbook of the Sociology of Health, Illness, and Healing: A Blueprint for the 21st Century*, ed. Bernice A. Pescosolido et al. (New York: Springer, 2011), 411–29.

9. Phelan and Link, "Is Racism a Fundamental Cause of Inequalities in Health?": David R. Williams and Chiquita Collins, "Racial Residential Segregation Project: A Fundamental Cause of Racial Disparities in Health," *Public Health Reports* 116, no. 5 (2001): 404–16: Brittany M. Harder and J. E. Sumerau, "Understanding Gender as a Fundamental Cause of Health: Simultaneous Linear Relationships between Gender, Mental Health, and Physical Health Over Time," *Sociological Spectrum* 38, no. 6 (November 2, 2018): 387–405, https://doi.org/10.1080/02732173.2018.1532366.

10. Young men who self-identify as involuntary celibate, often in online forums. Timothy Anderson et al., "Therapist Effects: Facilitative Interpersonal Skills as a Predictor of Therapist Success," *Journal of Clinical Psychology* 65, no. 7 (2009): 755–68, https://doi.org/10.1002/jclp.

11. Zach Beauchamp, "Our Incel Problem," *Vox*, April 23, 2019.

12. Gonzalez and Rodriguez y Gibson, *Humor and Latina/o Camp in* Ugly Betty: *Funny Looking*.

13. Mizejewski, *Pretty/Funny: Women Comedians and Body Politics*.

14. Judith Butler, *Gender Trouble: Feminism and the Subversion of Identity* (New York: Routledge, 1999).

15. Oppliger and Shouse, *The Dark Side of Standup Comedy*: Jeffries, *Behind the Laughs: Community and Inequality*.

16. Beauchamp, "Our Incel Problem."

17. Caryn Murphy, "'Is This the Era of the Woman?': SNL's Gender Politics in the New Millennium," in *Saturday Night Live and American TV*, ed. Nick Marx, Matt Sienkiewicz, and Ron Becker (Bloomington, IN: Indiana University Press, 2013).

18. Murphy, "'Is This the Era of the Woman?': SNL's Gender Politics in the New Millennium." Pg. 179

19. Yohana Desta, "Tig Notaro Distances Herself from Louis C.K., Says He Should 'Handle' Sexual Misconduct Rumors," *Vanity Fair*, August 2017: Jen Yamato, "Roseanne Barr Calls out Louis C.K.: 'I've Heard So Many Stories,'" *The Daily Beast*, June 30, 2016: Dave Itzkoff, "Marc Maron Reckons With Louis C.K.'s Misconduct," *New York Times*, November 13, 2017.

20. Marina Watts, "Comedians React to Allegations That Chris D'Elia Harassed Underage Girls," *Newsweek*, June 17, 2020.

21. Matt Giles and Nate Jones, "A Timeline of the Abuse Charges Against Bill Cosby [Updated]," *Vulture*, December 2015; Graham Bowley, "Prosecutors Want Cosby 'Spanish Fly' Comments as Evidence at Trial," *New York Times*, March 30, 2017.

Chapter 9

Lost Opportunities to Cope and Heal

Despite the evidence presented in this book and in many other studies, many people may continue to believe that anyone can do comedy. Some argue that all you need to do is be funny to get up and perform, as Leonel states: "If you are funny, you can't be denied." In theory, Leonel is correct; open mics are available to anyone who wants to speak their mind. Skill should be the only defining characteristic in finding success in standup comedy. "You just have to be funny," as Leonel says.

However, in practice, we know that's not the case. In many instances, comedians were outright denied access to the stage. Mateo explains that skills are the least of his worries. "When you are applying to festivals or late night or Comedy Central, you are not in competition with all the comedians. You are in competition with all the other Latinos because they are just going to pick one or two. That's it." Mateo didn't just lose parts of his truth on the stage, he lost access to the stage altogether before he even uttered a word. Yes, he absolutely must be funny. But he is also vying for one slot on any stage while others are competing for many. Because of artificial quotas, skill is not the only factor that matters; all minority comedians are competing with every other minority comedian for an equal number of spots. And just like Latinos, women are competing with other women, Black people are competing with other Black people, and LGBTQ+ comedians are competing with other LGBTQ+ comedians.

Furthermore, we must not overlook the community's structure. Standup seems to be a community rife with unhealthy behaviors, drug and alcohol abuse, mental health problems, exploitation, and even violence. While some comedians, like Rebecca, may feel better after performing, others are they are immediately inundated with worries about their next meal or paying rent once they step offstage. Remember, Rebecca's assault occurred at the same bar where she and other comedians frequently gathered after a show. That location, which once freed her voice, now triggers anxiety.

Why does all of this matter? It's not just about direct discrimination, which we've seen can happen. What's more important is the structural discrimination that discourages participation and equality. Discrimination is rarely a result of direct policies or laws (known as de jure discrimination). Instead, it's more commonly de facto discrimination, which happens as a result of customs or circumstances. One classic example of this is racial residential segregation.[1] De jure segregation happens when a law directly segregates people, such as redlining. On the other hand, de facto segregation is an "unintentional" result of other policies or traditions that separate races, such as financing school districts. This system, where education is funded by property taxes, compels wealthy white people to move to their own neighborhoods, which then takes money away from poor, predominantly minority neighborhoods, putting people of color at a disadvantage. Importantly, unintentional segregation is not illegal, and it is the dominant problem creating today's racial inequality. Research on stigma shows that denying people their voice is rarely a result of direct discrimination. Stigma conditions people into silence. From the beginning, the playing field isn't level, and optimal outcomes aren't possible. Specifically, within comedy, everyone may feel exploited, but some are harmed more than others, and open conversations aren't available to most. The next section explores how discrimination and inequality create missed opportunities.

FINANCIAL STRAIN: HARMING COMEDY AND HARMING FAMILIES.

Comedy has many problems, and much of it can be traced back to its culture of financial exploitation. The lack of benefits and the dogmatic view that comedy must be performed at night in bars and clubs create a lot of conflict with a financial undercurrent. Lydia experiences this conflict often as a full-time attorney who works over sixty hours a week. Despite her demanding job, she still puts in the time for comedy and was voted the funniest person in her major midwestern city, which led to an invitation to try out for a prestigious comedy club in Los Angeles. "It was a popular show," she recalls. "Really famous people are on it: people who have done Colbert and the other late-night shows."

Although the club earns hundreds of millions of dollars in profit each year, Lydia bore the financial burden of her invitation. She had to pay for her flight tickets, boarding, and food. While most struggling comedians couldn't afford such a trip, Lydia's job as an attorney happened to take her to Los Angeles.

"I was in LA a couple of weeks ago doing a show, but I was also there for work," she explained. "This is my double life." Unfortunately, juggling both jobs turned into a nightmare. "I was so stressed to get there. I flew out of Columbus at 4 a.m.," she continued. "I had a whole day of work on leadership development at a huge entertainment complex. I have to show up for my job so I can get paid and keep doing this comedy bullshit, and I was so stressed about getting to this club that night." Lydia also mentioned that she received little support from other performers. "Everyone there treated me like shit. I thought we were friends; I had opened for them in the Midwest. Nope." In the end, Lydia regretted making the trip. "I got back from the club at 2 a.m. I was in my hotel room weeping. Why am I doing this to myself?"

Lydia's experience was terrible, but it could have been worse. She has money and the means to take care of herself, thanks to her job that takes her around the country, a perk she relishes. Without the financial support, her situation would have been much more challenging. Lydia's financial stability allows her to offset or counter the stress of comedy, something that others without such means cannot do. According to Dahlia, money is the key to success in comedy. She explains that comedy success does not depend on meritocracy, as many successful standup comedians come from wealthy families and never had to work a day job. They were able to dedicate themselves fully to comedy. Dahlia also points out that poverty is exploited in standup, as club owners take advantage of comedians who are willing to perform for free rather than pay them.

Club owners may exploit low pay, making those with more constraints less likely to participate, especially those with family responsibilities. Trina, who works full-time and cares for a son with mental illness, is close to quitting comedy. "Sometimes, I'm over this comedy stuff. It's generally not comedy though. It's work. I'll miss a gig or something because of my job. A lot of the open mics don't start until 9 or 10 o'clock. I don't get off work till 9 or 9:30," Trina laments. "I get so angry and frustrated that I think, just forget it."

Comedy is a tough industry for parents and families. Due to their parental responsibilities, many parents struggle to find time to focus on their comedy career. This is why standup comedy is often dominated by men who are single and childless. Those who prioritize their family over their personal dreams of stardom often miss out on opportunities. Felipe, a Latino comedian with young children, shared his experience of balancing fatherhood with his comedy career. He said, "It's challenging. I want to go out and socialize, but I'm often too tired from the day before. I rarely spend Friday and Saturday nights away from my family. Sometimes when I'm with my kids, they look at me and they're so cute. It feels warm and I just decide to stay with them. I have that 'always working' mentality anyway, but I have to choose my family over work more often."

Similarly, Jeremy misses out on opportunities when he spends time with his family. He says, "I'm either doing standup or I'm with my family." However, he goes on to explain how missing time with his family harms his mental health. He says, "It's very important to me that I am there with the kids, putting them down for bed. I generally don't accept shows that are before 9:30 p.m., because when I am not there, I can feel it. When I go on the road, I feel it. I'm not someone who generally gets depressed, but it is depressing not being with them." Jeremy also described a recent show where he went to Montreal for the weekend. He says, "I got to Saturday after breakfast, and it's just me in a hotel room. As beautiful as that city is, it's just me in a hotel room, and I am not with my kids. When you are single, it's fine, but not when you are a father."

Performing comedy can be very difficult due to family commitments, which can harm the psychological well-being of many participants, as was the case with Jeremy. However, families are also equally affected. Many comedians describe how their familial relationships have deteriorated because of their comedy careers. For example, Dylan performs multiple times a week to maintain his comedy career while also trying to keep his full-time job. Balancing both careers leaves little time for his marriage, which is now on the brink of collapse:

> Me and my wife have conflict because of comedy. I'm out many nights, and we definitely fight a lot about that. There have been times when it got really intense. It's hard to balance family back home, my wife, a couple of friends, and doing comedy. It just gets too much, especially when I am booked. I was in a different city every other day. I'm out; I'm traveling. I'm managing my day job. All that's overwhelming; it's always a struggle.

While Dylan's marriage is strained due to his struggle to find time for comedy, others have found a balance with their family, largely due to the emotional support that their families provide, not just the financial. Dylan's wife supports his comedy, but is much less emotionally supportive of his career choice. In contrast, Mateo's relationship with his wife is different. He explains, "My wife is literally supporting me in doing this. If she didn't want me to go out at night, there is no way that this would be sustainable. One thing is going to give, and it's either going to be comedy or the relationship. Thank God she is very supportive. I don't care what her parents, my parents, or other relatives might think; she has to live with me because we're spouses. As long as my marriage is strong, the rest of it doesn't matter."

Comedians often face a tough choice between their career and family life due to financial constraints. Jamal, who had been struggling in his comedy career for two decades, had to make a decision. He had sacrificed many relationships in his youth for his career, but now he realized that he wanted to prioritize happiness and the love of his girlfriend, who is now his wife and the future mother of his child. It was a wise choice that brought him the contentment and fulfillment he had been missing:

> I used to tour, and I wanted to reach high. But then I got married, and I now we have a kid coming. All those things that I thought I was going to do in comedy, I would have had to have done them by now, and I didn't. It bummed me out. I spent so much of my time and money and sacrificed family and friends. I put all those to the side to chase what I wanted the most. And then, it didn't happen, so what do I do now? And then, I realized that I am okay with it. I would have had to sacrifice a lot more than I was not willing to. I was going to have to sacrifice her. I couldn't love her and pursue comedy. The amount of time I would have to spend away from her was wrong. It was either be happy in this relationship and still do standup for enjoyment on the side, which I still do, or try and beat the odds and lose this relationship. If I chose comedy, I know I'd find myself ten years out, alone with no success.

Comedy can be tough for all parents, but it can be especially challenging for mothers. Many of them drop out of the industry almost immediately after becoming pregnant, just like Dahlia. "I stopped doing standup," she said. "I took a break because I was pregnant and exhausted. They support some fathers, but not mothers. I know one person who gave up the first three years when she had her child, and she was able to get back in, but she's not happy at all with her career." Dahlia also pointed out that the age of the children can make a difference. "The moms I know have kids in middle school or high school. I just don't know comedian women with small children."

Olivia confirms Dahlia's observation about the different types of support that comedy provides for mothers and fathers. Decades ago, Olivia started doing comedy as a single mom trying to support her three kids, one of whom lived with a mental illness. "I thought comedy would be able to support me and my kids and the lifestyle we deserve. My son, who passed away," she reveals, "suffered from schizophrenia. He was my best audience member, and he desperately needed help. Because the circumstances were so painful, I had to keep my teaching job. I thought comedy was going to be the second job that could help get proper housing for my son."

Despite her best efforts, comedy was not the saving grace she had hoped for, and Olivia eventually quit comedy. She has only returned to it more than twenty years later now that her remaining children have become adults. Although Olivia is now finding some success, "I have a couple of casino gigs coming up," they could not provide for her and her family, considering that they are "350 miles away and pay 100 dollars." In fact, Olivia can't honestly call it a career. "It's not a career, because a career is something you earn a living in," she says. "It's still a struggle; an enormous financial struggle." She now recognizes that the lack of family support in comedy crippled her career: "I could have done more sooner, but I couldn't leave my kid."

Certainly, standup comedy is not intended to be a tool for building stronger families or relationships. In fact, it can often have the opposite effect, especially for those individuals who have significant financial resources or are single and unattached. Unfortunately, this can result in valuable resources being overlooked, which could otherwise contribute to an individual's overall health and well-being. As Hope pointed out, "I firmly believe that standup comedy played a significant role in why I am not married and do not have children today."

A DANGEROUS, VIOLENT COMMUNITY THAT DETERS.

In the previous chapter on the dark side of comedy, we explored a world of harmful behaviors, including poor diets, drug use, and substance abuse. We also discovered that comedy is a social game, as Bernard described, "You have to hang out. Connections are important." These two facts create real problems for recovering alcoholics like Lora. "A lot of people go out after the shows to the bar. I don't want to do that," she shakes her head. "I'd rather go home, read a book, and sleep."

And there is a range of responses, each creating harm. On one side, many people have to go through extra hoops to try to cultivate relationships, such as Lora, who organizes a brunch every week to "sit around and chat and exchange information." For some, like Bernard, they may hang out at bars while hiding their status, which creates more stressors. "I'll have a ginger beer," he explains, "but I won't call it a ginger beer." Bernard describes how he hangs out with comics at the bar but hides the fact that he's not drinking, admitting that he has to leave quickly to avoid temptations. "I'll sit down with them, and I'll have one, and then I'm going to go home with my wife." For others, they simply avoid everyone in the scene altogether, including Stephanie, who says "I do not hang out often with comics because a lot are a fucking mess, not taking care of themselves or active in their addiction."

More importantly, each of the three comics misses an opportunity, but they can still participate to some extent, even if they are more stressed. Other dangerous behaviors cannot be managed without withdrawing. For someone like Lawshawn, a gay Black man, violence is a real concern. Lawshawn often faces very stressful situations. "I have to navigate a world that was not designed for me," he explains. "I travel to the South a lot. I joke about not taking my personal safety into account, but honestly, I have to avoid thinking about it. I can't think, 'Oh my God, there were this number of hate crimes in this city last year.'" But remember, comedy does not pay much. Combined with financial exploitation, comedians are forced to take less-than-advisable jobs in unwelcoming places to try and make ends meet. "I look at a show's lineups of comics, and I know that I wouldn't gel with their styles or their audience," Lawshawn says. "Instead of going out there and getting attacked, I just avoid that space. Then again, I go to tons of cities, and when I'm booked, I won't say no to the show. I'm not trying to be a martyr, but I hate to say it," he laments, "Professional Lawshawn can't think about the Black, gay, me, because I need spots."

Financial exploitation forces comedians into situations they wouldn't willingly put themselves in, making them vulnerable to violence. For instance, many clubs still do not provide hotel accommodations even when invited, which compels comedians to resort to couch surfing as it is often the only way to make a profit. Comedian women, like Hope, are at a higher risk of sexual assault due to couch surfing. Hope shared her experience, "I was doing a show, and a horrendous ice blizzard was starting. Everybody told me I shouldn't drive all the way home. The club owner was like, 'You have to crash at our house. We have a couch.' I said, 'That's really generous; thank you very much.' I went to sleep, but around 3 a.m., I was awoken by him climbing onto me."

While financial exploitation may spur on more violence, the real catalyst is sexism that has institutionalized rape and sexual misconduct throughout comedy. All the standup comedian women who participated in this study, regardless of their geographic location or professional status, reported witnessing and experiencing sexual improprieties in their field. Their stories reveal that the abuse can come from anyone, including open-mic-ers and club owners. The possibility of sexual assault is always present, especially when touring. Hope explains:

> I've tried to split other hotel rooms with other comedians when there are four or five of us to try and cut costs. I have gotten to where I will volunteer to sleep on the floor or the couch, because I know if I am in the double bed, someone is going to try and touch me. I can't go into strangers' homes who are offering me a couch and trust that I am safe. I can't trust that just because someone offered me a gig, it's not going put me in a dangerous situation. I would love to have the luxury of knowing that if someone offers me a place to stay, they just want to give me a place to stay. Surprise, surprise, if I politely reject a housing invite, those people have never offered me a gig again.

Many comedian women take extra precautions to avoid sexual harassment in the entertainment industry. Holly, a comedian, explained that women are using social media to network and protect themselves. "I'm in a secret Facebook group for women in comedy," she said. "It's a buddy system to tell each other about shows and places that make us uncomfortable. I can't even tell you how many comedian women have been profoundly uncomfortable going to certain places, especially when certain people would be on those lineups. We go on that Facebook group to figure out if a place is bad, or we have to go, we see if any other women can just show up so we are in a group."

Yes, there were other issues related to sexism that influenced the decision to perform onstage. All of the women in the study also dealt with body image concerns to some extent. Hiromi asked, "Why aren't there more women in comedy?" She explained, "Most women struggle with their appearance because they are bombarded with lookism. That's just the way it is in this industry. You're standing onstage in front of an audience of three hundred people who are all looking at you. Why would any woman want to go through that?"

Many marginalized comedians were afraid of how their status, such as being Black or Latino, could affect their career. However, women in comedy often expressed a fear of violence that influenced their decisions. Sexual terrorism is a system that men use to control and dominate women by instilling fear of sexual violence in them,[2] and best encompasses why some women avoid participating in this industry. It also explains the extra psychologically stressful precautions that they have to take to manage those risks, like seeking help and sharing information through secret social media groups. Many others simply quit. Unfortunately, all of the ramifications mean that women miss out on opportunities that could advance their careers, such as invitations to tour, which is one of the most important things for a comedy career. Stephanie puts it best: "It's a constant battle to stay safe and still be able to do what we love."

> Why aren't I on tour? Because I don't want to get assaulted on a couch. I don't travel alone. I can't sleep in the back of my car or in a motel; that's not safe for me. People ask, what's your plan for being a full-time comedian? I don't know, because I can't go the normal route. I can't sleep in the back of my van for six months to try and find myself. It's a safety issue. My mental, physical, and emotional safety are more valuable to me than my career.

I want to note that although women are more likely to be victims, men who try to avoid affiliations with abusers or harassers can also be hurt by the culture. As comedian Valentino explained, "Anyone who has been an abuser or harasser, those are the people who I actively avoid. . . . One of my friends told me about it, and I didn't do the show." Valentino even approached the booker to explain that he did not want to be affiliated with a rapist. However, since speaking out, Valentino has found it harder to book shows.

LOSING SOCIAL CONNECTIONS AND DROPPING OUT OF COMEDY

To be successful in standup comedy, one needs to possess creativity, wit, and humor that's relevant to current events. However, despite the perception of comedy as a solitary art form, it's far from an individual pursuit. Social connections are perhaps the most critical resource for navigating the industry. As Demarcus aptly put it, "It's a relationship business." There's no clear-cut path to success, no internships or residencies to follow. Instead, it's all about meeting the right people and building positive relationships. "Come on the road with me. Come perform on this show," are invitations that can make all the difference.

Throughout this book, we have seen how stigma limits people's voices and forces them to hide parts of themselves. Financial constraints also limit access to the stage, as people must prioritize feeding themselves and their families. Additionally, unhealthy behaviors such as alcohol and substance use can discourage people from pursuing comedy. Harassment, bigotry, and violence further discourage comedians, particularly women, people of color, and those who are LGBTQ+. These factors can cause them to lose vital social connections that are crucial to their success in comedy. For example, even after performing for two decades on late night and television programming, including Comedy Central, Dahlia is still professionally isolated. She says, "I don't consider too many people in standup to be my real friends. I have two or three of those. But the broader community, I will not turn to. You have to be one of the cool kids to have people rally behind you, and I don't have that."

Similarly, Jamal has superficial relationships with other comedians in his community. He explains, "Just because you share a venue for an hour or two or because you keep meeting at the same place and performing at the same shows, that does not automatically put you in the friend pile. You are a person I work with. We share a bar tab, but that does not make us friends. Friendship requires something additional beyond stage time." Jamal lost social resources in a couple of ways. Firstly, he explicitly described the culture of harm as keeping him away. The comedy culture that facilitates drinking, drug use, poor diets, and bad sleep patterns was a major deterrent for his participation. In this way, unhealthy cultural norms act as a barrier, leading to an overall loss of social resources; those willing to drink heavily and associate themselves with the unhealthy lifestyle end up making more social connections in comedy. Secondly, Jamal described how he did not receive much support from other Black comedians in "urban" rooms. Other Black comedians do not support him or invite him to their stages because of who he is and how he presents. Nyah was more explicit when she said, "Urban rooms hate me." Discrimination is what they are both describing: the unjust or prejudicial treatment of different categories of people, especially on the grounds of race, age, or sex. That differential treatment goes beyond humor. One may be inclined to simply believe that Jamal and Nyah are not funny to those audiences. That may be true, but why are they not funny? It's not just because the jokes didn't land, it's because those groups of people do not even like who they are, which is the foundation of stigma.

One of the main problems that contributes to the isolation of marginalized individuals in comedy is the overwhelming lack of diversity in terms of race, gender, and sexuality. Even if there is no violence or overt discrimination occurring on a daily basis, there are very few welcoming stages where marginalized individuals can simply feel like people without being labeled. Even in diverse and liberal communities, these opportunities are scarce. Fernanda accurately describes this lack of diversity in Chicago's comedy scene when compared to other places outside of major metropolitans. "In Chicago, I have been very pleased to see niche open mics for just women, or queer peoples, or trans comedians. There may be a hyper supportive community within standup, and you may eventually find like-minded people. However," she adds, "that is not the norm."

Comedy, regardless of its location, is generally a homogeneous community that is mostly white and "bro-y." Anyone outside of that norm is immediately isolated upon entry, making women and minorities feel unwelcome. Lola explains, "Sometimes you can go to a show or an open mic and be the only woman there, and that can feel very isolating." Even the way she is introduced onstage is disconcerting. "The host might say, 'Are you ready for your next comic? It's a lady this time,' [wink]. It feels very unwelcoming."

Another problem with being such a homogeneous community is that it makes building key professional social relationships very difficult. It's not that interracial or intergender relationships can't be built, but the likelihood is slim because stigma and negative social perceptions proliferate among the dominant population. For instance, Zahra reveals, "Some older comics will bond with white guy comics that make mistakes. It is hard for them to connect with me because I'm a woman, Black, and gay. They are more likely to take those other persons under their wing," she sighs, "but I haven't really had anyone try to take me under their wing." After five years, she has yet to find a seasoned mentor in her white community, while other comics are quick to find help and opportunity.

Other women, including Dahlia, have described how they are not even given the same common courtesy as men. "It's even the little things like when

I go onstage," she explains, "none of them stay in the room to watch my set." According to Dahlia, "they don't even bother to find out if I'm funny or how I did. Then, they don't recommend me to managers in the industry." Her and other women's social isolation is a product of sexism that doesn't even give them the benefit of the doubt, which, she adds, "is all very demoralizing."

Women and marginalized individuals reported feeling isolated, while white men were more likely to describe a socially and emotionally supportive community. This contrast is most evident when comparing the experiences of one of the study's comedy power couples, Hope and Todd, who are both professional comedians that have headlined shows across the country. When asked about their relationships with other comedians, Todd described having very fulfilling friendships:

> We know so much about each other just from listening to each other onstage. If you've been on a road trip with another comic, or on tour, that's when true friendship is formed because you have to spend time and talk with these people. On Sunday, I was in a car for five hours with two guys and we had a great time. I've never had a conversation longer than a couple of minutes with them, but talks about everything. We talked about the shows we were on. We talked about where we came from and what our lives we're like. And I love that stuff.

The bonds between Todd and his fellow comedians run deep. Todd has even turned to them for support outside of comedy, and he says that help is always there when he needs it. Todd recounts a time when his dog passed away, leaving him with a pile of bills to pay. His friends in the comedy community rallied around him and put on a benefit show to help him cover the costs. They performed for free, and even people Todd barely knew donated money to help him out. Thanks to their generosity, Todd not only paid off his bills but was also able to donate leftover funds to the American Humane Society. It's clear that the comedy community is a tight-knit and supportive one for people like him

Now let's compare Todd to his partner, Hope. Remember how she was brutally harassed by her ex, with the help of comedian men. Although she has found camaraderie, "I have maybe two comic friends," it mostly comes from other women who share the stage. "I have such an affinity for comedian women because I don't have my guard up with them. Even if I don't know them," Hope adds, "if one asked me a personal question, I would tell them literally anything that they wanted to know. I just like to imagine that this is something she will experience sexism and she needs to hear the truth."

The difference between Todd and Hope highlights the disparate reality experienced by women and marginalized people compared to white men. Men often describe the comedy world as very fulfilling and find profound friendships that provide them ample support, even when they reach rock bottom in their personal lives. Women and minorities, on the other hand, are reticent to interact with the comedy community due to repeated threats and isolation. It's important to note that people like Hope can find meaningful social relationships. In fact, Todd and Hope share a valuable connection with another comedian couple. They have gone on double dates, trips to a pumpkin patch, and were guests at a wedding. However, the overall negative social interactions frame most of her experiences in comedy.

Furthermore, we must acknowledge that men can also be harmed by toxic relationships in comedy, particularly when it comes to substance use and drinking, as described in a previous section. Moreover, many recognize the barriers that their women peers face. Todd expressed his sympathy for the experiences of marginalized people in comedy, including his partner, Hope. "It's a time where we have to do a lot of listening, not a lot of talking," Todd reflects. "As a booker, I have to make a real effort. I have to use my position of power to empower those who don't have it."

However, the reality is that, like many men, Todd holds a positive view of the comedy community because he finds social fulfillment and deep emotional connections with his peers. Conversely, Hope, like most women, people of color, and LGBTQ+ individuals, keeps her distance because they face harm within the comedy industry. Without social, emotional, and financial support, comedians often experience significant psychological distress, with many eventually dropping out. For instance, Treyvaughn gave up comedy for over a decade in the early 1990s due to homophobia, with the worst hatred coming from his Black community. He only returned to the industry in recent years thanks to the support he received from a few comedian women, still reporting homophobia from Black comedian men. Comedy does not provide social support for many, limiting their opportunities for growth, and placing particular burdens on those who face issues like sexism both on and offstage. Due to how comedy is structured and who it caters to, women, people of color, LGBTQ+ individuals, and parents often struggle to build the necessary social resources, causing them to drop out. Like Treyvaughn three decades before her, who quit after a constant torrent of homophobia, Dahlia has reached a breaking point:

> I love standup, but why continue? I have been doing standup for about fourteen years. I have multiple TV credits. I have done college tours. I've been booked in major clubs as the headliners, sometimes for a month. But I'm not getting paid for any of it. I can't support a child with it. I've spent a year in therapy dealing with this, but I'm mad. I'm a professional comedian, but I have to go to bars and hang out, pay for drinks and then maybe they'll book me? I've proven myself. I'm funny. Then there are the horrible sexist comments when they bring

me onstage. And all those times when they say they'll take me on the road if I fuck them. I'm still doing sketch and writing, but I haven't decided if I will go back to standup. I miss performing, but the rest of it, I don't want that anymore.

BLAMING VICTIMS

Comedian women and minorities face many barriers that prevent them from being successful. In our quest to understand why many cannot access the stage, we have learned that discrimination creates a cycle of failure. Because of all the ways that some must contort their authentic selves in public, many not only lose their voice in the moment, but they also lose further opportunity to find solace and explore their ideas. Consider Barb, a lesbian woman who tries to use comedy to explore the meaning behind her sexual identity. In the comedy world that is often dominated by old, white men, her authentic self was not acceptable. She explains:

> I auditioned for a club not too long ago where two female, gay comics had auditioned previously. Strong comics who have been booked at other clubs. But the feedback they got there was although they are hilarious, the club booker/owner did not feel their material—gay material—was appropriate to be talking about onstage. So, I went to the audition I did not talk about being gay onstage. Not only did I do my weaker material, but I wasn't confident at all because I'm was hiding part of me. Long story short, the audition did not go well. The truth of the matter is this guy is like one hundred years old and probably just lives in the 1910s. He didn't say, "You're not funny because you are a woman" or "You're not funny because gay material is not funny." He said, "You're not funny because your jokes are not strong enough." But my jokes are not strong because I'm hiding everything about me.

Stigma, bigotry, and subsequent discrimination often lead to failure for many individuals. Barb faced this issue when she tried to perform in a club owned by a homophobic person. In an attempt to please the owner, she removed the best parts of her set, which ultimately made her performance weaker. Then, because her material was deemed "objectively" not funny, the comedy community blamed her for her failure. As Demarcus explains, growth comes from opportunities that are often denied to many people. "Most of us suck most of the time and we only get good over time," he says. "But you can't get good if you're not given opportunities to get better. That's why most women are shut down, patted on the head, and told to go away. They don't get the opportunity to be bad at comedy."

Many people who benefit from unequal opportunities in the comedy industry are aware of how the culture and structure of comedy cater to their background while limiting others. Cyrus explains, "A lot of people are bitter about that rich kid whose parents pay for everything. They have all the time. Obviously, they have better opportunities than most people, but don't feel bad about the money. They have the money, but it's still up to them to work hard." Similarly, Leonel has observed people of color, including his best friend, being denied stages outright. He acknowledges the disproportionate difficulties faced by women and marginalized groups. "You have to work ten times as hard," he explains. "Maybe it's a form of oppression. We're ahead of the game. Women are barely at that level."

But, while both Cyrus and Leonel acknowledge the hardships that marginalized groups face in a world of systemic discrimination, they also place the responsibility on the shoulders of those who are disadvantaged, rather than on the homophobic, racist, or bigoted owners who make it difficult for many to get ahead. Cyrus sees the lack of representation among women and other marginalized people as a math problem rather than recognizing the discrimination that prevents them from advancing. Leonel is even more blunt in his assessment. Despite witnessing prejudice firsthand when his darker-skinned friend was denied entry to a club, he blames women for their own failures. "Women struggle a little bit more with humor because they grow up differently than us," he rationalizes. "I hate to say it, but women struggle more with being funny." He suggests that women can rely on their looks, saying, "I have nothing to offer. But women? They don't have to have a killer instinct. They really don't."

Worse, many comedians claim reverse discrimination. Nathaniel, a man who lives with cerebral palsy and is confined to a wheelchair, is unable to access many comedy clubs that lack wheelchair accommodations. He has encountered other standup comedians who believe that he has an easier time navigating standup because of his disability. Nathaniel said, "Some people think that I always have an easier way through comedy. I've had it all my life. You get an A+ on a paper, and people are like, 'That's just because you are disabled.' They think we have easier jokes because we have material about a particular obstacle." Cyrus confirmed Nathaniel's sentiment and argued that the oversaturation of men in comedy "makes it easier for them [women] to get the gig."

The positions taken by individuals like Cyrus and Leonel are perplexing because they previously acknowledged the uphill battle of discrimination faced by women and minorities in comedy. However, despite being aware of this truth, they conveniently forget these realities and blame marginalized individuals for their lack of humor. Their stance disregards individuals like Barb, who are set up to fail because homophobic owners do not want her to mention her sexuality. They fail to recognize the numerous instances where women cannot practice due to sexual harassment. They also fail to acknowledge that people of color are often pigeonholed into performing stereotypical acts, which limits their access to other stages. Their positions also ignore the blatant discrimination that prevents incredibly talented comedians from succeeding. For example, Bianca, who has been performing for almost two decades, has been passed over for men who are not headlining material. As she explains:

> There are women out there who are killing it and we are just treated differently. I was working at this famous comedy club in Las Vegas. I should have been opening, but they made me MC. There was a heckler in the audience, and as the MC, my job is to shut them up before the main acts. I did that. But when it was the opener's turn, the heckler started up again and it's now his turn to shut him up, he's on the stage. But he couldn't. He went to the other side of the stage, ignored half the audience, because he didn't know what to do. And the headliner and I were in the green room watching this on TV. He turns to me and asks, "Why are you not headlining? Or at least my feature? What is going on?" And I go, "Oh, it's because I ovulate every month. I don't know if you know that, but I have boobs, so that guy gets priority."

Positions like those of Cyrus and Leonel are pervasive and destructive as they reinforce bigoted ideas and discriminatory practices.[3] Women and marginalized individuals experience inequality due to structural forces, which perpetuate psychologically bigoted beliefs that they are inferior and that domination by men is necessary. Dahlia describes the feedback loop between fear of violence, missed opportunities to socialize, and subsequent denial of access to the stage. "There are places I won't hang out because it is such a boys' club, and I'm not welcome there," she explains. "And then because I don't want to hang out there because of how they treat me, I can't get into that club because they don't see me perform."

We also cannot forget that stigma exists both inside and outside of comedy. It's important to note that the stigma that affects life outside of comedy will also affect the inside, specifically the availability of comedy resources. For example, there are many gendered expectations around family life. Women and mothers face disproportionate pressure to sacrifice their happiness, well-being, and career for the family, while men are allowed to reap the benefits. Lydia described the disadvantages that many women face outside of comedy, obstacles that privileged men like Cyrus get to avoid. "I know a lot of male comedians who are in relationships where the woman is the breadwinner," she added, "and the dude is a deadbeat comedian, writer, podcaster. I've never seen the other way around where the man is supporting the woman. If you see it in your study, please let me know."

Lydia was correct. I did not find any men who were financially supporting their female partners in the same way that women supported men in standup comedy. Men, on the other hand, were more likely to quit their day jobs and devote their entire time to comedy with the financial support of their spouses or families, including Cyrus. Cyrus's wife works full-time and supports both of them for six months out of the year, allowing him to be a full-time comic. "That's when I do my best," Cyrus explains. "That's when I write my most material. That's when I am out doing the most shows, and I'm able to be a full-time comic." Women and minorities, on the other hand, were more likely to be well-educated, balancing a full-time job, and supporting immediate and extended family, such as Hope, who was the child of slaves. Women and minorities were more likely to give support while men, and white men, were more likely to take it. Rather than suggesting that women need to work hard to be successful in comedy, perhaps people like Cyrus should ask why he doesn't have to work as hard as others. Rather than suggesting that women can rely on their looks, perhaps people like Leonel should consider the privilege that allows unattractive men to be starving artists.

THE FOUNDATION OF HEALTH
INEQUALITY IS DISCRIMINATION

If comedy were solely based on skill, then why aren't more women and minorities overcoming their fears of performing onstage? The truth is that comedy is not equal and skill is not the only factor that determines success. The fact that there is a lack of representation of women and minorities in comedy suggests that discrimination is preventing or discouraging their participation. Structural factors allow some individuals to dominate resources and prevent others from accessing them. Sexism, racism, and bigotry all contribute to a lack of resources, which decreases the likelihood of a successful outcome. Marginalized individuals face exploitation and violence, and those who are able to enter these spaces with less risk are typically white, single men.

In recent years, comedians have faced reckoning for their behaviors. However, they often face swift backlash and ample defenses. For instance, to justify Chris D'Elia's sexually inappropriate behavior toward underage women, many in the comedy community argued that although he was a creep, he did not do anything illegal.[4] A similar defense was used for Louis C.K. on multiple occasions. Joe Rogan argued on his podcast with Andrew Santino that what Louis C.K. did was "not a crime."[5] Santino agreed with Rogan's assertion that Louis did not sexually "assault" anyone; "no one said no" to Louis's request to masturbate in front of them, so he did it anyway. Rogan continued the defense of Louis C.K. on another podcast with Joe List by arguing that C.K. "did not block the door."[6] Then there was Dave Chappelle, who defended Louis C.K. by attacking his victims. One victim stated that her encounter with Louis C.K. dashed her dreams of being a comedian. If she were going to have to endure being sexually objectified by powerful men, she would not continue in the comedy profession. Dave Chappelle's retort was to use a Martin Luther King Jr. analogy to claim that those assaulted by Louis were weak women; "Well, then I dare say, madam, you may have never had a dream."[7] Even more pathetically, perpetrators have claimed that they are victims. According to Rogan, C.K. is a victim who has "suffered enough."[8] Prominent comedian Lenny Clark agreed by attacking the women who, according to him, betrayed Louis because he "gave them jobs."[9]

Being a white man certainly has its challenges, but our comedians have revealed that they often have the luxury of just existing on a stage. This means they have more time and opportunity to focus on the issues that are important to them. In contrast, marginalized people must manage the audience's feelings from the moment they step onstage. They must be selective with their stages, words, and details, all of which limit their opportunities to be seen.

Most importantly, the damage that women and minorities have suffered is ingrained deep in their psychology, creating self-stigma. Take Joji's perspective on his career, for example. Joji has been performing for over fifteen years, headlining across the country, and based on his current income level, is in the upper class. As a trans man, he is more professionally successful than most other comedians, including some of his white, cisgender male counterparts. However, when asked to rate his professional level in comedy, he could not give himself a perfect score. Joji does not rank himself at the most professional level, while many others with less experience and fewer comedy credentials ranked themselves higher. When asked why, with all his success, he still doesn't rank himself as the most professional, Joji explained that as a transgender man of color, he is treated as lesser than and denied many mainstream opportunities:

> From the outside looking in, it's like damn; you are killing it. Yes, but not in the same hustle and grind of most other people. Think about it. Even five years ago, queer and trans people didn't have any presence in the media or society. There weren't any positive conversations around the trans community. So, fresh out of college, twenty years ago, I wasn't even thinking about comedy. I was a record producer because that's where I could make money as a gender-nonconforming queer person. Then I saw John Leguizamo and I said I could do that. I tried my hardest to get onto those mainstream stages in New York, to take every gig and show for as many agents as I could, but it never happened. And I couldn't do those open mics with a bunch of racist, sexist, misogynist, queerphobic, white men who were talking all sorts of hate in mainstream, comedy rooms. I couldn't subject myself to this torture. So, I stayed in the university/college system. But

here, you are performing for the same demographic over and over and over again and your craft is not maturing. So no, I haven't had success.

The obstacles that comedians face teach us an important lesson about the challenges of managing stigma. Stigma is a powerful barrier, but it's not the only one that people face. For many, finding a way to manage stigma is difficult because they also have to deal with racism, sexism, and homophobia both internally and externally. Unfortunately, we tend to oversimplify problems and look for a single solution. We believe that doing just one thing will make us healthier, but we don't acknowledge the many obstacles that make it difficult to achieve good health. Obesity and COVID are examples of this. When people pointed out that obesity is a major risk factor for COVID-related complications and death, some responded with "take responsibility for yourself." However, this stance ignores the many other factors that contribute to obesity. People with low socioeconomic status may have multiple jobs and limited time to exercise. Poor neighborhoods may be unsafe for outdoor exercise due to crumbling infrastructure and extreme heat. Public transportation may be unreliable, making it difficult to travel to safer areas for exercise. Gyms may be too expensive for those living below the poverty line. People with low socioeconomic status may also have physically demanding jobs and higher rates of chronic pain, which can make healthy living difficult. Nutritious food may be expensive and hard to find in low-income neighborhoods. Misinformation about nutrition is common, and segregation makes it less likely that poor people will ever learn the truth. Even if one issue is solved, every other risk factor for obesity remains.

The ability to address a stigma is restricted by many risk factors, much like obesity. When I finally began to actively cope with my trauma after twenty years of suppression, it wasn't as simple as "starting a conversation." As I confronted my childhood sexual abuse, masculinity was ringing in my ears. I was also navigating the trauma as a Latino man, facing many stereotypes that directly influenced the public's perception of a childhood victim. Minorities, in general, are constantly thought of as poor, weak, and foreign. When Donald Trump was elected president, many of my colleagues reached out to check if we were doing okay, as if we were going to crumble into dust. We are also seen as a threat. I recall one time during my college education when I was spending time with a group of fellow students. When I revealed that I was Latino, one woman's face sank, and she hiked her purse up closer to her body as if I were going to mug her on the spot. If I discussed trauma or mental illness, it would most certainly trigger someone's bias against Latinos. Therefore, it's a safer choice to avoid it altogether.

How can someone dream of healing one wound when they are living with so many wounds and a world that keeps cutting them? The evidence is clear:

every drop in socioeconomic status is linked to more trauma, more obstacles to care, and less access to valuable resources. The reality is that most people live a life of hardship that makes healing seem almost impossible. I will now let Nathaniel close out this chapter. Speaking from his motorized chair in an assisted living home, he recounted all the obstacles he faces living with cerebral palsy. These include stages that are not wheelchair accessible, a lack of healthcare that hinders his ability to pursue comedy in Los Angeles or New York, bookers who "miss" his calls to avoid making legal accommodations, and an audience that is uncomfortable with his use of the word "retarded." Comedy is an insurmountable mountain for him. Despite these difficulties, Nathaniel had the clarity to see himself in the lives of everyone who has experienced marginalization: "Women can relate. Or people of color; they can relate too. They know how it feels. It's like they are disabled."

NOTES

1. Douglas S. Massey, "Residential Segregation and Neighborhood Conditions in U.S. Metropolitan Areas," in *America Becoming: Racial Trends and Their Consequences*, ed. Neil J. Smelse, William Julius Wilson, and Faith Mitchel, vol. 1 (Washington, D.C.: National Academies Press, 2001), 391–434: Williams and Collins, "Racial Residential Segregation Project: A Fundamental Cause of Racial Disparities in Health."

2. Elizabeth Grauerholz and Mary A. Koralewski, "Feminist Explanations: Male Power, Hostility, and Sexual Coercion," in *Sexual Coercion: A Sourcebook on Its Nature, Causes, and Prevention* (New York: Lexington Books, 1991), 61–73.

3. Cecilia L. Ridgeway and Shelley J. Correll, "Unpacking the Gender System a Theoretical Perspective on Gender Beliefs and Social Relations," *Gender and Society* 18, no. 4 (2004): 511, https://doi.org/10.1177/0891243204265269.

4. Kristy Puchko, "Bold Move: Chris D'Elia Defends Himself by Releasing Emails That Show He Is a Creep," *Pajaba*, June 20, 2020.

5. *The Joe Rogan Experience #1317—Andrew Santino* (United States: JRE Podcast, 2019).

6. *The Joe Rogan Experience #1296—Joe List* (United States: JRE Podcast, 2019).

7. Kirsten Chuba, "Dave Chappelle Calls Louis C.K. Accusers 'Weak' and 'Brittle' in New Special," *Variety*, January 2018.

8. *The Joe Rogan Experience #1296—Joe List.*

9. *The Joe Rogan Experience #1270: Lenny Clark* (United States: JRE Podcast, 2019).

Conclusion

Lessons Learned

Some believe that the comedy stage is a place where success is determined solely by one's skills, and anyone can get up and speak. Many comedians indeed take advantage of the power of the microphone to discuss deeply personal and troubling experiences. Some use the stage to address issues of racism and sexism, while others use it to air their grievances about the homophobia that still exists in many parts of society. For some, the stage provides a space to present themselves as they truly are, something they may not be able to do in other aspects of their lives. The ideal comedy stage allows people to be fully seen, heard, and embraced as equals.

For many comedians seeking emotional catharsis onstage, the optimal stage provides several key features. It allows comedians to be completely open about a subject. It allows them to discuss and disclose information in an uninterrupted manner. It invites positive feedback. It provides ample time, either during a long set or over several months, to reflect on their ideas and gain a new understanding of their stigma.

However, like many other fields, the world of comedy is not equal and does not liberate most people. While comedy may be liberal at the top of the economic ladder, it's far from that at the bottom. This book supports other studies that have found comedy venues function as both enablers and constrainers of social difference.[1] Access to the stage is being denied in two different directions, internally and externally (e.g., self-stigma and public stigma). To have an open and productive conversation, the issue can only be moderately stigmatized for the audience. The most difficult issues to discuss include mental illness, cancer, and child abuse. The audience also doesn't want to feel attacked or implicated in harm that the comedian experienced, which makes discussing race, sexism, and homophobia treacherous. Some audiences simply aren't ready for those conversations, no matter how perfectly crafted the joke or skilled the performer.

"Starting a conversation" is too narrow of a goal and cannot be universally applied. Rarely do people like Rebecca, who framed this book, have the conditions to fully access their voice. In reality, individuals must weigh the pros and cons of coming "out" of the closet when revealing a stigma through taboo conversation. Harm can come to those who "start a conversation" or "break the silence." Social isolation, discrimination, and even violence are real possibilities—I can attest to that. As anti-stigma advocates, we must recognize the real world that most people live in. Ending stigma is critical, but fundamentally, we are trying to save lives.

Comedians often require distance from an event to have productive discussions. This comes after long reflection, a deep understanding of the implications of the experience, and in many circumstances, some closure. Comedians practice repeatedly for different audiences, refining their ideas until they are funny. People test and recognize boundaries in their social lives to understand the best approach for having a conversation. Although these testing and communication strategies are unequal in their effectiveness, they still create some benefits. People may challenge stigma, hide, lead others along long conversations to help educate, or sometimes retreat because the alternative is more painful. For some, hiding becomes the best survival tactic to avoid discrimination, a process that both closes us off to potential healing and buffers potential harm. We cannot deny that shouting and shocking can make a person feel better in the moment, although it won't decrease stigma. A single tactic is often not enough. Rather, the best outcomes come from a myriad of tactics in different conditions that complement each other and lead to empowerment.

Conversations can be powerful, but comedians are often denied access to their voice due to various stigmas. Coping with multiple stigmas and managing self-presentation, words, and ideas means they are not being completely truthful or fully seen. Discrimination based on gender, race, ethnicity, skin color, mental or physical health conditions, or LGBTQ+ status defines the barriers that prevent them from speaking. Additionally, many comedians face obstacles to access the stage. The stage is only open at night, which competes with raising a family or having a job that pays the bills. Comedians may have access to the stage, but they are often paid little and cannot afford nutritious food or safe housing. They may also be immersed in a culture of drugs and alcohol, which can affect their sleep, exercise, and overall health. Furthermore, they may be expected to perform racist or sexist caricatures of themselves to be accepted. Even if they avoid these harmful situations, they are often blamed for not speaking up. Financial exploitation, poverty, drug and alcohol use, poor sleep habits, harassment, violence, and rape are all barriers to equality that disproportionately affect women, people of color, parents, and those who are LGBTQ+. For many, open conversations are a minor levee; the waters of their inequality still flow in the same direction. How can someone gain liberation when they do not have full access to the most basic of resources: their voice?

Despite many people being unable to have open and fruitful conversations to manage their stigma, many still gained positive resources through the process. In this closing chapter, I will discuss a few general takeaways. First, I will address the deeper, fundamental issue that plays a critical role in stigma: segregation. It is important for people to have alternative safe spaces, especially during times of crisis and harm. However, if we want to eliminate biases that are the foundation of stigma, those who discriminate must have positive exposure to those whom they harm. Why does segregation matter? How does it further facilitate discrimination and inequality? And why is diversity good for everyone?

Taking into account the larger sociocultural factors that influence various patterns, I will then discuss effective methods for addressing stigma in people's daily lives. It's important to consider intermediary processes, like veiled disclosure, that may offer some advantages. Our comedians, for example, need to approach the possibility of a conversation not going well with a positive attitude. Many comedians fail repeatedly but continue to take the stage. We also need to explore ways to help individuals build their self-confidence and skills, regardless of whether we can eliminate the stigma completely. Developing interpersonal skills may be crucial for both having productive conversations and knowing how to bounce back when things don't go as planned.

I will address a major limitation of this study: I did not interview the audience. This study places a lot of blame on the audience for causing conversations to fail due to stigma, but is discrimination the only reason for communication breakdown? There may be other underlying reasons why some members of the public are not ready for conversations.

Finally, I will conclude with some closing thoughts on comedy and the purpose of this book. These issues are complex, but comedy provides insight into why it is challenging for many to find liberation and how we can create equality for others. It is a tool to analyze and understand stigma. However, those who face mental illness, stigma, or other issues should seek help from places designed to assist them, rather than relying on chance.

THE FUNDAMENTAL PROBLEM CREATING STIGMA: SEGREGATION

People may find ways to personally achieve equality and find their voice, but it's important to acknowledge the community's role in creating inequality.

Researchers and advocates should recognize the limitations of their resources, while the community should recognize its responsibility in creating inequalities. This is a crucial lesson that lies beneath all coping processes, as health is not only individual, but also social.

Although it may seem like I am blaming comedy, that is not the case. This book is using standup comedy to understand inequality and stigma, but discrimination is a universal issue. While some suggest that comedy is uniquely violent and unequal, there are many other violent and unequal places out there. Military women, for instance, would certainly argue that the comedy community is not the worst offender.

In recent times, comedy has become more inclusive due to the democratization of comedy through the internet. However, equity movements are not uniform, and they do not affect all people equally, even within the same group. Women, people of color, and LGBTQ+ individuals are poorly represented in most of the comedy world. Even if alternative stages and venues make up for the lack of representation prevalent in clubs, one can only claim that comedy is separate but equal at best. Within most comedy venues, especially the most famous ones, white men still dominate. While alternative venues have allowed minority voices to flourish, the quality and quantity of such places are limited, particularly outside liberal cities.

The only known cure for stigma is social contact, and segregation is the antithesis of social contact. To have social contact, there must be diversity. Unfortunately, when there is a discussion of inclusion, many people quickly become defensive. As Holly explains, "They feel so threatened and censored, and they turn to animosity. No one is trying to exclude them," she adds, "they are just being asked to evolve."

Holly is correct; men should not become defensive when asked to share, especially because it benefits them too. Men who live in more racially and gender-egalitarian societies have lower rates of mental illness and are less likely to commit suicide.[2] The military is a prime example of this, with its high suicide rates. Where there is segregation, physical and mental health is worse for everyone.[3] Gatekeepers, those who pull the strings and make the most money, should understand that a sick society is an economically unproductive community. The evidence is clear that businesses that are more diverse are more profitable than those that are not.[4] Desegregation will make the community healthier and help the bottom line. Most importantly, it will help because comedy is losing many talented people. Hiromi, for instance, wanted to be a comedian from a young age. "At eight or nine years old, I thought I could be a standup," she explains. "But then when I was 19, I went with my mom to a comedy club, and we saw an old white comedian. And when my mom went to the bathroom, he made fun of me for being fat while I was in the audience. At that moment, I thought comedy is not really a thing anymore. It's not a job. If it is, not for someone like me, obviously." Today, Hiromi is selling out shows and headlining major stages, which is revenue that comedy lost for decades due to how they treated her.

Moreover, segregation is a major problem in the comedy world because it drives away paying audiences who don't have a performer to connect with. As an example, in 2018, there were almost 5 million expectant mothers and 33.6 million families with children under the age of 18.[5] That's a huge paying population that the comedy world is missing out on. It may take a little more effort and resources to get mothers and pregnant women onstage, such as hosting comedy shows at reasonable hours or in places not full of drunks. But by having more women and expecting mothers, the comedy world could tap into a vast market of paying customers, as Nyah pointed out:

> When I first started, I thought that as a forty-year-old divorcee, nobody is going to want to listen to me because when I went to open mics, all I would see are young white kids talking about their dicks. I thought that's what everyone wants because that's all I was seeing. And then the more I perform, the more I hear "Oh my God, I'm so glad you are not a young white dude talking about his penis." I thought I was some militant infiltrator subverting the narrative, but no, people want hear stories from people like me. They want real people who have dealt with their kids and have seen a little bit of the world. Typically, over half the audiences are women, moms having their moms' night out.

Above all, the patterns outlined earlier aren't merely those in comedy; they're present wherever there is health inequality. The question that lingers is: how can we promote diversity in communities and combat the segregation that leads to inequality?

GROWING DIVERSITY IS AN ACTIVE PROCESS

Chattoo and Feldman argue that, in addition to grassroots efforts and support from industry allies, Hollywood must find new ways to promote inclusivity and move beyond tokenism. This book reaches the same conclusion, but emphasizes that creating a more diverse, egalitarian, and integrated society requires active effort, not passivity. It's important to distinguish between equity and equality. While equality means treating everyone the same and allowing free entry to comedy clubs, equity recognizes that people face different barriers due to cultural backgrounds.[6] The reality is that many people cannot reach the stage, and because standup venues can be hostile environments, many are afraid to even try. The first step toward equity is to listen to the ideas of minority comedians in the industry. Many of them have good ideas, like Candace, who says, "In New York, there are hundreds of Black women performers and thousands of white men. Bookers only book one Black women and hope that they don't cancel so that they don't look racist. My solution: fill your lineups with Black women on a regular basis, and then if one cancels, there are more ready in the wings. Stack the deck a little, and then maybe more of us will join."

Communities must actively work to eliminate violence that discourages participation. This issue is illustrated by those who left the comedy scene due to Louis C.K.'s sexual misconduct. Would they have continued in comedy if those in power looked like them, understood their experiences, and put a stop to C.K.'s predatory behavior years ago when he was just an open-mic performer? Renowned comedians such as Roseanne Barr and Tig Notaro spoke out against C.K.'s predatory behavior as early as 2015. Despite someone as influential as Roseanne Barr warning that Louis C.K. was "about to get busted," it still took almost two years for the truth to come out.[7] Many people in the comedy community, including some in this study, knew about Louis's behavior but were afraid of retaliation if they spoke up.

However, behaviors don't arise in a vacuum. Ideas nurture them. Destructive behaviors result from negative ideas and prejudiced beliefs, which are overflowing in the standup comedy industry.[8] While comedy can be empowering, humor has often been used to belittle others. Transphobic comedy is now at the forefront of the fight for equality, as demonstrated by Dave Chappelle.[9] In his Netflix special *Equanimity*, Chappelle referred to Caitlyn Jenner as "yuck," referred to her genitalia as a "man-pussy," and equated gender reassignment surgery with "cutting off your dick."[10]

Moreover, there is a clear link between the messages at the top and what comedians are experiencing in the trenches, out of the limelight, as described by Candice. "We have to address things like Kevin Hart's homophobic material," she says. "We can't overlook it because, guess what, I'm backstage with comedians who are still arguing, 'Why can't I say faggot? It's such an easy word. It's got hard syllables.' One woman told me she's upset that she can't do her really good Asian woman impression. This stuff isn't funny, and they think it's still acceptable."

While it may be easy to dismiss the spread of bad ideas in places like comedy as simply "jokes," that idea flies in the face of the evidence which finds that negative ideas in comedy can create real-world harm. Researchers have been studying the effects of humor on health and well-being for many years and have found that exposing people to disparaging humor fosters prejudice against the targeted groups, including racism.[11] Experimental research has also shown that humor that mentally denigrates, physically objectifies, and belittles women leads to negative opinions of women at higher levels.[12] Sexist humor fosters the refusal to admit discrimination against women, antagonism toward women's equality movements, and resentment against affirmative action. It also reinforces the belief that women are helpless or sexual objects and that men's value comes from conquering and subjugating women. Overall, those who observe the ridicule of others, even in comedy, are likely to internalize those ideas and engage in further discriminatory behaviors.[13]

Unfortunately, evidence suggests that subversive humor that challenges bigotry is often misunderstood. Research shows that even when the speaker intends the joke to be subversive, disparaging humor that is sexist, racist, homophobic, or bigoted in any way is most often used as affirmation for prejudiced feelings.[14] Consequently, not only does explicitly racist or sexist humor lead to bigoted beliefs, but even socially conscious comedy can promote bigotry and harmful behaviors if it is not carefully constructed. Lastly, those who find bigoted humor amusing are less likely to empathize with those whom bigoted humor targets. They are less likely to oppose violence and more likely to support or excuse violence against those targeted by bigoted humor.[15] In other words, bigots only hear bigoted ideas and not nuances. Racist and sexist ideas, even through jokes, can lead to racial and sexual violence.

Furthermore, humor that revolves around bad ideas can be harmful to both the audience and the comedian. Engaging in self-defeating humor, which involves minimizing or tearing oneself down, can lead to worse psychological well-being.[16] On the other hand, self-affirming humor can be beneficial for one's health. This may explain why comedian men often struggle with their mental health, as they are more likely to use self-defeating, sexist, and aggressive humor as a coping mechanism. Women, on the other hand, are more likely to use self-affirming humor.[17]

Addressing bigoted ideas, even in comedy, is essential in the cultural shift needed to combat stigma. A culture that promotes harmful ideas not only harms individuals but also reinforces intolerance. When it comes to comedy, accepting bigoted humor means accepting individuals who are openly hostile and potentially violent toward marginalized groups such as women. However, pushing out terrible ideas is not the same as silencing people. It's about being smarter, tactful, and inclusive. Even if comedy becomes a "nicer" place, it does not mean that comedy is no longer funny, as Holly sums up: "Comedy does not lose its edge when you stop literally verbally abusing someone. I don't know where that idea came from. To be edgy, you have to be vitriolic. Whole careers have been built on hate speech. That's insane to me because I don't believe in political correctness. There are ways to talk about race, sexuality, religion, but it doesn't have to be in hate speech. Be direct, but don't be violent."

Comedy gatekeepers at the top must recognize their active role in ending discrimination. They are not passive observers and can take steps to stop the proliferation of bigotry. Local norms play a significant role in the acceptance of bigoted humor. People are more likely to accept and agree with bigoted ideas in places that "tacitly communicate local norms about the acceptance of sexist humor."[18] It is an uphill battle, especially when fighting sexism in comedy. Sexist jokes are rated as less offensive than racist jokes, making it harder to combat.[19] However, diversity can increase comedy's bottom dollar, even if health and well-being are not a priority for gatekeepers. Shows would be more interesting and attract a wider audience, which is lacking in comedy according to some.

Sensitivity training alone is not sufficient to address the stigma surrounding mental illness, as highlighted at the beginning of the book. To facilitate integration, institutions like comedy should create policies that promote inclusivity. Communities should reevaluate their structures that discourage participation and promote segregation. For comedy, this could mean paying performers fair wages to enable those with outside responsibilities to participate. As independent contractors, most comedians do not have workplace protections, which can lead to financial and gender/ethnic exploitation. Comedy clubs should also prioritize performers' health by, at the very least, restricting access to the stage for those who are not sober.

Comedy needs to reconsider its literal places of business, which are often dark and seedy environments. Perhaps the reason why bad ideas are festering in the highest echelons of comedy is that it is being fostered in terrible places. Other art forms embrace the opportunity to perform in the light and reach diverse audiences, but not comedy. Comedy tends to practice in rooms with darkened windows, at night, and in front of mostly drunk people and a disproportionately male audience. By their very structure, comedy venues often exclude families, parents, and those who do not drink. Why not perform in daylight, at a coffee shop during brunch, or at cultural events like Día De Los Muertos or Juneteenth? Other artists venture into different places, expose people to unfamiliar ideas, and bridge gaps. If a comedian can only perform in one type of place for one type of person, then perhaps those comedians are not that funny to begin with; they are certainly not growing their craft. As described by Valentino, a lot of the hate filled comedy is simply being lazy:

> All these sexist, racist jokes, everybody knows them and where that line of thinking goes. It's more interesting for me not to do that kind of shit. And if you are making those jokes, why are you in standup? This is not the '50s and '60s. It's 2020. Why do the same shit that everyone has been doing since the start?

Some comedians are brave enough to push comedy in new and diverse directions. However, the stigma surrounding certain topics is a product of our culture. This book emphasizes that the burden of eliminating stigma cannot fall solely on the individual who is stigmatized. Similarly, if we rely solely on individual efforts to achieve equality in areas like comedy, inequality will persist.

SLOW CHANGES AND BACKLASH

It's not all doom and gloom. There have been incredible shifts in our society that are reflected in comedy. Comedy has not only given voice to traditionally excluded groups such as Latinos, African Americans, women, and even gay, lesbian, and transgender comedians, but it has also given voice to those hidden stigmas that even people at the top suffer through. For instance, diversity has allowed Simon to be more personal, show emotion, and even connect with other comedian men—a connection that was unheard of in the past. He describes it as a comedy revolution:

> When I started, it was white men making fun of smaller groups of minorities. That was the dominant theme, even if they didn't know it. Comedy has gotten a lot better since I started. Leaps and bounds better. I've had friends call me up and express to me real emotion. Tears and everything. But back in 1995. No way. You would have been mocked so badly. If someone went onstage and talked about how much they loved comic books, told an amazing joke about a comic book that really meant something to them, I bet 100 dollars that the next comic up after that person would go "All right, let's hear it for the faggot." Here is a line that was said every single night when I started. A comic would go up and say, "All right, lets here it for so and so; I knew him when he was straight." I remember one of the first sets that I did; I said that my sister is gay, and I think she should be allowed to marry whoever she wants. They pulled me off the stage. They stopped me from talking. They were furious with me.

The cultural shift is most noticeable in how people in positions of power are held accountable for their bad ideas, even in comedy. Shane Gillis is a prime example, as he was hired by *Saturday Night Live* until his past podcast episodes were discovered, in which he used homophobic, racial, and ethnic slurs.[20] However, a better example of this shift is the changing acceptability of using the n-word in comedy. Sixty years ago, Lenny Bruce advocated for racial justice onstage while using the "n" word.[21] Nowadays, any use of the word by white people is met with quick criticism, as seen in Bill Maher's use of it on his show, *Real Time*.[22] After the backlash against Maher, a clip resurfaced of Chris Rock and Louis C.K. using the word, with Rock giving C.K. a pass as a "down" white guy.[23] However, both C.K. and Rock faced criticism, with some referencing Rock's 1995 comedy routine, "Niggas vs. Black People," which was described as anti-Black contempt held by "certain quarters of Black folks." The scrutiny of bad ideas is now universal, regard-less of who spreads them.

But, it's important to remember that this process is slow, it is still not equal, and there will continue to be egregious discrimination and backlash. For example, when The Laughing Skull Comedy Festival in Atlanta, Georgia, a predominantly Black city, revealed their lineup, the public quickly realized that it did not feature a single Black woman.[24] After an uproar from comedi-ans across the country, the festival eventually invited four Black women, but not without backlash against the push for equity. The festival defended itself by attacking critics and stating that fewer than ten Black women submitted [applications] for the festival, arguing that it was the Black women's fault for not applying.

Moreover, the club's excuse for snubbing Black women is misguided for a few reasons, all of which can be traced back to structural discrimination. First, although it may be true that few Black women entered the Laughing Skull Comedy Festival (unknown because they did not give actual names), it is equally possible that there was a demographic issue among the judges (there was). Humor is in the eye of the beholder, and a panel of white judges cannot fully empathize or connect with the experience of Black women and the lives that create their comedy. Those Black women comedians would have been received more positively if more people of color were on the Laughing Skull selection committee. Second, when people experience and expect bias, they will not pursue opportunities, which means a lack of entrants suggests that Black women did not feel welcome within the Laughing Skull Comedy community. Lastly, discrimination begets discrimination. By denying these women access to the stage, they also dissuade Black women from being spec-tators, creating a self-fulfilling prophecy for women of color's marketability.

There is hope for the next generation to witness progress, but it will require a conscious effort.

INTERMEDIARY COPING TACTICS, INTERPERSONAL SKILLS, AND COMPARTMENTALIZING PROBLEMS

Despite the enormous challenge of addressing those cultural factors contrib-uting to health inequalities, there are still valuable lessons to be learned. As society drives these patterns, we may need to focus on achieving more attain-able outcomes rather than simply striving for the most desirable outcomes. This is why we use the term "living with mental illness" rather than "curing mental illness." For some, living with mental illness may mean having access to all necessary social support and resources. For others, living with mental illness may mean a more modest quality of life.

Foremost, we need to recognize the purpose of any potential health resource. Therefore, let's consider the reality of comedy. In their analysis of social justice opportunities in comedy, Chattoo and Feldman[25] argue that "the nature of capitalist entertainment is to make money—it's not to end racism or promote social equity or solve the world's problems." This same concept applies to comedy and mental illness. Just like "charged comedy," which is severely limited in its ability to draw attention to economic, political, or social inequality,[26] we must question whether comedy can truly free voices and destigmatize mental illness. While some people may find healing through comedy, it is not designed for this purpose and can even be an unhealthy world. Most importantly, comedy is meant to entertain, while therapy is explicitly designed to provide help.

Comedians who use comedy as a coping mechanism must confront the uncomfortable truth about the industry, as outlined in a study on comedy and equality. According to Jeffries,[27] comedy is not a meritocracy, and the economic structure of professional standup comedy is a pyramid scheme. Only a few comedians at the top of the pyramid will achieve economic success, while executives and club owners, who pay performers very little, sit at the very top. The comedy industry is based on free labor, with the promise of success if comedians continue to work hard and bring in customers who spend money on drinks that go directly into the owner's pocket. However, many comedians, including some in the study, are at the top of their game but still live in poverty. They perform in shows across the country while living below the poverty line in small apartments with other struggling artists. By not being honest about the economic reality of the industry, comedians are tricked into investing their lives in a system that may not reward them.

I am not trying to discourage anyone from pursuing their dreams in comedy or blame those who are in the arts. No one should have to struggle so much or be harmed in the ways that many comedians are, as Jamal aptly describes: "Many comics are in a spiral of sadness. Taking care of your physical health is below taking care of your mental health, and sometimes mental health doesn't even make a list." Those at the top of the comedy industry need to recognize how their culture is directly harming their performers. I am simply trying to manage perceptions for both comedians and anyone else who wants to reduce stigma. For productive conversations to occur, conditions need to be perfect, including having resources to fall back on.

For instance, consider those who have come out to their families as LGBTQ+ people. Evidence suggests that those who had the most positive coming-out experience had been testing and understanding their identity with many people, including friends and coworkers, well before that coming-out conversation.[28] Before coming out, they had a general knowledge of acceptance, ways to discuss their identity, and most importantly, social support that was ready to provide aid. They had built a wide safety net that blunted potential negative outcomes.

Similarly, one of the most important findings from the study on comedians who manage stigma is the importance of intermediary processes before having an open conversation about highly controversial topics. Effective communication requires a variety of skills, including building relationships, exchanging thoughts and emotions, active listening, and conflict resolution.[29] The comedy world provides a unique opportunity for individuals to develop these skills, which can lead to personal growth and better mental health. Comedians often repeat their stories onstage until they find the right description, building their skills along the way. This is particularly important for addressing public ridicule, as humor is often constructed on elements of incongruity or paradox, allowing comedians to deflect the ramifications of embarrassment.[30] They may also use interpersonal skills to deflect negative social consequences by arguing that what they revealed was purely fictitious. The most productive comedians were also the most patient, a crucial component of good interpersonal skills, especially when giving constructive criticism to those who discriminate. Recognizing the views of others as valid, even if only because of their socialization, is an important step in leading them to a more open-minded perspective.

When we acknowledge the intentions of the industry and interpersonal abilities, we can better understand why compartmentalizers may have the best of both worlds results. They are actively prioritizing their health and seeking resources that can assist them. They understand that comedy can be harmful and avoid those issues as best they can. Moreover, even though they don't aim to gain advantages, like most comedians in the study, by interacting with the audience, many compartmentalizers are enhancing their interpersonal abilities. As a result, they can use those skills when necessary to handle the stigma they face in their daily lives.

Compartmentalizing and developing interpersonal skills are crucial for productive conversations, and I can attest to that fact. After years of struggling with my trauma, which was partially helped by conversations with comedians, I decided it was time to reveal the truth to my family. My intention was to manage the stigma that had haunted me for so many years. I first spoke to my wife, who was very supportive, and then to my parents, who were not. While I wanted that conversation to help me heal, unfortunately, it had the opposite effect. After that conversation, my relationship with my parents completely deteriorated. I tried again, and it ended in tears once more. I was then faced with two choices: attempt to have another conversation that only seemed to make things worse, or cut them out of my life. I chose to compartmentalize and take charge of my health in other ways. I spent time exercising, eating right, and building positive relationships to offset the absence of a negative one with my parents. I worked on building a healthy relationship with my wife and sought out relatives who could provide an understanding of my parents' lived experiences within poverty. I also talked to a professional counselor to express my deep, hidden pain. While I was focusing on my health, I was simultaneously developing my interpersonal skills. College professors are very similar to comedians in the amount of oratory practice we undertake. Educators need enhanced public speaking skills to positively convey complex ideas to students. Standing in front of a classroom of diverse students, we test our ideas repeatedly until we can effectively transfer them to our students. Moreover, as a professor who has spent a lot of time discussing and analyzing health inequality, it has helped me understand the social circumstances surrounding my trauma.

Then incidentally, after two years of silence, my parents reached out to me. I was about to participate in the commencement for my PhD Of course, COVID prohibited guests from attending, but anyone could watch online including my parents. After the ceremony, my father sent me a text and asked if he could brag about me to his friends. Soon thereafter, my mother congratulated both me and Amanda—who was also graduating with her PhD.

After a few more polite texts exchanged, my mother and I talked on the phone. Cordial and mundane at first, by the second conversation, I dove into what I needed to say. Two years earlier, our conversation was fraught with blame and shame. This time, I devised a new strategy based on my understanding brought forth by this study. I understood that I as the stigmatized person was not driving the conversation, she was. I began by making her comfortable; letting her know that I was no longer angry or even sad about those issues; both true. I told her that I understood how difficult it was for her and my father to raise kids as teenagers in poverty. I discussed the poverty and violent culture of the military that they were engrained within. I was able to connect my suffering to suffering that extended generationally through my grandparents (she had no idea that my grandmother was a child victim of sexual abuse). I told her that I knew she and my father were fundamentally good and that poverty placed her children in bad circumstances that were out of her control. Tragically, poverty breeds child abuse. If anything, it was inevitable. And then I told her that although she couldn't say it, I knew she and my father were ashamed that harm came to her kids; she didn't have to apologize.

My mother listened intently with no emotions. When I finished, she cried and unexpectedly, took responsibility. Our conversation was productive not because I "started a conversation"; starting a conversation two years earlier ended in disaster. It was productive because of the skills that I had built over the years. It was productive because I had other social support that was readily available if that relationship fell apart again. While I am glad that she is in my life, my liberation was not dependent on my relationship with them or even the productive conversation.

Compartmentalizers have the right idea, and we should all take note. In their book *The Humor Code*, McGraw and Warner argue that laughter can help us cope with illnesses, but it's not necessarily the best medicine.[31] I would emphasize the reverse of that statement. While laughter can sometimes heal, there are many better alternatives. Communal coping can work, but it should be used as a complement to more rigorously designed health strategies, not as the primary coping mechanism. We need to help people find places that are designed to help, not just places that might help by chance. It's selfish to place the burden of an open and productive conversation on distressed people. Asking for a positive attitude in the face of failure is like telling a depressed person to be happy. Managing those conversations can be a minefield, and it's even worse for someone in the midst of an internal crisis. Instead of putting all our "health" eggs in one basket, how can we compartmentalize coping in one place and simultaneously seek the best complementary alternatives? Religious coping offers a clear example. Although increased religious participation is consistently associated with better health, those who are religious and simultaneously use mental healthcare services thrive the most.[32] An open and productive conversation is a great goal, but the journey is just as important.

IT TAKES TWO TO CONVO

One limitation of this study is that the data is based on the participants' perceptions, which, although rich, may not necessarily reflect the reality of the situation. It's important to note that in conversations, the audience ultimately has the power to steer the direction of the discussion, not the comedian or speaker. Those who stigmatize hold the power to derail the conversation if they choose to do so. For example, if a comedian wants to talk about mental health but the audience is more fixated on the comedian's race or appearance, the conversation may shift to those topics instead. This highlights the significant power imbalance between those who stigmatize and those who are stigmatized. Comedians can only go as far as their community allows them, and their ability to be seen is shaped by the public's reactions.

However, I did not interview the audience, even though they are intertwined within this story. It's important to understand why the audience may react in certain ways. This limitation raises an important question: why are these issues too taboo to talk about? While we have hypothesized that discrimination is the driving force, other motivations can equally shut down conversation. Participants often described misunderstandings as the driving force behind negative reactions, rather than malice. Rarely, comedians were trying to get a rise out of the audience or push buttons. It is their job to entertain those who want to be entertained. For example, Fernanda has been invited to children's hospitals with other performers to cheer up sick children. One time, at the request of a child with cancer, Fernanda performed a song for a young girl who was a huge fan of theater.

> Her favorite musical that she had just performed in was the *Addams Family Musical*, which I had also played in a while back. And she was like, "Oh my God, can you sing 'Just Around the Corner?' I love that song. It's my favorite." I remembered the melody, that it wasn't vulgar; there was nothing about sex so it should be appropriate. So, I pulled up the lyrics and started singing it acapella. I forgot how the joke is about how death is just around the corner. That's literally the chorus; "death is just around the corner." And the whole song is all the different ways you can die. One of the lines is "turning off the respirator, with a simple click." I was singing this in a cancer ward around a bunch of kids that were dying. And I was thinking, If I stop singing it, it's going to make it more of a thing because obviously, look around, they are all dying. And she had explicitly asked for it. If you know the Addams Family, you know it's totally lighthearted, tongue in cheek. But out of context, it's horrifying.

Fernanda's experience may not be based on a comedy performance, but it sheds light on the importance of simple misunderstandings. Misunderstandings can lead to offense and conflict, which can cast a shadow on a person's healing process. However, it's essential to understand that others may be offended not because of hatred or discrimination but because of their own lived experiences. No one would be surprised if those kids or their families were offended by Fernanda's performance, even though she meant no harm.

Comedians perform in front of a lay audience, not medical professionals. It's not the job of the audience to heal the comedians or anyone else trying to cope with their struggles outside of a professional medical relationship. Take Evelyn, for instance, a schoolteacher who lives with the fear of gun violence. She wants to address this fear onstage, but she holds back because she knows many parents in the audience struggle with the same fear. "I want to make humor out of something that scares me to deal with that. I have a niece in school. So, this thing kind of terrifies me. But I have to talk about things more vaguely."

Yes, the audience's limitations on Evelyn's conversation are significant, but it's also essential to understand why they limit her. The audience may be prejudiced, sexist, or racist, as we have seen throughout this book. However, they also have their own lives and experiences, some of which may be very painful. For instance, Lydia uses comedy to talk about the mistreatment she faced growing up as a queer girl in a conservative, Catholic family. One night, her mother was in the audience, and Lydia shares, "She got really wasted afterward. She couldn't handle it. I think she blames herself because she thought of herself as a great mom. I don't think she is a bad mom, but she is a part of the Catholic church. So that was a hard show for her. That was a hard show for me too."

We should not expect those who are being stigmatized to bear the burden of managing that stigma alone. However, it's important to acknowledge that trauma can be present in unexpected places. Comedians, for example, face a difficult challenge in navigating potentially hurtful topics. Even when they make a conscious effort to avoid controversy, audience members may still be triggered and forced to relive past traumas. This was the case for George, who believed he was telling a harmless joke about parenting.

> I did one joke about not having kids. I used to do a lot on it. People have come up to me and been like, "yeah, I'm in my late thirties, and I don't have any kids either. I can relate to what you are talking about because I don't feel like I should have to have children." Men and women have said that to me. But one time this woman told me, "At first I was not having a good time. You were just making all these jokes about not having kids. I just had my fourth miscarriage. I would do anything to have a kid. So, it was just hard to hear." And then she said, "I kept watching, and I loved the rest of your set. I started off being triggered and reminded of a bad thing for me. And then I ended up having a good time and forgetting about that. And I just wanted to let you know that." She was really sweet; she wasn't offended, she was just very sad.

Jamison had a similar experience when, during a show, he chose not to engage with a very stoic patron.

> There's a gentleman who is sitting up front, by himself. Very stern-looking man. Short, cropped haircut, very fit guy. Absolutely piercing eyes. His arms are crossed and he is just staring at me, eye contact the entire time. I'd normally interact and I'd draw attention to it, but I was so intimidated, I couldn't. Something told me just not to go there—spider sense. After the show, I'm outside meeting people and he comes up when I am by myself. Oh God, here it comes. I'm ready to throw down and he goes, "That was the best time I've ever had in my life." And I go, "What? You didn't laugh. You didn't crack a smile. You just stared at me." He then explains, "I'm here celebrating retirement." I said, "really? Congratulations." He goes, "I didn't want to retire. I was forced to retire." He explains he was a Marine, active duty, and he was in a transport vehicle in Afghanistan and he got hit by a missile. Everyone in his truck was killed except him. They discharged him because he had seen too much. He said, "This is the first time I've gone out to do anything since that happened. And every night when I go to bed, I see that explosion, and I see the bodies." He

shows me pictures on his phone of this transport. And he says, "Tonight really made me happy. I didn't show it, but I don't know if I can show that right now."

Neither George nor Jamison harmed those people, and their jokes were pretty mild and playful, unlike other standups who engage in charged humor that discusses controversial topics. However, during the discussion, they could have deeply harmed others without an ounce of malice in their hearts. Although they did not harm anyone, there was a real potential for harm. Jamison cried that night when he realized how impactful his comedy can be, and for George, his effect on that woman still brings him to tears.

The experiences of these people demonstrate that many individuals have their own hidden traumatic experiences, and most are not prepared for those discussions. Asking strangers to laugh at trauma can be difficult, especially if they are silently grieving themselves. There are often traumatic reasons why people find it hard to engage in difficult conversations, which was a major explanation for the disaster conversation between my parents and me. After we stopped communicating, I opened up to a few close relatives who slowly revealed more about my parents' upbringing. Both of my parents came from Latino families on the south side of San Antonio, which was not unknown. However, I was surprised to find out some of the tragic details of their childhoods. My father's childhood was hard, to say the least. My grandmother married her first husband (my father's real father) at the age of fourteen. Eloping was her strategy to escape sexual abuse by her stepfather. She never returned to school, having her first daughter at the age of fifteen and my father at seventeen. For the first few years of my father's life, his father was in Vietnam, effectively leaving my grandmother as an impoverished, single, underaged, and low-educated Latina to care for two children in the dangerous west side of San Antonio. Her first marriage fell apart due to emotional abuse, and it took many years for her second marriage to build into the loving and compassionate marriage that it is today. While she doesn't regret having children, my grandmother admits that having them at her age was not fair to them; she was a child in poverty having children in poverty. She spent those early years as a mother learning through trial and error. If she had been a little older and wiser, she may have been able to provide them the support they needed and safeguard them from the abuse that they experienced.

The audience, like my parents, carries their own baggage. They may not be ready to relive their pain, so those who are coping may be less successful. Social context is also important, including the context of those who stigmatize or abuse. However, I don't mean to suggest that people should remain silent. Some conversations need to be had. Additionally, for some marginalized people, the stage may be the only place where they can express their views uninterrupted. In fact, several comedians explicitly described how the stage was the only place where they could explain their feminist ideas or thoughts on racism.

Rather, I am simply pointing out why so many conversations may be silenced and emphasizing the importance of the relationship between the stigmatized and those who stigmatize. We must recognize that two parties are involved in this conversation. As Jamison puts it, "comedy should be the solution for people's day, not the cause of their pain." Similarly, personal liberation should not cause harm to others. If someone seeks to be seen and inadvertently harms strangers or family, there may be conflict that could hinder future healing. Take Demarcus, whose art reflects his experiences as a father and the social pressures that many Black men face in marriage and parenthood.

> People expected that you, as a Black man, would be the most toxic part of your family. I feel like I grew up in an environment that degraded the concept of being committed to a woman and raising children with them. To me, as a Black man growing up in America, you have a couple of options. You have to either avoid prison. You have to avoid an early death or a violent death. And you have to avoid becoming a baby daddy or like a toxic lover. If you just go with the flow and do whatever everybody else did, walk that regular path that everyone else walks, you are going to end up in one of those spots. You could be a very reserved kind of guy or an outgoing kind of guy, but someone is going to accuse you of stealing a backpack, and you're going to go to prison, period. That could happen to any of us. When I was a teenage, it seems like all the women that I knew were holding the families together. And all the guys that I knew were struggling to be in their kid's lives. They are going to court. Or they disappeared. My dad was the anomaly, living in our house taking care of the family.

Demarcus uses comedy to advocate for other Black people, particularly Black fathers, and tries to counter the stereotypes attached to Black fatherhood. He feels pained when thinking about the pressures to empower his community and the internalized stereotypes. "In life, when I have felt these feelings, I have literally had panic attacks," he reveals. "I would spend big chunks of the day just sitting in one spot crying and being really distant with my family. And all that feels really helpless. Overwhelmingly. I've always been fighting against that. It was like Oedipus. I was introduced to it so early that I was going to be a problem for my kids. But I'm going to make other choices and become a different kind of person."

No matter how "funny" a person may be, they also need to be standing in front of the right audience who is willing to have that conversation because they either have never experienced the trauma or have found some closure. If someone like Demarcus found out he had harmed others in his art—particularly Black men and women he is trying to help—there is no way he would be able to stand and be seen.

This study generally agrees with others who argue that to be funny, jokes need to be simple and clear.[33] But equally important is that the audience is not so wrapped up in their own trauma that they are blinded to the intent of the conversation.

FINAL THOUGHTS ON COMEDY

I am very grateful that comedians invited me into their community and discussed intimate details of their lives with me. I hope that I introduced a new perspective on their craft that they had not previously considered. I also hope that you saw yourself in their experiences even if you are not a comedian.

With that praise of comedy, I'm compelled to identify a final caveat. While I am grateful for the opportunity to listen and share comedians' experiences, I am also not endorsing the idea of using comedy to cope or even celebrating comedy in general. Rather, I am researching stigma and inequality. Comedy may promote positive social change by making complex social issues more accessible and highlighting their severity.[34] Indeed, it has a long history of critiquing those in power, as seen in Charlie Chaplin's ridicule of Hitler in *The Great Dictator*. Additionally, there are documented benefits for health and well-being.

We should be cautious when people give too much importance to comedy or claim that it is equivalent to modern-day philosophy.[35] Philosophy is the "love of wisdom" and involves seeking fundamental truths about ourselves, the world we live in, and our relationships with it and with others.[36] While some comedians have spent years reflecting on their lives and navigating society to come to terms with their pain, it may be appropriate to describe their work as philosophical.[37]

But, simply stringing together a series of ideas and getting others to agree with them does not necessarily mean that the ideas are good. Comedians, for example, possess excellent analogical reasoning skills that are also essential in the legal and scientific professions. As part of the comedy process, comedians build an argument through a series of jokes, elicit agreement from the audience (which is confirmed through laughter), and then transfer that agreement to other cases. However, it is important to note that public agreement does not automatically make an idea a fact, and eloquence is not a measure of intelligence. Comedians can receive positive public reactions even when their ideas are flawed, violent, or harmful. This phenomenon can be best explained through the concept of collective effervescence. Collective effervescence is a social phenomenon often occurring at religious ceremonies, where group members experience a feeling of loss of individuality and growth in the sense of unity with God through the group.[38] This phenomenon is also observed in other mundane, nonreligious group settings such as music concerts and sporting events. It intensifies group togetherness, reaffirms moral solidarity, and brings harmony between group members. Collective effervescence explains how groups of people can come together and bond emotionally, even if it means embracing dangerous ideas and causing harm to others. It's the driving force behind grotesque behaviors such as burning witches, lynching people of color, and even committing genocide, as Charlie Chaplin highlighted in *The Great Dictator*.

It's important to consider the ideas presented by comedians based on their merit alone, despite the collective setting in which they practice their craft. Comedy is often performed in bars and clubs at night, with drunk people in the audience. While it's difficult to determine the sociodemographics of the comedy world, it's reasonable to question whether many of the ideas presented are factually informed. Does standup comedy truly delve into the fundamental nature of knowledge, reality, and existence, as the study of philosophy aims to do? Can standup comedy lead society toward progress? It's possible, but it's also important to acknowledge that comedians may simply be skilled at exploiting human characteristics like greed, vanity, and naivety to create a sense of group closeness.

I'm not suggesting that comedians are a threat or that we should ignore them. In fact, I've spent most of this book explaining why they deserve more respect than they currently receive. Comedians have been valuable in helping us understand issues related to stigma and health, and they could be useful in other areas as well. Therefore, researchers should not be too quick to dismiss comedy as a potential source of insight.

But, good ideas are good ideas, and bad ideas are bad ideas, regardless of how eloquently they are presented. The primary objective of this research is to uncover new ways to cultivate empathy, which is essential in reducing inequality. The goal is not to promote comedy, but rather to use it as a tool to inform both scholars and readers. Comedians are unique in that they embrace embarrassment as part of their culture, which makes them ideal subjects for this research. Does this study answer all the questions? No, but if it is successful, readers will gain a better understanding of the complexities that make addressing stigma difficult, potential approaches to overcoming stigma, and an appreciation for the intricate ways in which individual lives interact with social and structural forces. At the very least, I hope you enjoyed listening to the stories behind the laughter, and I apologize if this book on comedy had too few jokes and was not that funny.

NOTES

1. Thomas, *Working to Laugh: Assembling Difference in American Standup Comedy Venues.*

2. Øystein Gullvåg Holter, "'What's in It for Men?': Old Question, New Data," *Men and Masculinities* 17, no. 5 (2014): 515–48, https://doi.org/10.1177/1097184X14558237.

3. Vickie M. Mays, Susan D. Cochran, and Namdi W. Barnes, "Race, Race-Based Discrimination, and Health Outcomes Among African Americans," *Annual Review of Psychology* 58, no. 1 (2007): 201–25, https://doi.org/10.1146/annurev.psych.57.102904.190212.

4. Vivian Hunt, Dennis Layton, and Sara Prince, "Diversity Matters" (McKinsey & Company, 2015), https://doi.org/10.1177/0003319715611826: Vivian Hunt et al., "Delivering through Diversity" (Mckinsey & Company, 2018): Marcus Noland, Tyler Moran, and Barbara Kotschwar, "Is Gender Diversity Profitable? Evidence from a Global Survey" (Washington, DC: Peterson Institute for International Economics, 2016).

5. Joyce A. Martin et al., "Births: Final Data for 2018," *National Vital Statistics Reports*, vol. 68 (Washington DC: US Department Of Health And Human Services Centers for Disease Control and Prevention, 2015); US Bureau of Labor Statistics, "Economic News Release: Employment Characteristics of Families Summary" (Washington DC: US Department of Labor, 2018), https://www.bls.gov/news.release/famee.nr0.htm.

6. Sven Ove Hansson, "Equity, Equality, and Egalitarianism," *Archives for Philosophy of Law and Social Philosophy* 87, no. 4 (2001): 529–41; Robert J. Havighurst, "Opportunity, Equity, or Equality," *The School Review* 81, no. 4 (1973): 618–33; Karen S. Cook and Karen A. Hegtvedt, "Distributive Justice, Equity, and Equality," *Annual Review of Sociology*, no. 9 (1983): 217–41.

7. Yamato, "Roseanne Barr Calls out Louis C.K.: 'I've Heard So Many Stories.'"

8. Rosenthal, Bindman, and Randolph, *No Laughing Matter Visual Humor in Ideas of Race, Nationality, and Ethnicity.*

9. Brian Logan, "Dave Chappelle's 'reckless' #MeToo and Trans Jokes Have Real After-Effects," *The Guardian*, January 4, 2018, https://www.theguardian.com/stage/2018/jan/04/dave-chappelle-comedy-standup-transgender-netflix.

10. Samantha Allen, "Being Transgender Can Be Funny, but Not for the Reasons Dave Chappelle Thinks," *The Daily Beast*, January 5, 2018.

11. Donald A. Saucier et al., "'What Do You Call a Black Guy Who Flies a Plane?': The Effects and Understanding of Disparagement and Confrontational Racial Humor," *Humor* 31, no. 1 (2018): 105–28, https://doi.org/10.1515/humor-2017-0107; Thomas E. Ford, Kyle Richardson, and Whitney E. Petit, "Disparagement Humor and Prejudice: Contemporary Theory and Research," *Humor* 28, no. 2 (2015): 171–86, https://doi.org/10.1515/humor-2015-0017.

12. Chrysalis L. Wright et al., "'Boy's Club': Examining Sexist Humor on Types of Sexism and Femininity Ideology Using Two Research Approaches," *Humor* 31, no. 1 (2018): 129–50, https://doi.org/10.1515/humor-2017-0108.

13. Leslie Janes and James Olson, "Humor as an Abrasive or a Lubricant in Social Situations: Martineau Revisited," *Humor* 28, no. 2 (2015): 271–88, https://doi.org/10.1515/humor-2015-0021.

14. Strain, Saucier, and Martens, "Sexist Humor in Facebook Profiles: Perceptions of Humor Targeting Women and Men."

15. Annie O. Kochersberger et al., "The Role of Identification with Women as a Determinant of Amusement with Sexist Humor," *Humor* 27, no. 3 (2014): 441–60, https://doi.org/10.1515/humor-2014-0071.

16. Gloria Grases Colom et al., "Study of The Effect of Positive Humour As A Variable That Reduces Stress. Relationship of Humour With Personality and Performance Variables," *Psychology in Spain* 15, no. 1 (2011): 9–21.

17. Martin Führ, Tracy Platt, and René T. Proyer, "Testing the Relations of Gelotophobia with Humour as a Coping Strategy, Self-Ascribed Loneliness, Reflectivity, Attractiveness, Self-Acceptance, and Life Expectations," *European Journal of Humour Research* 3, no. 1 (2015): 84–97, https://doi.org/10.7592/ejhr2015.3.1.fuhr.

18. Jared Alan Gray and Thomas E. Ford, "The Role of Social Context in the Interpretation of Sexist Humor," *Humor* 26, no. 2 (2013): 289, https://doi.org/10.1515/humor-2013-0017.

19. Julie A. Woodzicka et al., "It's Just a (Sexist) Joke: Comparing Reactions to Sexist versus Racist Communications," *Humor* 28, no. 2 (2015): 289–309, https://doi.org/10.1515/humor-2015-0025.

20. Dave Itzkoff, "Shane Gillis Dropped From 'S.N.L.' Cast Amid Criticism of Racist Slurs," *The New York Times*, September 16, 2019.

21. Lheal, "Lenny Bruce: 'Are There Any Niggers Here Tonight?'"

22. German Lopez, "Bill Maher Dropped the N-Word on Live TV," *Vox*, June 3, 2017.

23. Stereo Williams, "Chris Rock's N-Word Controversy with Louis C.K. and the Myth of the 'Down Ass White Guy,'" *The Daily Beast*, December 23, 2018.

24. Marshall Chiles, "Atlanta's Laughing Skull Comedy Festival Has Booked No Black Women This Year," *Paste*, March 2019.

25. Chattoo and Feldman, *A Comedian and an Activist Walk into a Bar: The Serious Role of Comedy in Social Justice*, 120

26. Krefting, *All Joking Aside: American Humor and Its Discontents*.

27. Jeffries, *Behind the Laughs: Community and Inequality*.

28. Paul Taylor, "A Survey of LGBT Americans Attitudes, Experiences and Values in Changing" (Pew Research Center, 2013).

29. Cloitre et al., "Skills Training in Affective and Interpersonal Regulation Followed by Exposure: A Phase-Based Treatment for PTSD Related to Childhood Abuse."

30. Glenn E. Weisfeld and Miriam B. Weisfeld, "Does a Humorous Element Characterize Embarrassment?," *Humor* 27, no. 1 (2014): 71, https://doi.org/10.1515/humor-2013-0050.

31. McGraw and Warner, *The Humor Code: A Global Search for What Makes Things Funny*.

32. Terrence D. Hill et al., "Religious Attendance and The Health Behaviors of Texas Adults," *Preventive Medicine* 42, no. 4 (2006): 309–12, https://doi.org/10.1016/j.ypmed.2005.12.005; Christopher G. Ellison, "Race, Religious Involvement and Depressive Symptomatology in a Southeastern US Community," *Social Science & Medicine* 40, no. 11 (1995): 1561–72, https://doi.org/10.1016/0277-9536(94)00273-V; Christopher G. Ellison and Andrea K. Henderson, "Religious and Mental Health: Through the Lens of the Stress Process," in *Toward a Sociological Theory of Religion and Health*, ed. Anthony J. Blasi (Boston, MA: Brill, 2011), 11–43; Harold G. Koenig, "Religion, Spirituality, and Health: A Review and Update," *Advances in Mind Body Medicine* 29, no. 3 (2015): 19–26.

33. McGraw and Warner, *The Humor Code: A Global Search for What Makes Things Funny.*

34. Caty Borum Chattoo, "How Comedy Works [to Change the World]" (Washington, DC: American University: Center for Media & Social Impact, 2019).

35. Chris Weller, "Aziz Ansari's 'Master of None' Proves America's Best Philosophers Are All Comedians," *Business Insider*, November 15, 2015; Dana Gabrielle Espinosa, "Comedians Are Our Modern Day Philosophers: You Can Learn More than You'd Think from a Dirty Joke.," *The Odyssey*, February 2016.

36. Florida State University, "What Is Philosophy?," n.d., https://doi.org/10.1111/theo.12163.

37. John Morreall, *The Philosophy of Laughter and Humor* (Albany: SUNY Press, 1987).

38. Émile Durkheim, "The Elementary Forms of Religious Life," *Sociology of Religion* 57, no. 3 (n.d.), https://doi.org/10.2307/3712165.

Appendix A

Questionnaire

SECTION A: GETTING INTO STANDUP

I'd like to begin by discussing your standup comedy career.

1. First, how would you describe your comedy?
2. What are your aspirations for standup?

For each performer, there was a moment when they first thought they could do standup.

1. Can you describe when you first considered doing standup?
2. Can you describe your first time?
3. What was the audience's reaction and how did they make you feel?
4. What were the other comedians' reaction and how did they make you feel?
5. Did you have any friends or family there?
   a. [If Yes] How did they react and how did that make you feel?
   b. [If No] Why not? Explain your feelings?
6. If you did poorly, why did you do it again?
7. At what point did you feel that you were on the right track?

SECTION B: CHILDHOOD

Children have multiple social groups and relationships that shape their lives as they grow up. Some of those relationships could include family, friends, and church groups.

1. First, how would you describe yourself as a child? For instance, would you say you were outgoing, introverted, popular, excitable, lonely, athletic, something else?
2. How would you describe your family and friends when you were growing up?
3. What were some other important relationships or social groups you had as a child? Can you tell me the most important few?
   a. Briefly, what did they mean or do for you?

SECTION C: QUALITY TIME

There seems to be a lot of interest in the need to spend "quality time" with others.

1. What does the term "quality time" mean to you?
2. Tell me about how you spend quality time with family and friends outside of the standup community?
3. Tell me about how you spend quality time with your fellow performers?

SECTION D: PERSONAL STRESS AND COPING

Comedians, like all people, can sometimes feel overwhelmed or stressed.

1. Can you tell me about a time you felt stressed or overwhelmed?
2. How do you usually cope or what do you usually do to make yourself feel better at times like that?
3. How does performing add and remove stress to your life?
4. Do you ever decide not to perform for yourself?

SECTION E: EXPERIENCES THAT INFLUENCE STANDUP.

A foundation of some comedy is to draw upon experiences when performing. Some of those experiences can be positive, while others can be negative or even traumatic.

1. Can you describe any personal experiences you draw upon when performing?
   a. *If no personal issues, probe for social issues that may cause distress.*

2. How do you feel talking about those issues during a performance?
   a. How did the audience react?
   b. How did other performers react?
3. Was your family present when you talked about that issue during a performance?
   a. How did you feel with them present?
   b. How did they feel?
4. Have you ever talked about that issue to your family, one-on-one, outside of a performance?
   a. How did you feel during that conversation?
   b. How did they feel during that conversation?

Your family [*now knows/does not know*] about that NEGATIVE issue.

5. How has comedy helped or hindered your ability to address those experiences with them?
   a. How do you feel now that they [*know/don't know*]?
   b. What would you do differently?
6. How does that experience shape people's perception of you? [Stigma]
   a. How does comedy change that perception?

SECTION F: CURRENT SOCIAL NETWORKS

Now that I have a picture of who you were when you were growing up, how you spend quality time with others, what stresses you, and what inspires you, I would like to know about your current social groups and relationships that you turn to during stressful times.

1. First, can you identify your current and most important relationships or social groups outside of the standup community that you turn to for help? Please tell me a few.

[Ask questions 2-7 for the MOST important relationship or social group]

2. What does [*Group/Relationship*] mean to you or do for you?
3. What stressful issues do you turn to them for help or guidance [*Group/Relationship*]
4. What stressful issues do you find it difficult to turn to them for help or guidance?

5. Was there ever a time that you needed support from [*Group/Relationship*] and they weren't there?
   a. Are they usually there when you need them?
   b. Who did you turn to for help?
6. Has [*Group/Relationship*] seen you perform?
   a. [*If YES*] How did you feel when they FIRST saw you?
   b. [*IF NO*] Why not?
      i. How does that make you feel?
7. How would you feel if [*Group/Relationship*] saw you perform TODAY?

SECTION G: COMEDY COMMUNITY SUPPORTS

Now, I'd like to know about the support you may receive from your fellow performers.

1. What are stressful issues that you turn to your fellow performers for help or guidance?
2. What are stressful issues that you find it difficult or cannot turn to your fellow performers for help or guidance?
3. Was there ever a time that you needed support from your fellow performers and they weren't there?
   a. Are they usually there when you need them?
   b. Who did you turn to for help?

[*If race/gender WAS/WAS NOT salient during the conversation*]

Finally, I noticed that your experience DID/DID NOT seem to reflect you as a [*race/gender/sexual orientation*].

1. How does being a [*race/gender/sexual orientation*] affect your experiences as a comedian?
2. Are there any other questions or issues that are important to you or the standup comedy community that you would like to talk about or discuss?

Appendix B

Supporting Table

Descriptive Statistics Reporting Sociodemographic and Health Statistics

Interview Length			
Min	24 m		
Max	2h 4 m		
Average	1h 20m		

Demographics	*n*		*n*
Age		*Education*	
20–29	31	High school	11
30–39	39	Some college	28
40–49	23	Bachelor's	47
50–59	6	Graduate degree or higher	13
Gender		*Employment Status*	
Woman	49	Full-time employed	47
Man	45	Self-employed	29
Trans man	2	Part-time employed	10
Trans woman	3	Students	7
Race/Ethnicity		Not working	6
White, non-Hispanic	66	*Average Personal Income*	
Black or African American	17	$29,999 or less	48
Hispanic or Latino	17	$30,000–49,999	35
Asian or Pacific Islander	10	$50,000–99,999	13
American Indian	3	$100,000+	3
Middle Eastern	3	*Income from Comedy*	
Marital Status		All	4
Married	27	A great deal	12
Single	38	Some	18
Cohabiting	13	Very little	43
Dating/in a relationship	13	None	22
Divorced	8		

(*Continued*)

Demographics	n		n
Parental Status (Yes)	23	Region of Residency	
Sexual Orientation		Northeast	13
Straight	63	Midwest	47
Gay or lesbian	13	Pacific	28
Bisexual	17	South	9
Queer	13	Southwest	12
Perception of Comedy Career		Years Performing	
1= Beginner	2	Min	>1
2	7	Max	33
3	23	Average	7.34
4	24		
5	20		
6 = Professional	23		
Perception of Health		Anxiety or Panic Disorder	
Excellent	5	Formal diagnosis	35
Very good	30	Informal diagnosis	13
Good	34	Depression	
Fair	27	Formal diagnosis	42
Poor	3	Informal diagnosis	13
Level of Psychological Distress in the Past 30 Days(K10)		Post-Traumatic Stress Disorder	
Severe	11	Formal diagnosis	14
Moderate	23	Informal diagnosis	16
Mild	34	Alcohol Use Disorder	
Low	31	Formal diagnosis	2
Hazardous Drinker (AUDIT-C)		Informal diagnosis	8
Men (yes)	25		
Men (no)	22		
Women (yes)	25		
Women (no)	27		

Note: Descriptive statistics are based on self-identified information. While there appear to be some inconsistencies in the total number of participants and total category, those inconsistencies are explained by the overlap in which participants indicated multiple categories. For instance, some people are multiracial, and some people indicated multiple sexual orientations (e.g., queer and lesbian)

Bibliography

Acosta, Joie, Amariah Becker, Jennifer L. Cerully, Michael P. Fisher, Laurie T. Martin, Raffaele Vardavas, Mary Ellen Slaughter, and Terry L. Schell. 2014. *Mental Health Stigma in the Military*. RAND Corporation. Santa Monica, California.

Afzal, Anam Rana. 2018. "How Lucille Ball Fought the Patriarchy, While Lucy Ricardo (Indirectly) Contributed to Second-Wave (White) Feminism." City University of New York.

Agnes, Flavia. 2012. "From Shahbano to Kausar Bano—Contextualizing the 'Muslim Woman' within a Communalised Polity." *South Asian Feminisms*, 33–53.

Allen, Samantha. 2018. "Being Transgender Can Be Funny, but Not for the Reasons Dave Chappelle Thinks." *Daily Beast*, January 5, 2018.

Anderson, Timothy, Benjamin M. Ogles, Candace L. Patterson, Michael J. Lambert, and David A. Vermeersch. 2009. "Therapist Effects: Facilitative Interpersonal Skills as a Predictor of Therapist Success." *Journal of Clinical Psychology* 65 (7): 755–68.

Augoustinos, Martha, and Stephanie De Garis. 2012. "'Too Black or Not Black Enough': Social Identity Complexity in the Political Rhetoric of Barack Obama." *European Journal of Social Psychology* 42 (5): 564–77.

Bailey, April H., Marianne LaFrance, and John F. Dovidio. 2019. "Is Man the Measure of All Things? A Social Cognitive Account of Androcentrism." *Personality and Social Psychology Review* 23 (4): 307–31.

Batalion, Judy, ed. 2011. *The Laughing Stalk: Live Comedy and Its Audiences*. Anderson, SC: Parlor Press.

Beauchamp, Zach. 2019. "Our Incel Problem." *Vox*, April 23, 2019.

Beitin, Ben K. "Interview and Sampling." In *The SAGE Handbook of Interview Research: The Complexity of the Craft*, edited by David Pilgrim, Anne Rogers, and Bernice Pescosolido, 243–52. Thousand Oaks, CA: Sage Publication, 2012.

Bell, Margret E., Jessica A. Turchik, and Julie A. Karpenko. 2014. "Impact of Gender on Reactions to Military Sexual Assault and Harassment." *Health and Social Work* 39 (1): 25–33.

Bem, Sandra Lipsitz. 1993. *The Lenses of Gender: Transforming the Debate on Sexual Inequality*. New Haven, CT: Yale University Press.

Benko, Steven A. 2020. *Ethics in Comedy: Essays on Crossing the Line.* Jefferson, NC: McFarland.

Berkman, Lisa F. 1985. "The Relationship of Social Networks and Social Support to Morbidity and Mortality." In *Social Support and Health,* edited by Sheldon Cohen and S. Leonard Syme. New York: Academic Press.

———. 2008. "Social Networks and Health." *Annual Review of Sociology* 34 (2008): 405–18.

Berman, Judy. 2018. "'Nanette' Is the Most Discussed Comedy Special in Ages. Here's What to Read About It." *New York Times,* July 13, 2018.

Bomboy, Scott. 2019. "Looking Back: George Carlin and the Supreme Court." National Constitution Center. 2019. https://constitutioncenter.org/blog/a-controversial-order -leads-to-internment-camps.

Borenstein, Jeffrey. 2020. "Stigma, Prejudice and Discrimination Against People with Mental Illness." American Psychiatric Association. 2020. https://www.psychiatry .org/patients-families/stigma-and-discrimination.

Bormann, Jill E., Lin Liu, Steven R. Thorp, and Ariel J. Lang. 2012. "Spiritual Wellbeing Mediates PTSD Change in Veterans with Military-Related PTSD." *International Journal of Behavioral Medicine* 19 (4): 496–502.

Bowley, Graham. 2017. "Prosecutors Want Cosby 'Spanish Fly' Comments as Evidence at Trial." *New York Times,* March 30, 2017.

Bradshaw, Matt, and Christopher G. Ellison. 2010. "Financial Hardship and Psychological Distress: Exploring the Buffering Effects of Religion." *Social Science & Medicine* 71 (1): 196–204.

Brewer, Mike, and Alita Nandi. 2014. "Partnership Dissolution: How Does It Affect Income, Employment and Well-Being?"

Brodie, Ian. 2014. *A Vulgar Art: A New Approach to Stand-Up Comedy.* Jackson, MS: University Press of Mississippi.

Brown, Cecil. 2013. *Pryor Lives!: How Richard Pryor Became Richard Pryor Or Kiss My Rich, Happy Black . . . Ass! A Memoir.* CreateSpace Independent Publishing Platform.

Bryant, Wesley W. 2011. "Internalized Racism's Association With African American Male Youth's Propensity for Violence." *Journal of Black Studies* 42 (4): 690–707.

Butler, Judith. 1999. *Gender Trouble: Feminism and the Subversion of Identity.* Tenth anniversary edition. New York: Routledge.

Campion, Karis. 2019. "'You Think You're Black?' Exploring Black Mixed-Race Experiences of Black Rejection." *Ethnic and Racial Studies* 42 (16): 196–213.

Carver, Charles S., Michael F. Scheier, and Jagdish K Weintraub. 1989. "Assessing Coping Strategies: A Theoretically Based Approach." *Journal of Personality and Social Psychology* 56 (2): 267–83.

Cater, Janet K, and Jerry Leach. 2011. "Veterans, Military Sexual Trauma and PTSD: Rehabilitation Planning Implications." *Journal of Applied Rehabilitation Counseling* 42 (2): 33–41.

Chae, David H., Amani M. Nuru-Jeter, Karen D. Lincoln, and Darlene D. Francis. 2011. "Conceptualizing Racial Disparities in Health: Advancement of a Socio-Psychobiological Approach." *Du Bois Review* 8 (1): 63–77.

Chattoo, Caty Borum. 2019. "How Comedy Works [to Change the World]." Washington, DC.

Chattoo, Caty Borum, and Lauren Feldman. 2020. *A Comedian and an Activist Walk into a Bar: The Serious Role of Comedy in Social Justice.* Oakland: University of California Press.

Chiles, Marshall. 2019. "Atlanta's Laughing Skull Comedy Festival Has Booked No Black Women This Year." *Paste*, March 2019.

Chuba, Kirsten. 2018. "Dave Chappelle Calls Louis C.K. Accusers 'Weak' and 'Brittle' in New Special." *Variety*, January 2018.

Cloitre, Marylene, Karestan C. Koenen, Lisa R. Cohen, and Hyemee Han. 2002. "Skills Training in Affective and Interpersonal Regulation Followed by Exposure: A Phase-Based Treatment for PTSD Related to Childhood Abuse." *Journal of Consulting and Clinical Psychology* 70 (5): 1067–74.

Cole, Elizabeth R, and Alyssa N Zucker. 2007. "Black and White Women's Perspectives on Femininity." *Cultural Diversity and Ethnic Minority Psychology* 13 (1): 1–9.

Coleman, Libby. 2018. "These Major Trends Are Driving Comedy Club Growth." *Forbes*, September 18, 2018.

Collins, Pamela Y., Hella von Unger, and Adria Armbrister. 2008. "Church Ladies, Good Girls, and Locas: Stigma and the Intersection of Gender, Ethnicity, Mental Illness, and Sexuality in Relation to HIV Risk." *Social Science & Medicine* 67 (3): 389–97.

Collins, Patricia Hill. 2015. "Intersectionality's Definitional Dilemmas." *Annual Review of Public Health* 41: 1–20.

Collins, Patricia Hill, and Sirma Bilge. 2016. *Intersectionality*. Cambridge, MA: Polity Press.

Colom, Gloria Grases, Cristina Trias Alcover, Cristian Sanchez-Curto, and Juan Zarate-Osuma. 2011. "Study of the Effect of Positive Humour as a Variable That Reduces Stress: Relationship of Humour with Personality and Performance Variables." *Psychology in Spain* 15 (1): 9–21.

Combahee River Collective. 1983. "The Combahee River Collective Statement." In *Home Girls: A Black Feminist Anthology*, edited by Barbara Smith, 29–37. New York: Kitchen Table: Women of Color Press.

Connell, R. W., and James W. Messerschmidt. 2005. "Hegemonic Masculinity: Rethinking the Concept." *Gender and Society* 19 (6): 829–59.

Cook, Karen S., and Karen A. Hegtvedt. 1983. "Distributive Justice, Equity, and Equality." *Annual Review of Sociology*, no. 9: 217–41.

Cooley, Charles. 1902. *Human Nature and The Social Order.* New York: Charles Scribner's Sons.

Correll, Shelley J., Stephen Benard, and In Paik. 2007. "Getting a Job: Is There a Motherhood Penalty?" *American Journal of Sociology* 112 (5): 1297–1339.

Corrigan, Patrick W. 2004. "How Stigma Interferes With Mental Health Care." *American Psychologist* 59 (7): 614–25.

Corrigan, Patrick W., Jonathon E. Larson, and Nicolas Rüsch. 2009. "Self-Stigma and the 'Why Try' Effect: Impact on Life Goals and Evidence-Based Practices." *World Psychiatry* 8 (2): 75–81.

Corrigan, Patrick W., and Amy C. Watson. 2002. "The Paradox of Self-Stigma and Mental Illness." *Clinical Psychology: Science and Practice* 9 (1): 35–53.

Crenshaw, Kimberlé. 1991. "Mapping the Margins: Intersectionality, Identity Politics, and Violence against Women of Color." *Stanford Law Review* 43 (6): 1241–99.

Criss, Doug. 2018. "Comedian Louis C.K. Mocks Parkland Shooting Survivors in Leaked Audio: Parkland Survivors Respond." CNN, 2018.

Decamp, Elise. 2015. "Humoring the Audience: Performance Strategies and Persuasion in Midwestern American Stand-up Comedy." *Humor* 28 (3): 449–67.

DeRochers, Rick. 2014. *The Comic Offense from Vaudeville to Contemporary Comedy: Larry David, Tina Fey, Stephen Colbert, and Dave Chappelle*. New York: Bloomsbury.

Desta, Yohana. 2017. "Tig Notaro Distances Herself from Louis C.K., Says He Should 'Handle' Sexual Misconduct Rumors." *Vanity Fair* 2, August 2017.

Dickenson, Peter, Anne Higgens, Paul Matthew st. Pierre, Diana Solomon, and Sean Zwagerman, eds. 2017. *Women and Comedy: History, Theory, Practice*. Vancouver: Fairleigh Dickinson University Press.

Driessen, Ellen, Steven D. Hollon, Claudi L. H. Bockting, Pim Cuijpers, Erick H. Turner, and Lin Lu. 2015. "Does Publication Bias Inflate the Apparent Efficacy of Psychological Treatment for Major Depressive Disorder? A Systematic Review and Meta-Analysis of US National Institutes of Health-Funded Trials." *PLoS ONE* 10 (9): 1–23.

Dry, Jude. 2017. "Stephen Colbert's Most Anti-Trump Act Is Giving Diverse Stand-Up a Platform." *Indie Wire*, August 4, 2017.

Durkheim, Émile. n.d. "The Elementary Forms of Religious Life." *Sociology of Religion*. New York: The Free Press.

Dyson, Michael Eric. 2016. "Whose President Was He?" *Politico*, the Obama Issue: 1–5.

Ellison, Christopher G. 1995. "Race, Religious Involvement and Depressive Symptomatology in a Southeastern U.S. Community." *Social Science & Medicine* 40 (11): 1561–72.

Ellison, Christopher G., and Andrea K. Henderson. 2011. "Religious and Mental Health: Through the Lens of the Stress Process." In *Toward a Sociological Theory of Religion and Health*, edited by Anthony J. Blasi, 11–43. Boston: Brill.

England, Paula, Jonathan Bearak, Michelle J. Budig, and Melissa J. Hodges. 2016. "Do Highly Paid, Highly Skilled Women Experience the Largest Motherhood Penalty?" *American Sociological Review* 81 (6): 1161–89.

Espinosa, Dana Gabrielle. 2016. "Comedians Are Our Modern Day Philosophers: You Can Learn More than You'd Think from a Dirty Joke." *The Odyssey*, February 2016.

Fazio, Elena M. 2010. "Sense of Mattering in Late Life." In *Advances in the Conceptualization of the Stress Process: Essays in Honor of Leonard I. Pearlin,* edited by William R. Avison, Carol S. Aneshensel, Scott Schieman, and Blair Wheaton, 149–76. New York: Springer.

Florida State University. n.d. "What Is Philosophy?" https://philosophy.fsu.edu/undergraduate-study/why-philosophy/What-is-Philosophy.

Folkman, Susan, and Judith Tedlie Moskowitz. 2004. "Coping: Pitfalls and Promise." *Annual Review of Psychology* 55: 745–74.

Ford, Thomas E., Kyle Richardson, and Whitney E. Petit. 2015. "Disparagement Humor and Prejudice: Contemporary Theory and Research." *Humor* 28 (2): 171–86.

Fox, Jess David. 2015. "How the Internet and a New Generation of Superfans Helped Create the Second Comedy Boom." *Vulture*, March 30, 2015.

Fredriksen-Goldsen, Karen I., Loree Cook-Daniels, Hyun Jun Kim, Elena A. Erosheva, Charles A. Emlet, Charles P. Hoy-Ellis, Jayn Goldsen, and Anna Muraco. 2014. "Physical and Mental Health of Transgender Older Adults: An At-Risk and Underserved Population." *The Gerontologist* 54 (3): 488–500.

Führ, Martin. 2002. "Coping Humor in Early Adolescence." *Humor* 15 (3): 283–304.

Gates, Rachel. 2013. "Bringing the Black: Eddie Murphy and African American Humor on Saturday Night Live." In N. Marx, M. Sienkiewicz, and R. Becker (Eds.), *Saturday Night Live and TV*. Bloomington: Indiana University Press.

Gee, Gilbert C., and Chandra L. Ford. 2011. "Structural Racism and Health Inequality: Old Issues, New Directions." *Du Bois Review* 8 (1): 115–32.

Gilbert, Joanne R. 2004. *Performing Marginality: Humor, Gender, and Cultural Critique.* Detroit: Wayne State University Press.

Giles, Matt, and Nate Jones. 2015. "A Timeline of the Abuse Charges Against Bill Cosby [Updated]." *Vulture*, December 2015.

Gilman, Charlotte Perkins. 1911. *The Man-Made World, or, Our Androcentric Culture*. New York: Charlton Company.

Gleeson, Patrick. 2018. "Statistics on People Getting Famous in Acting." *Chron*, June 27, 2018.

Glick, Peter, and Susan T. Fiske. 1996. "The Ambivalent Sexism Inventory: Differentiating Hostile and Benevolent Sexism." *Journal of Personality and Social Psychology* 70 (3): 491–512.

Goff, Phillip Atiba, and Kimberly Barsamian Kahn. 2013. "How Psychological Science Impedes Intersectional Thinking." *Du Bois Review* 10 (2): 365–84.

Goffman, Erving. 1963. *Stigma: Notes on the Management of Spoiled Identity*. New York: Simon & Schuster, Inc.

Gonzalez, Tanya, and Eliza Rodriguez y Gibson. 2015. *Humor and Latina/o Camp in Ugly Betty: Funny Looking*. New York: Lexington Books.

Gorman, Bridget K., Justin T. Denney, Hilary Dowdy, and Rose Anne Medeiros. 2015. "A New Piece of the Puzzle: Sexual Orientation, Gender, and Physical Health Status." *Demography* 52 (4): 1357–82.

Grauerholz, Elizabeth, and Mary A. Koralewski. "Feminist Explanations: Male Power, Hostility, and Sexual Coercion." In *Sexual Coercion: A Sourcebook on Its Nature, Causes, and Prevention*, 61–73. New York: Lexington Books, 1991.

Gray, Jared Alan, and Thomas E. Ford. 2013. "The Role of Social Context in the Interpretation of Sexist Humor." *Humor* 26 (2): 277–93.

Gross, Terry. 2022. "Comic Jerrod Carmichael Bares His Secrets in 'Rothaniel.'" *Fresh Air*, December 28. NPR.

Haggins, Bambi. 2007. *Laughing Mad: The Black Comic Persona in Post-Soul America.* New Brunswick, NJ: Rutgers University Press.

Hammersley, Martyn, and Paul Atkinson. *Ethnography.* New York: Taylor & Francis, 2007.

Hansson, Sven Ove. 2001. "Equity, Equality, and Egalitarianism." *Archives for Philosophy of Law and Social Philosophy* 87 (4): 529–41.

Harder, Brittany M., and J. E. Sumerau. 2018. "Understanding Gender as a Fundamental Cause of Health: Simultaneous Linear Relationships between Gender, Mental Health, and Physical Health over Time." *Sociological Spectrum* 38 (6): 387–405.

Harrington, C. Lee. 2008. "Talk About Embarrassment: Exploring the Taboo-Repression-Denial Hypothesis." *Symbolic Interaction* 15 (2): 203–25.

Harris, Elizabeth A. "Amy Schumer, Ali Wong and the Rise of Pregnant Stand-Up." *New York Times*, April 19, 2019.

Havighurst, Robert J. 1973. "Opportunity, Equity, or Equality." *The School Review* 81 (4): 618–33.

Heflick, Nathan A. 2013. "Why Are People Mean?" *Psychology Today.* 2013.

Henslin, James M. 2019. *Essentials of Sociology: A Down-to-Earth Approach.* 13th ed. New York: Pearson.

Higate, Paul. 2007. "Peacekeepers, Masculinities and Sexual Exploitation." *Men and Masculinities* 10 (1): 99–119.

Hill, Terrence D., Amy M. Burdette, Christopher G. Ellison, and Marc A. Musick. 2006. "Religious Attendance and the Health Behaviors of Texas Adults." *Preventive Medicine* 42 (4): 309–12.

Hoge, Charles W., Jennifer L. Auchterlonie, and Charles S. Milliken. 2006. "Mental Health Problems, Use of Mental Health Services, and Attrition From Military Service After Returning From Deployment to Iraq or Afghanistan." *JAMA* 295 (9): 1023–32.

Hollister, Frederick J. 1969. "Skin Color and Life Chances of Puerto Ricans." *Caribbean Studies* 9 (3): 87–94.

Holter, Øystein Gullvåg. 2014. "'What's in It for Men?': Old Question, New Data." *Men and Masculinities* 17 (5): 515–48.

Hunt, Vivian, Dennis Layton, and Sara Prince. 2015. "Diversity Matters."

Hunt, Vivian, Sara Prince, Sundiatu Dixon-Fyle, and Lareina Yee. 2018. "Delivering through Diversity."

Itzkoff, Dave. 2017. "Marc Maron Reckons With Louis C.K.'s Misconduct." *New York Times*, November 13, 2017.

———. 2019. "Shane Gillis Dropped From 'S.N.L.' Cast Amid Criticism of Racist Slurs." *New York Times*, September 16, 2019.

Jackson, Stevi. 2006. "Gender, Sexuality and Heterosexuality: The Complexity (and Limits) of Heteronormativity." *Feminist Theory* 7 (1): 105–21.

Janes, Leslie, and James Olson. 2015. "Humor as an Abrasive or a Lubricant in Social Situations: Martineau Revisited." *Humor* 28 (2): 271–88.

Jeffries, Michael P. 2018. *Behind the Laughs: Community and Inequality*. Stanford, CA: Stanford University Press.

Jones, Jeffrey P. 2009. *Entertaining Politics: Satiric Television and Political Engagement (Communication, Media, and Politics)*, second edition. Lanham, MD: Rowman & Littlefield Publishers.

Jones, Norman, Maya Twardzicki, John Ryan, Theresa Jackson, Mohammed Fertout, Claire Henderson, and Neil Greenberg. 2014. "Modifying Attitudes to Mental Health Using Comedy as a Delivery Medium." *Social Psychiatry and Psychiatric Epidemiology* 49: 1667–76.

Kachel, Meredith, and Austin Sheaffer. 2017. "What's the Deal with Standup Comedy Bookings?:Using Data to Show Discrepancies in Gender in Chicago's Stand-Up Comedy Scene." Meredith Kachel. 2017.

Kaufman, Amy. 2020a. "After Twitter Outcry, Five Women Detail Chris D'Elia's Alleged Sexual Improprieties." *L.A. Times,* June 20, 2020.

———. 2020b. "Actor Bryan Callen Accused of Sexual Assault, Misconduct." *L.A. Times*, July 20, 2020.

Kaufman, Will. 2019. *The Comedian as Confidence Man: Studies in Irony Fatigue*. Wayne State University Press.

Kenny, David A., Wemke Veldhuijzen, Trudy van der Weijden, Annie LeBlanc, Jocelyn Lockyer, France Légaré, and Craig Campbell. 2010. "Interpersonal Perception in the Context of Doctor-Patient Relationships: A Dyadic Analysis of Doctor-Patient Communication." *Social Science & Medicine* 70 (5): 763–68.

Killewald, Alexandra, and Margaret Gough. 2013. "Does Specialization Explain Marriage Penalties and Premiums?" *American Sociological Review* 78 (3): 477–502.

Kimmel, Michael. 2005. "Men, Masculinity, and the Rape Culture." In *Transforming a Rape Culture*, edited by Emilie Buchwald, Pamela R. Fletcher, and Martha Roth, Revised, 139–57. Minneapolis, MN: Milkweed Editions.

Kochersberger, Annie O., Thomas E. Ford, Julie A. Woodzicka, Monica Romero-Sanchez, and Hugo Carretero-Dios. 2014. "The Role of Identification with Women as a Determinant of Amusement with Sexist Humor." *Humor* 27 (3): 441–60.

Koenig, Harold G. 2015. "Religion, Spirituality, and Health: A Review and Update." *Advances in Mind Body Medicine* 29 (3): 19–26.

Kohpeima Jahromi, Vahid, Seyed Saeed Tabatabaee, Zahra Esmaeili Abdar, and Mahboobeh Rajabi. 2016. "Active Listening: The Key of Successful Communication in Hospital Managers." *Electronic Physician* 8 (3): 2123–28.

Krefting, Rebecca. 2014. *All Joking Aside: American Humor and Its Discontents*. Baltimore: Johns Hopkins University Press.

Ledermann, Thomas, Guy Bodenmann, Myriam Rudaz, and Thomas N. Bradbury. 2010. "Stress, Communication, and Marital Quality in Couples." *Family Relations* 59 (2): 195–206.

Lehman, Joseph G. "A Brief Explanation of the Overton Window." *Mackinac Center*, 2019. https://www.mackinac.org/OvertonWindow.

Levant, Ronald, Katherine Richmond, Stephen Cook, A. Tanner House, and Maryse Aupont. 2007. "The Femininity Ideology Scale: Factor Structure, Reliability, Convergent and Discriminant Validity, and Social Contextual Variation." *Sex Roles* 57 (5–6): 373–83.

Lheal, Kulvir. 2016. "Lenny Bruce: 'Are There Any Niggers Here Tonight?'" *Medium*, September 2016.

Lin, Nan, and Walter M. Ensel. 1989. "Life Stress and Health: Stressors and Resources." *American Sociological Review* 54 (3): 382–99.

Link, Bruce G, and Jo C. Phelan. 1995. "Social Conditions as Fundamental Causes of Disease." *Journal of Health and Social Behavior* 35 (Extra Issue: Forty Years of Medical Sociology: The State of the Art and Directions for the Future): 80–94.

———. 2009. "Social Conditions As Fundamental Causes of Disease." *Journal of Health and Social Behavior* 35 (1995): 80–94.

Livingston, James D., and Jennifer E. Boyd. 2010. "Correlates and Consequences of Internalized Stigma for People Living with Mental Illness: A Systematic Review and Meta-Analysis." *Social Science & Medicine* 71 (12): 2150–61.

Logan, Brian. 2018. "Dave Chappelle's 'Reckless' #MeToo and Trans Jokes Have Real after-Effects." *The Guardian*, January 4, 2018.

Lopez, German. 2017. "Bill Maher Dropped the N-Word on Live TV." *Vox*, June 3, 2017.

Lyons, Renee F., Kristin D. Mickelson, Michael J. L. Sullivan, and James C. Coyne. 1998. "Coping As A Communal Process." *Journal of Social and Personal Relationships* 15 (5): 579–605.

Mallenbaum, Carly, Patrick Ryan, and Maria Puente. 2018. "A Complete List of the 60 Bill Cosby Accusers and Their Reactions to His Prison Sentence." *USA Today*, September 26, 2018.

Martin, Jack K., Bernice A. Pescosolido, and Steven A. Tuch. 2000. "Of Fear and Loathing: The Role of 'Disturbing Behavior,' Labels, and Causal Attributions in Shaping Public Attitudes toward People with Mental Illness." *Journal of Health and Social Behavior* 41 (2): 208–23.

Martin, Jack K., Steven A. Tuch, and Paul M. Roman. 2003. "Problem Drinking Patterns among African Americans: The Impacts of Reports of Discrimination, Perceptions of Prejudice, and 'Risky' Coping Strategies." *Journal of Health and Social Behavior* 44 (3): 408–25.

Martin, Joyce A., Brady E. Hamilton, Michelle J. K. Osterman, and Anne K. Driscoll. 2015. "Births: Final Data for 2018." *National Vital Statistics Reports*. Vol. 68. Washington D.C.

Marx, Nick, Matt Sienkiewicz, and Ron Becker, eds. 2013. *Saturday Night Live and American TV*. Bloomington: Indiana University Press.

Maserejian, Nancy N., Carol L. Link, Karen L. Lutfey, Lisa D. Marceau, and John B. McKinlay. 2009. "Disparities in Physicians' Interpretations of Heart Disease Symptoms by Patient Gender: Results of a Video Vignette Factorial Experiment." *Journal of Women's Health* 18 (10): 1661–67.

Mason, L., E. Peters, S. C. Williams, and V. Kumari. 2017. "Brain Connectivity Changes Occurring Following Cognitive Behavioural Therapy for Psychosis Predict Long-Term Recovery." *Translational Psychiatry* 7 (1).

Massey, Douglas S. 2001. "Residential Segregation and Neighborhood Conditions in U.S. Metropolitan Areas." In *America Becoming: Racial Trends and Their Consequences*, edited by Neil J. Smelse, William Julius Wilson, and Faith Mitchel, 1:391–434. Washington, D.C.: National Academies Press.

Mays, Vickie M., Susan D. Cochran, and Namdi W. Barnes. 2007. "Race, Race-Based Discrimination, and Health Outcomes Among African Americans." *Annual Review of Psychology* 58 (1): 201–25.

McDermott, Annette. 2018. "Did World War II Launch the Civil Rights Movement?" *History*. 2018. https://www.history.com/news/did-world-war-ii-launch-the-civil-rights-movement.

McFarland, Sam. 2010. "Authoritarianism, Social Dominance, and Other Roots of Generalized Prejudice." *Political Psychology* 31 (3): 453–77.

McGraw, Peter, and Joel Warner. 2014. *The Humor Code: A Global Search for What Makes Things Funny*. New York: Simon & Schuster.

McLeod, Jane D. 2012. "The Meanings of Stress: Expanding the Stress Process Model." *Society and Mental Health* 2 (3): 172–86.

———. 2013. "Social Stratification and Inequality." In *Handbook of the Sociology of Mental Health*, edited by Carol S. Aneshensel, Jo C. Phelan, and Alex Bierman, 229–53. Dordrecht: Springer Netherlands.

Meier, Matthew R., and Casey R. Schimtt, eds. 2017. *Standing Up, Speaking Out: Stand-Up Comedy and the Rhetoric of Social Change*. New York: Routledge.

Mills, Brett, and Sarah Ralph. 2015. "'I Think Women Are Possibly Judged More Harshly with Comedy': Women and British Television Comedy Production." *Critical Studies in Television: The International Journal of Television Studies* 10 (2): 102–17.

Mirowsky, John, and Catherine E. Ross. 2002. "Measurement for a Human Science." *Journal of Health and Social Behavior* 43: 152–70.

Mizekewski, Linda. 2014. *Pretty/Funny: Women Comedians and Body Politics*. Austin: University of Texas Press.

Mizejewski, Linda, and Victoria Sturtevant, eds. 2017. *Hysterical!: Women in American Comedy*. Austin: University of Texas Press.

Molina, Kristine M., and Drexler James. 2017. "Discrimination, Internalized Racism, and Depression: A Comparative Study of African American and Afro-Caribbean Adults in the US." *Group Process and Intergroup Relations* 19 (4): 439–61.

Momen, Mehnaaz. 2018. *Political Satire, Postmodern Reality, and the Trump Presidency*. Lanham, MD: Rowman & Littlefield.

Monod, David. 2020. *Vaudeville and the Making of Modern Entertainment, 1890–1925*. Chapel Hill: University of North Caroline Press.

Morreall, John. 1987. *The Philosophy of Laughter and Humor*. Albany: SUNY Press.

Morse, Janice M. 2012. "The Implications of Interview Type and Structure in Mixed-Methods Design." In *The SAGE Handbook of Interview Research*: The

Complexity of the Craft, edited by Jaber F. Gubrium, James A. Holstein, Amir B. Marvasti, and Karyn D. McKinney, 193–204. Thousand Oaks, CA: Sage.

Murphy, Caryn. 2013. "'Is This the Era of the Woman?': SNL's Gender Politics in the New Millennium." In *Saturday Night Live and American TV*, edited by Nick Marx, Matt Sienkiewicz, and Ron Becker. Bloomington: Indiana University Press.

National Alliance on Mental Illness. 2016. "Starting the Conversation: College and Your Mental Health." National Alliance on Mental Illness. Arlington, VA.

———. 2022. "Annual Report 2021."Arlington, VA.

NC State University Counseling Center. n.d. "Interpersonal Skills." Accessed January 8, 2020. https://counseling.dasa.ncsu.edu/interpersonal-skills/.

Noland, Marcus, Tyler Moran, and Barbara Kotschwar. 2016. "Is Gender Diversity Profitable? Evidence from a Global Survey." Washington, D.C.

O'Brien, Carol, Jessica Keith, and Lisa Shoemaker. 2015. "Don't Tell: Military Culture and Male Rape." *Psychological Services* 12 (4): 357–65.

Opie, Tina R., and Katherine W. Phillips. 2015. "Hair Penalties: The Negative Influence of Afrocentric Hair on Ratings of Black Women's Dominance and Professionalism." *Frontiers in Psychology* 6 (August): 1–14.

Oppliger, Patrice A., and Eric Shouse, eds. 2020. *The Dark Side of Stand-Up Comedy*. London: Palgrave.

Oricchio, Michael. 1995. "Pryor Wrote the Book on Comedy and Now, a Memoir of His Tumultuous Life." *The Baltimore Sun*, May 31, 1995. https://www.baltimoresun.com/news/bs-xpm-1995-05-31-1995151149-story.html.

Pager, Devah. "The Mark of a Criminal Record." *American Sociological Review* 103, no. March (2003): 937–75.

Parker, Bethany. 2008. "Probing Question: What Are the Roots of Stand-up Comedy?" https://www.psu.edu/news/research/story/probing-question-what-are-roots-stand-comedy/.

Pascoe, C. J. 2005. "'Dude, You're a Fag': Adolescent Masculinity and the Fag Discourse." *Sexualities* 8 (3): 329–46.

Pearlin, Leonard I. 1989. "The Sociological Study of Stress." *Journal of Health and Social Behavior* 30 (3): 241–56.

Pearlin, Leonard I., and Alex Bierman. 2013. "Current Issues and Future Directions in Research into the Stress Process." In *Handbook of the Sociology of Mental Health*, edited by Carol S. Aneshensel, Jo C. Phelan, and Alex Bierman, 325–40. Dordrecht: Springer Netherlands.

Pearlin, Leonard I., Elizabeth G. Menaghan, Morton A. Lieberman, and Joseph T. Mullan. 1981. "The Stress Process." *Journal of Health and Social Behavior* 22 (4): 337–56.

Pearlin, Leonard I., and Carmi Schooler. 1978. "The Structure of Coping." *Journal of Health and Social Behavior* 19 (1): 2–21.

Pedulla, David S., and Sarah Thébaud. 2015. "Can We Finish the Revolution? Gender, Work-Family Ideals, and Institutional Constraint." *American Sociological Review* 39 (1): 116–39.

Pérez, Raúl. 2013. "Learning to Make Racism Funny in the 'Color-Blind' Era: Stand-up Comedy Students, Performance Strategies, and the (Re)Production of Racist Jokes in Public." *Discourse and Society* 24 (4): 478–503.

Pescosolido, Bernice A. 2013. "The Public Stigma of Mental Illness: What Do We Think; What Do We Know; What Can We Prove?" *Journal of Health and Social Behavior* 54 (1): 1–21.

Pescosolido, Bernice A., Andrew Halpern-Manners, Liying Luo, and Brea Perry. 2021. "Trends in Public Stigma of Mental Illness in the US, 1996–2018." *JAMA Network Open* 4 (12): e2140202.

Pescosolido, Bernice A., Bianca Manago, and John Monahan. 2019. "Evolving Public Views on the Likelihood of Violence from People with Mental Illness: Stigma and Its Consequences." *Health Affairs* 38 (10): 1735–43.

Pescosolido, Bernice A., Jack K. Martin, J. Scott Long, Tait R. Medina, Jo C. Phelan, and Bruce G. Link. 2010. "'A Disease Like Any Other'? A Decade of Change in Public Reactions to Schizophrenia, Depression, and Alcohol Dependence." *American Journal of Psychiatry* 167 (11): 1321–30.

Pescosolido, Bernice A., Tait R. Medina, Jack K. Martin, and J. Scott Long. 2013. "The 'Backbone' of Stigma: Identifying the Global Core of Public Prejudice Associated With Mental Illness." *American Journal of Public Health* 103 (5): 853–60.

Pescosolido, Bernice A., Brea L. Perry, and Anne C. Krendl. 2020. "Empowering the Next Generation to End Stigma by Starting the Conversation: Bring Change to Mind and the College Toolbox Project." *Journal of the American Academy of Child and Adolescent Psychiatry* 59 (4): 519–30.

Phelan, Jo C., and Bruce G. Link. 2015. "Is Racism a Fundamental Cause of Inequalities in Health?" *Annual Review of Sociology* 41: 311–30.

Phelan, Jo C., Bruce G. Link, and Parisa Tehranifar. 2010. "Social Conditions as Fundamental Causes of Health Inequalities: Theory, Evidence, and Policy Implications." *Journal of Health and Social Behavior* 51 (S): S28–40.

Proulx, Christine M., and Linley A. Snyder-Rivas. 2013. "The Longitudinal Associations Between Marital Happiness, Problems, and Self-Rated Health." *Journal of Family Psychology* 27 (2): 194–202.

Puchko, Kristy. 2020. "Bold Move: Chris D'Elia Defends Himself by Releasing Emails That Show He Is a Creep." *Pajaba*, June 20, 2020.

Pudrovska, Tetyana, Scott Schieman, Leonard I. Pearlin, and Kim B. Nguyen. 2005. "The Sense of Mastery as a Mediator and Moderator in the Association Between Economic Hardship and Health in Late Life." *Journal of Aging and Health* 17 (5): 634–60.

Pyke, Karen D. 2010. "What Is Internalized Racial Oppression and Why Don't We Study It? Acknowledging Racism's Hidden Injuries." *Sociological Perspectives* 53 (4): 551–72.

Quadlin, Natasha. "The Mark of a Woman's Record: Gender and Academic Performance in Hiring." *American Sociological Review* 83, no. 2 (April 15, 2018): 331–60.

Read, Jen'nan Ghazal, and Bridget K. Gorman. 2010. "Gender and Health Inequality." *Annual Review of Sociology* 36 (2010): 371–86.

———. 2011. "Gender and Health Revisited." In *Handbook of the Sociology of Health, Illness, and Healing: A Blueprint for the 21st Century*, edited by Bernice A. Pescosolido, Jack K. Martin, Jane D. McLeod, and Rogers Anne, 411–29. New York: Springer.

Redden, Molly. 2017. "Louis CK Accused by Five Women of Sexual Misconduct in New Report." *The Guardian*, November 9, 2017.

Reinhart, M., D. Fritze, and T. Nguyen. 2021. "The State of Mental Health in America." Alexandria, VA.

Ridgeway, Cecilia L., and Shelley J. Correll. 2004. "Unpacking the Gender System: A Theoretical Perspective on Gender Beliefs and Social Relations." *Gender and Society* 18 (4): 92–126.

Robins, Jo Lynne W., Laura Kiken, Melissa Holt, and Nancy L. Mccain. 2014. "Mindfulness: An Effective Coaching Tool for Improving Physical and Mental Health." *Journal of the American Association of Nurse Practitioners* 26 (9): 511–18.

Rogan, Joe. 2019a. *The Joe Rogan Experience #1270*: Lenny Clark (podcast).

———. 2019b. *The Joe Rogan Experience #1296*: Joe List (podcast).

———. 2019c. *The Joe Rogan Experience #1317*: Andrew Santino (podcast).

Rosenberg, Morris, and B. Claire McCullough. 1981. "Mattering: Inferred Significance and Mental Health among Adolescents." *Research in Community and Mental Health* 2: 163–82.

Rosenblum, Karen Elaine, and Toni-Michelle Travis. 2012. *The Meaning of Difference: American Construction of Race, Sex and Gender, Social Class, Sexual Orientation, and Disability*. 6th ed. New York: McGraw-Hill.

Rosenfield, Sarah. 2012. "Triple Jeopardy? Mental Health at the Intersection of Gender, Race, and Class." *Social Science & Medicine* 74 (11): 1791–1801.

Rosenfield, Sarah, and Dawne M. Mouzon. 2013. "Gender and Mental Health." In *Handbook of the Sociology of Mental Health*, edited by Carol S. Aneshensel, Jo C. Phelan, and Alex Bierman, second edition, 277–96. Dordrecht: Springer Netherlands.

Rosenthal, Angela, David Bindman, and Adrian W. B. Randolph, eds., n.d. *No Laughing Matter: Visual Humor in Ideas of Race, Nationality, and Ethnicity*. Chicago: Chicago University Press.

Rubin, Herbert J., and Irene S. Rubin. *Qualitative Interviewing: The Art of Hearing Data*. Thousand Oaks, CA: Sage, 2002.

———. "Why We Do What We Do: Philosophy of Qualitative Interviewing." In *Qualitative Interviewing: The Art of Hearing Data*, 19–38. Thousand Oaks, CA: Sage, 2005.

Rudnick, Abraham, Paul M. Kohn, Kim R. Edwards, David Podnar, and Sara Caird. 2014. "Humour-Related Interventions for People with Mental Illness: A Randomized Controlled Pilot Study." *Community Mental Health Journal* 50: 737–42.

S.2938 - Bipartisan Safer Communities Act. Public Law 117–159. Sponsor: Sen. Rubio, Marco [R-FL].

Sammond, Nicholas. 2015. *Birth of an Industry: Blackface Minstrelsy and the Rise of American Animation.* Durham, NC: Duke University Press.

Saucier, Donald A., Megan L. Strain, Stuart S. Miller, Conor J. O'Dea, and Derrick F. Till. 2018. "'What Do You Call a Black Guy Who Flies a Plane?': The Effects and Understanding of Disparagement and Confrontational Racial Humor." *Humor* 31 (1): 105–28.

Scambler, Graham. 2011. "Stigma and Mental Disorder." In *The Sage Handbook of Mental Health and Illness*, no. 2008: 218–38.

Schieman, Scott, Tetyana Pudrovska, and Melissa A. Milkie. 2005. "The Sense of Divine Control and the Self-Concept: A Study of Race Differences in Late Life.*" Research on Aging* 27 (2): 165–96.

Schomerus, George, S.Van der Auwera, S. E. Baumeister, and Matthias C. Angermeyer. 2015. "Do Attitudes towards Persons with Mental Illness Worsen During the Course of Life? An Age-Period-Cohort Analysis." *Acta Psychiatrica Scandinavica* 132 (5): 357–64.

Schrock, Douglas, and Michael Schwalbe. 2018. "Men, Masculinity, and Manhood Acts." *Annual Review of Sociology* 35 (2009): 277–95.

Schwartz, Lisa M., and Steven Woloshin. 2019. "Medical Marketing in the United States, 1997–2016." *JAMA* 321 (1): 80.

Seeman, Teresa E. 1996. "Social Ties and Health: The Benefits of Social Integration." *Annals of Epidemiology* 6 (5): 442–51.

Seidman, Irving. 2006. *Interviewing as Qualitative Research: A Guide for Researchers in Education and the Social Sciences.* New York: Teachers College Press.

Seizer, Susan. 2011. "On the Uses of Obscenity in Live Stand-Up Comedy." *Anthropological Quarterly* 84 (1): 209–34.

———. 2017. "Dialogic Catharsis in Standup Comedy: Stewart Huff Plays a Bigot." *Humor* 30 (2): 211–37.

Smith, Patricia M., Janet M. Herold, Ian Eliasoph, and Marc Pilotin. Office of Federal Contract Compliance Programs, *United States Department of Labor v. Google, Inc.* (January 4, 2017).

Snowden, Lonnie R. 2001. "Social Embeddedness and Psychological Well-Being among African Americans and Whites." *American Journal of Community Psychology* 29 (4): 519–36.

Soloski, Alexis. 2017. "The (Elegant, Brazen, Brainy) Pioneering Women of Comedy." *New York Times*, November 21, 2017.

Swim, Janet K., Kathryn J. Aikin, Wayne S. Hall, and Barbara A. Hunter. 1995. "Sexism and Racism: Old-Fashioned and Modern Prejudices." *Journal of Personality and Social Psychology* 68 (2): 199–214.

Takeuchi, David T., Emily Walton, and ManChui Leung. 2010. "Race, Social Contexts, and Health: Examining Geographic Spaces and Places." In *Handbook of Medical Sociology*, edited by Chloe E. Bird, Peter Conrad, Allen M. Fremont, and Stefan Timmermans, 6th ed., 92–105. Nashville, TN: Vanderbilt University Press.

Taylor, John, and R. Jay Turner. 2001. "A Longitudinal Study of the Role and Significance of Mattering to Others for Depressive Symptoms." *Journal of Health and Social Behavior* 42 (3): 310–25.

Taylor, Paul. 2013. "A Survey of LGBT Americans Attitudes, Experiences and Values in Changing."

The Telegraph. 2008. "Obituaries: George Carlin." *The Telegraph*, June 23.

Thoits, Peggy A. 1995. "Stress, Coping, and Social Support Processes: Where Are We? What Next?" *Journal of Health and Social Behavior Extra Issue* (1995): 53–79.

———. 2011. "Resisting the Stigma of Mental Illness." *Social Psychology Quarterly* 74 (1): 6–28.

Thoits, Peggy A., and Bruce G. Link. 2016. "Stigma Resistance and Well-Being among People in Treatment for Psychosis." *Society and Mental Health* 6 (1): 1–20.

Thomas, James M. 2015. *Working to Laugh: Assembling Difference in American Stand-Up Comedy Venues.* Lanham, MD: Lexington Books.

Thornicroft, Graham, Nisha Mehta, Sarah Clement, Sara Evans-Lacko, Mary Doherty, Diana Rose, Mirja Koschorke, Rahul Shidhaye, Claire O'Reilly, and Claire Henderson. 2016. "Evidence for Effective Interventions to Reduce Mental-Health-Related Stigma and Discrimination." *The Lancet* 387 (10023): 1123–32.

THR staff. 2014. "Hollywood Salaries Revealed, From Movie Stars to Agents." *The Hollywood Reporter*, October 2, 2014.

Tucker, Terrence T. 2018. *Furiously Funny: Comic Rage from Ralph Ellison to Chris Rock.* Tallahassee: University Press of Florida.

Twardzicki, Maya, and Norman Jones. 2017. "'Have You Heard the One about . . . ' Using Comedy to Tackle Mental Health–Related Stigma with UK Military Personnel?" *Journal of Public Mental Health* 16 (1): 9–11.

U.S. Bureau of Labor Statistics. 2018. "Economic News Release: Employment Characteristics of Families Summary." Washington D.C.

U.S. Department of Health and Human Services. 2019. "Lesbian, Gay, Bisexual, and Transgender Health New Why Is LGBT Health Important?" HealthyPeople.Gov. 2019. https://www.healthypeople.gov/2020/topics-objectives/topic/lesbian-gay-bisexual-and-transgender-health.

Villarreal, Andrés. 2010. "Stratification by Skin Color in Contemporary Mexico." *American Sociological Review* 75 (5): 652–78.

Watts, Marina. 2020. "Comedians React to Allegations That Chris D'Elia Harassed Underage Girls." *Newsweek*, June 17, 2020.

Weisfeld, Glenn E., and Miriam B. Weisfeld. 2014. "Does a Humorous Element Characterize Embarrassment?" *Humor* 27 (1): 65–85.

Weller, Chris. 2015. "Aziz Ansari's 'Master of None' Proves America's Best Philosophers Are All Comedians." *Business Insider*, November 15, 2015.

Wheaton, Blair. 1985. "Models for the Stress-Buffering Functions of Coping Resources." *Journal of Health and Social Behavior* 26 (4): 352–64.

White, Judith B., and Ellen J. Langer. 1999. "Horizontal Hostility: Relations between Similar Minority Groups." *Journal of Social Issues* 55 (3): 537–59.

Willett, Cynthia, and Julie Willett. 2019. *Uproarious: How Feminists and Other Subversive Comics Speak Truth.* Minneapolis: University of Minnesota Press.

Williams, David R., and Chiquita Collins. 2001. "Racial Residential Segregation Project: A Fundamental Cause of Racial Disparities in Health." *Public Health Reports* 116 (5): 404–16.

Williams, Stereo. 2018. "Chris Rock's N-Word Controversy with Louis C.K. and the Myth of the 'Down Ass White Guy.'" *Daily Beast*, December 23, 2018. https://www.thedailybeast.com/chris-rocks-n-word-controversy-with-louis-ck-and-the-myth-of-the-down-ass-white-guy.

Williams, Teeomm K. 2012. "Understanding Internalized Oppression: A Theoretical Conceptualization of Internalized Subordination." Open Access Dissertations.

W.K. Kellogg Foundation. Truth, Racial Healing & Transformation. April 18, 2023. https://healourcommunities.org/

Woodzicka, Julie A., Robyn K. Mallett, Shelbi Hendricks, and Astrid V. Pruitt. 2015. "It's Just a (Sexist) Joke: Comparing Reactions to Sexist versus Racist Communications." *Humor* 28 (2): 289–309.

Wright, Chrysalis L., Taylor Defrancesco, Carissa Hamiltonbi, and Natasha Vashist. 2018. "'Boy's Club': Examining Sexist Humor on Types of Sexism and Femininity Ideology Using Two Research Approaches." *Humor* 31 (1): 129–50.

Wright, Steve, Maya Twardzicki, Fabio Gomez, and Claire Henderson. 2014. "Evaluation of a Comedy Intervention to Improve Coping and Help-Seeking for Mental Health Problems in a Women's Prison." *International Review of Psychiatry* 26 (4): 423–29.

Wuster, Tracy. 2006. "Comedy Jokes: Steve Martin and the Limits of Stand-Up Comedy." *Studies in American Humor* 14 (3): 23–45.

Yamato, Jen. 2016. "Roseanne Barr Calls out Louis C.K.: 'I've Heard so Many Stories.'" *Daily Beast*, June 30, 2016.

Young, Dannagal Goltwaite. 2019. *Irony and Outrage: The Polarized Landscape of Rage, Fear, and Laughter in the United States.* New York: Oxford University Press.

Yu, Wei-Hsin, and Janet Chen-Lan Kuo. 2017. "The Motherhood Wage Penalty by Work Conditions: How Do Occupational Characteristics Hinder or Empower Mothers?" *American Sociological Review* 82 (4): 744–69.

Zippia. "Standup Comedian Demographics and Statistics." Zippia: The Career Expert. April 18, 2023. (https://www.zippia.com/stand-up-comedian-jobs/demographics/).

Index

INDEX OF SUBJECTS

collective effervescence, 205–206
Comedy Attic, 152
coping, 22, 34, 83–84, 93, 121–122
   emotional catharsis, 187
   negative coping, 93–95. *See also*
     drug abuse
   religious coping, 121, 200

discrimination, 3–4, 151–162, 17–182,
   184–185, 188–189
   disability, 52, 151–152, 180, 185
   equity movement
     backlash, 195–196
   gender, 157–158, 155–
     156, 176–179
   LGBTQ+, 153
   race/ethnicity, 154–155
     Murphy, Eddie, 116
   structural discrimination/
     inequality, segregation, 17,
     142–143, 167–168, 175–
     177, 189–191
drug abuse, 94, 146–148

financial exploitation, 162, 168–172
   workplace discrimination, 16–17

fundamental cause of health inequality,
   22, 142–143

hegemonic masculinity, 66–68
   incels (involuntary
     celibates), 150, 162
   toxic masculinity, 54–55,
     68, 163, 178

interpersonal skills, 137, 189, 196–200
intersectionality, 62–66,
   99–100, 116–117

Laughing Skull Comedy Festival, 196

methodology, 18–25
   data/demographics, 4, 20
   limitations, 21–23
   philosophy, 205
   positionality, 24–25, 48–49,
     67–68, 80–81, 95–96,
     137–138, 166, 184–185, 199–
     200, 203–204

Overton Window, 17

performer/audience
   relationship, 200–205

Saturday Night Live, 17, 116, 162–163, 195
psychological resources, 121–122, 133
    mattering, 121–122
    self-efficacy, mastery, 121–123, 128–131
    self-esteem, 122–125
    sexual exploitation, harassment, violence, 124, 159–161
    social isolation, 175–177
    social resources, 122

standup comedy
    blue comedy. *See* shocking the audience
    charged comedy, 13, 83, 121, 197, 203
    current demographics, 15–16
    discrimination history 12–18, 193
    diversity, 9
    history of mental illness, 15
        Gadsby, Hannah, 9, 15, 18–19
    history of sexism and homophobia, 12–15
    The Humor Code, 12, 200
    Latino stereotypes, 154–155
    modern day minstrelsy, 66–67
    political capital in comedy, 66–67
    political conversations, 17–18
        Bruce, Lenny, 13, 18, 195
        Pryor, Richard, 13–14, 18
        Carlin, George, 13, 18, 36
        Chaplain, Charlie, The Great Dictator, 205–206
    pre–Civil War history, 9, 13
    sexual violence history
        Barr, Roseanne, 163, 192
        Chappelle, Dave, 9, 79, 182, 192
        CK, Louis, 79, 163 182–183, 192
        Cosby, Billy, 17–18, 163
        D'Elia, Chris, 17, 163, 182
        Larry King Live, 163
        Maron, Marc, 163
        Notaro, Tig, 163, 192

Rogan, Joe, 182–183
stigma reduction and health improvement potential, 11–12
structural changes for equality, 193–195
on television, 4 15, 143, 167, 175, 192
    Comedy Central, 15, 143, 167, 175
    Conan Obrien Show, 15
    HBO 4, 15, 143
    Jimmy Kimmel Live, 15
    Netflix, 15, 143, 192
    TBS, 15
    The Tonight Show with Jimmy Fallon, 15
unhealthy diets, 146–151, 172, 175, 188
Stigma, 9–11
    blaming victims, 79
    invisible stigma, 71
    master status, 51–52
    public stigma, 187
    reduction, 8, 191–195, 197
        starting a conversation, 184, 188
        empathy and social contact, 11, 200–205
    resistance tactics, 95, 188
        advocacy, 72–73, 91–93
        candid conversations, 84–85
        compartmentalization, 135–136, 198–200
        concealing and withdrawing, 93–95
        existing without talking, 88–90
        veiled conversations, 85–88
    self-stigma, 52, 107, 116, 183, 187
    societal costs, 7
    visible stigma, 51–53
selective disclosure, 71–71, 80
    disarming the audience, 75–77
    leading the audience, 72–75
    shocking the audience, 77–79

Majory Stoneman Douglas
High School, 79
humor that is disparaging,
self-defeating, or
subversive, 192–193

INDEX OF RESEARCH
PARTICIPANTS

Alejandra, 34–35, 108
Alvin, 89–90, 132–134
Amelia, 93–94, 148

Barb, 75–77, 153, 179–180
Benicio, 54–55
Bernard, 72–73, 172
Blake, 56–59
Booker, 10–11

Cam, 57–61, 153
Candice, 64–65, 102–103, 192
Cara, 129–130, 153, 159
Carmen, 43–44, 113
Carson, 20
Chacha, 33–34, 145–146
Chase, 88–89
Chaz, 59–60, 90
Ciara, 101–101, 115, 151, 156–157
Claire, 48, 52–53, 103
Colleen, 45–46
Connor, 87–89
Cyrus, 16, 180–182

Demarcus, 64, 155–156, 161,
    175, 179, 205
Diego, 42–43
Doug, 54–55
Dylan, 36–40, 147, 151, 170

Emilio, 75–77, 89, 111
Ethan, 57–61, 132–134
Evelyn, 84–85, 44, 201

Felipe, 144, 154–156, 169
Fernanda, 111, 114, 129, 141–142,
    158, 176, 201
Franklin, 135

Gabby, 38–39
George, 202–203

Hazel, 123–136
Heather, 95, 126
Hiromi, 48–49, 50, 95, 174, 190–191
Holly, 10–11, 58–59, 154, 173, 190, 193
Hope, 73–74, 124–125, 133–134, 159,
    172–173, 177–178,

Ignacio, 108
Isabella, 107–110

Jada, 41–42, 112–115, 152
Jamal, 86–88, 99–100, 105–107, 112,
    146–149, 170, 175–176, 197
Jamison, 202–204
Jasmine, 53–54
Jeremy, 63, 145, 170
Jessi, 84–85
Joji, 123, 134–135, 183–184
Judith, 38–39
Justus, 85–86, 105, 150, 162

Lance, 61–63, 144
Lawshawn, 20, 153, 172–173
Leonel, 41, 77–78, 112, 180–181
Liam, 128–129
Lola, 109, 126–129, 157
Lora, 91–92, 143, 172
Luna, 114
Lydia, 56–59, 67 158, 168–
    168, 181, 202

Marcus, 104–105, 127–128, 131
Mark, 93–95
Marvin, 41
Mateo, 108, 123, 127, 130–
    132, 167, 170

Meghan, 62–63, 91
Mika, 39–40
Molly, 62

Nathaniel, 15, 51–52, 152, 180, 185,
Nora, 9–11,
Nyah, 43–44, 103–105, 107, 112,
    147, 176, 191

Oliver, 46–47
Olivia, 171–172

Pallavi, 44–48, 90
Pierson, 83–84, 147

Rafa, 80, 107, 110–111, 115, 133–134
Rebecca, 1–4, 9, 21, 24, 68, 121,
    161, 167, 188
Ross, 35–36, 38, 40 65,

Sef, 83–84
Sharice, 157–158
Simon, 92–93, 145, 195,
Sophia, 47, 150–151,
Stephanie, 135, 149–150, 172, 174

Tiana, 101–102
Tiffany, 78–79, 106
Todd, 177–178
Tracy, 101
Treyvaughn, 2–4, 11, 61, 95, 178
Trina, 65–66, 113, 169

Valentino, 109–110, 130–131, 149,
    174–175, 194
Vivian, 33–34

Yazmin, 46–47

Zachary, 34–35
Zahra, 122, 176
Zoey, 143, 160

INDEX OF PARTICIPANTS CONVERSATION SUBJECTS

audience misunderstanding, 201–206
    Addams family, 201

Black lives
    Black audiences, 101, 105–107
    Black celebrities, 155
    Black femininity, 112–115
    Black homophobia, 2–4, 11
    Black mother of
      interracial child, 65
    gender differences, 155–157
    mental illness, 65–66
    parenthood (motherhood,
      fatherhood), 64–66
    police violence / criminal
      justice, 54, 65–66
    privileges, 116
    racism/violence, 84–85, 92–93,
      104, 105, 156, 173
    romantic relationships,
      11, 101–102
    social justice, 92–93,
      100–101, 105
    stereotypes, 10, 102, 204–205
    White conservative audiences,
      36–37, 103, 104, 115, 172–173
    White liberal audiences, 85–86,
      99–100, 102–103, 104

cancer, 46–47, 90, 124, 201
car accidents, 20
comedy culture
    comedy attracts unhealthy
      people, 148–151
    incels, 150, 162
    mental illness
      Stevens, Brody, 150–151

opportunities for equality, 15
performance high, 123–124
Screen Actors Guild, 145
sexism. *See* sexism
substance abuse, 146–149
unhealthy diets, 146–148
White privilege, 179–180

death
Armenian Genocide, 91–92
child death, 43, 171
family member death, 124, 42–44
parental death, 41–43
disability, 51–52, 54–55
discrimination, 151–152
domestic violence, 41, 33–34, 42, 123–124, 133–134
childhood abuse, 43–44, 77–79, 86–88, 123–124, 132–133, 136, 141

family life, 75–77, 91–93, 124, 144
parent / child relationships, 33–38, 41, 72–73, 80, 132–135, 136
religion. *See* religion
financial exploitation, 20, 143–146, 168–169, 178–179
food stamps, 143–144
homelessness, 78
Late Night with Stephen Colbert, 144
family strain, 169–172

gender inequality
ballet, 141–142
body image issues/politics, eating disorders, 48–49, 141–142, 172
sexism, 53–56, 67, 91, 129, 114, 157–159, 181
sexual harassment/assault, 1–3, 52–53, 78, 85, 133–134, 145–146, 159–162, 173–175

Latino lives, 42–44
bigotry, 77, 109
Latina femininity, 112–115
Latino masculinity threat, 115
managing stereotypes, 76 77, 107–111, 154–155, 167–172
skin tone, 111–112
Southwest, 109–112
LGBTQ+
Boy Scouts, 60
coming out of the closet, 75, 88–89, 122–123, 132,
education, 58
gay masculinity, 59–62
gay safe spaces, 57
gender divisions, 58
Grindr, 57
HIV, 132
homophobia/discrimination, 73, 153–154, 179, 183–184
political resistance, 90
religious conflict, 56–57, 89, 202
romantic relationships, 10
transgender stereotypes, 10, 56–57, 58
violence, 57, 59, 123

masculinity, 41, 54–56, 77
mental illness, 44–48, 93, 136, 150–151
alcohol abuse/use, 83, 147–148,
alternative coping (i.e., therapy, meditation), 134–136
drug abuse, 147–148
suicide, 47, 93–94, 124–125, 150
substance use, 93–94, 172
military, 75–77, 131, 204–205

parenthood, 62–66
baby's Gender, 39
conceiving, 84
gender Expectation, 62–63, 91
motherhood, 10, 62, 191

motherhood vs.
  fatherhood, 62–64
teen parents, 40
psychological resources
  mastery, 126–128
  navigating the audience, 127

religious conflict, 35–38, 40, 56–57, 202
romantic relationship
  breakups, 38–39
  dating, 40

divorce, 23, 33 42, 53–54,
  104, 136, 191
marriage, 84

sex, 38
  sex work, 78–79
  fetishes, 130–131
social resources, 128–131
  improving family
    relationships, 132–135
  losing social
    connections, 175–177

About the Author

Dr. Sean Viña began his sociology career at Huston-Tillotson University, a historically Black college in Austin, Texas. After two years, he transferred to the University of Texas at San Antonio, where he completed his bachelor's and master of science degrees in sociology. He then pursued his PhD in sociology at Indiana University, focusing on health and stigma. His research has explored the relationship between religion and health, mental illness among service members and their spouses, and the stigma associated with PTSD. Sean is currently pursuing research on the sociology of psychedelics.

Currently, Sean is assistant professor of sociology at the University of the Incarnate Word in San Antonio.

Furthermore, Sean is passionate about public service and volunteers for multiple boards and commissions for the City of San Antonio. He is married to Dr. Amanda Stephens, Esq., and after five years, they still enjoy actively dating and going on long walks with their two dogs along the River Walk.